I0093038

Culture Secrets

Secrets Leaders Use to Build A V.A.L.U.E. Culture

Culture Secrets: Secrets Leaders Use to Build A V.A.L.U.E. Culture
Copyright © Chellie W. Phillips

Publisher's Note: Ignite Publishing is proud and excited to bring you this book by internationally best-selling author Chellie W. Phillips, Culture Secrets: Secrets Leaders Use to Build A V.A.L.U.E. Culture

As the leader in Empowerment publishing, Ignite's mission is to produce inspiring, motivational, and empowering books that will Ignite the reader's life.They are of the highest caliber to offer engaging, profound, and life-changing information that will impact the reader. Our mandate is to build a conscious, positive, and supportive community through our books. We welcome new book ideas and new authors onto our platform. Should you desire to be published, please apply at www.igniteyou.life/apply or reach out to us at info@igniteyou.life.

All rights reserved. No part of this publication may be reproduced, distributed, or transmitted in any form or by any means, including photocopying, recording, or other electronic or mechanical methods, without the prior written permission of the author, except in the case of brief quotations embodied in critical articles or reviews, and certain other noncommercial uses permitted by copyright law. For permission requests, write to the publisher, addressed "Attention: Permissions Coordinator," at the address below.

Limitation of Liability: Under no circumstances shall the author, contributors, or publisher be liable for any indirect, incidental, consequential, special, or exemplary damages arising out of or in connection with your use of any exercises or information contained in this book. Please be advised that if you follow any of the suggestions offered by the author, you do so of your own accord. It is up to you to seek professional advice before you implement any lifestyle changes. The views, thoughts, and opinions expressed in this text belong solely to the individual author and not necessarily to the publisher, editorial team, or the experts the authors may reference.

Published and printed by Ignite Publishing, a division of JBO Global Inc.
5569-47th Street Red Deer, AB
Canada, T4N1S1 1-877-677-6115

Cover design by Dania Zafar and Katie Smetherman
Book design by Dania Zafar, Katie Smetherman, and JB Owen
Edited by JB Owen, Mimi Safiyah, Zoe Wong
Designed in Canada
ISBN: 979-8-9872121-2-7
First edition:

Ordering Information: Quantity sales. Special discounts are available on quantity purchases by corporations, associations, and others. For details, contact the publisher at the above address. Programs, products, or services provided by the author are found by contacting them directly. Resources named in the book are found in the resources pages at the back of the book.
Author Details: Chellie W. Phillips, https://www.chelliephillips.com, contact@chelliephillips.com

GREAT PLACE TO WORK is a trademark of Great Place to Work Institute Inc.
PANASONIC is a trademark of PANASONIC CORPORATION.
GTA THE CO-OP WAY is a trademark of CHS Inc.
YAMAHA is a trademark of YAMAHA CORPORATION
MENLO is a trademark of Menlo Therapeutics Inc
TEDX is a trademark of TED CONFERENCES, LLC.
TOUCHSTONE ENERGY BUSINESS ONLINE AUDIT is a trademark owned by National Rural NATIONAL RURAL ELECTRIC COOPERATIVE ASSOCIATION is a trademark owned by NATIONAL RURAL ELECTRIC COOPERATIVE ASSOCIATION
TRUSUM VISIONS is a trademark of Trusum Visions, LLC.
AMB is a trademark of Bryant Ventures LLC.
GAP is a trademark of GAP (APPAREL), LLC.
HP is a trademark of HP Hewlett Packard Group LLC.
MICROSOFT is a trademark of MICROSOFT CORPORATION.
GLASSDOOR is a trademark of GLASSDOOR, INC..
FB is a trademark of Facebook, Inc
ZOOM is a trademark of Zoom Video Communications, Inc.
The USPTO has given the INDEED trademark a serial number of 85655398.
REVEAL GLOBAL INTELLIGENCE is a trademark and brand of Reveal Intelligence Services, LLC.
CLICKFUNNELS is a trademark of Etison LLC.
ATLANTA FALCONS is a trademark of Atlanta Falcons Football Club, LLC.
ATLANTA UNITED FC is a trademark of Major League Soccer, L.L.C.
MERCEDES-BENZ is a trademark of DAIMLER AG.
PGA TOUR is a trademark of PGA TOUR, Inc.
AMB is a trademark of Bogdanovich Maksym Eduardovych.
LINKEDIN is a trademark of LinkedIn Corporation.
HILTON is a trademark of HILTON INTERNATIONAL HOLDING LLC.
BARRYWEHMILLER is a trademark of Barry-Wehmiller Companies, Inc..
NAT GEO is a trademark of National Geographic Society

CERTIFIED SCRUMMASTER is a trademark of Scrum Alliance, Inc.
HILTON is a trademark of HILTON INTERNATIONAL HOLDING LLC.
The Etsy Marks are trademarks and trade dress of Etsy, Inc.
The NIKE trademark was assigned an Application Number #UK00000758078 by the UK Intellectual Property Office (UKIPO).
3M is a trademark of 3M Company.
PGA TOUR, PGA TOUR Champions, and the Swinging Golfer design are registered trademarks.
Apple and iPhone are trademarks of Apple Inc.,
IPOD is a trademark of APPLE INC..
THE WIZARD OF OZ is a trademark of Turner Entertainment Co..
NRECA is a trademark of National Rural Electric Cooperative
KING OF POPS is a trademark of King of Pops, Inc..
SLACK is a trademark of SLACK TECHNOLOGIES, INC.
MICROSOFT TEAMS is a trademark of Microsoft Corporation.
The TIKTOK trademark was assigned a Serial Number #88386243 – by the United States Patent and Trademark Office (USPTO).
GALLUP is a trademark and brand of Gallup, Inc.
SUPER BOWL is a trademark of NFL.
Little League Baseball, Little League, the medallion, and the keystone are registered trademarks and service marks belonging exclusively to Little League
WD-40 is a trademark of WD-40 Manufacturing Company.
ZINGERMAN'S is a trademark of Zing IP, LLC. Filed in July 28 (2022
KING OF POPS is a trademark of King of Pops, Inc.
CRAIGSLIST is a trademark of CRAIGSLIST, INC.
A ALABAMA CRIMSON TIDE is a trademark of Board of Trustees of the University of Alabama.
J.P. MORGAN is a trademark of JPMorgan Chase Bank, N.A
ATLANTA UNITED FC is a trademark of Major League Soccer, L.L.C.
IVY LEAGUE is a trademark of Council of Ivy Group Presidents.

Culture Secrets

Secrets Leaders Use to Build A
V.A.L.U.E. Culture

By
CHELLIE PHILLIPS
Business Coach & International Bestselling Author

Published by Ignite Publishing, a division of JBO Globle Inc.
IGNITEYOU.LIFE

Contents

Testimonials

"Culture Secrets" by Chellie Philips is a must-read. In today's fast-changing hybrid workplace dynamics, companies need to solve the culture challenge. Chellie's newest book provides insights and ideas on creating a people-first culture that thrives in today's competitive landscape.
– Cheryl Cran, Bestselling Author of "The Art of Change Leadership" and "Super. Crucial. Human"

If you've ever wanted to be a fly on the wall while leaders and executives are digging deep into what matters and what moves the needle, you're in the right place. Chellie doesn't espouse her theories or give anecdotal evidence to back up her suspicions. She brings you into the room while she's drilling deep into leadership and growth mindsets regarding work and a culture of excellence with those in the trenches.

This brilliant approach gives you a seat at the table and brings you into the conversation, rather than relying on hearsay or speculation. What a breath of fresh air, and a breadth of experience in these pages! Your organization will be enriched after reading this, or better yet, having Chellie address these ideas in person!
— Carrie Wilkerson, Author & Business Consultant, CarrieWilkerson.com

It's not often you come across a book that leaves you this informed and inspired to stay fresh, stay agile, and yet grounded to your values in business. The next time I'm asked for advice on how to succeed in business, 'Read Chellie Phillips' book, *'Culture Secrets'* will be the next words out of my mouth."
— Mike Kim, Wall St. Journal bestselling author of You Are the Brand

Chellie Phillips has captured the secret of any CEO's success to build an engaged workforce that is fiercely loyal and has the best work outcomes. Why? The employees feel VALUED, and that motivation allows their energy to remain engaged in the workforce. That is how I felt as I read *Culture Secrets*. As a leader in the workforce, I apply what I have learned from this book and the individuals I serve in return are so dedicated to the heart of the work that their energy is catching! This book has the power to do that for you as well.

— *April Tribe Giauque MSED, Author of Pinpoints of Light: Escaping the Abyss of Abuse & Out of Darkness: Find, Fuel, and Live in Your Light*

Share the limelight with your team," was a pearl of wisdom Chellie shared with me on the *UnNoticed Entrepreneur* show. This book contains so many precious insights that will reassure, guide, and inspire the reader to create a V.A.L.U.E. Culture based organization that will engage employees with both their hearts and minds.

— *Jim James, EASTWEST Public Relations, Author, Host of The UnNoticed Entrepreneur Show™*

Culture is such a critical part of any organization's success. No one knows more about culture and how to create a winning one than Chellie Phillips. *Culture Secrets* will give you the winning formula.

— *David Branderhorst, Business Coach and Founder of Design Launch Grow™*

If you want to learn great insight about co-op culture, how to define it, and how to influence it, Chellie Phillips is your best bet. Her experience and her knack for asking the right

questions has made Chellie a treasure for the cooperative community and for anyone interested in developing and impacting the culture of their organization.
— *Jana Adams, Executive Director of Touchstone Energy™*

Chellie has put together an incredible book that delivers actionable techniques any business leader can use to increase employee engagement quickly.
— *Jessica Rhodes, Founder of Interview Connections™*

For current or aspiring leaders tasked with developing or fixing a failing workplace culture - this book is a must-have. With inspiring stories, candid conversations, and a simple V.A.L.U.E. framework, it provides a unique overview to get you started.
— *Grant Baldwin, Founder and CEO at The Speaker Lab™*

Success in business starts and ends with people. **Culture Secrets: Secrets Leaders Use to Build A V.A.L.U.E. Culture** is an actionable guide for people-first organizations to create cultures of sustainable success.
—*George Grombacher, Top 100 Financial Advisor, Speaker*

Society, and the business world, teach us that our needs, wants, and desires disappear when we turn 21 and become adults. They turn off, and it is you, the human, who must address the needs, wants, and desires of the business. They supersede you. A V.A.L.U.E.-based culture says both the company and the employees have needs, wants, and desires and BOTH are important to the success of our mission. Chellie hits the nail on the head with "**Culture Secrets: Secrets Leaders Use to Build A V.A.L.U.E. Culture**" as she illustrates for you why your culture is your internal brand and how just one bad

apple in top leadership can have a SIGNIFICANT impact on the success of your company in all the ways you can measure it. The pages inside the covers of this book are a must-read for all corporate Executives and Business Owners.
— *Andy McDowell, Leadership/Business Coach/ Host of Generate Your Value Podcast™*

Chellie Phillips, has hit a home run with "*Culture Secrets*"! The wisdom she shares from her own research and experience, as well as from the insights of those she interviewed, packs this book full of gold nuggets. This is a must-read if you are serious about creating a culture that attracts and retains top talent!
— *Chris McClure, Executive Leadership Coach, Author*

Chellie's unique branding perspective, her V.A.L.U.E.-based approach to culture, and the insights her interviews provide, make this book THE KEY to unlocking a breakthrough for your company's Culture.
— *Christopher McCoy, VP of Business Development, Trusum Visions™*

As a business consultant focused on business transformation, I will be using Chellie's advice in "**Culture Secrets: Secrets Any Leaders Use to Build A V.A.L.U.E. Culture**" as an essential building block of both business planning and transformations. Without employee engagement from the beginning, growth and change are far more likely to fail. Having the roadmap provided by Chellie's book, employees will be far more productive and truly operate as a team. Chellie has put together a guide that delivers practical and straightforward techniques any business leader can use to begin positively impacting employee engagement.
— *Robert Towle, Founder, 636 Advisors™*

Chellie Phillips is a highly respected leader and knows first-hand how to impact culture to ensure a thriving workplace. This book is a MUST-READ in your leadership arsenal.
— *Marlo Huggins, Founder and Executive Coach*

The culture problem is a tough nut, and Chellie cracks it: understand what motivates the individual, and your cultural comprehension will follow. Lots of practical advice here she's extracted from those who are making it work right now. Smart stuff from cover to cover.
— *Michael Long, Co-author, The Molecule of More*

Today's leaders struggle to navigate a new marketplace. People want more than a wage to survive. They want to be valued for who they are and respected for their talents. Chellie highlights a new type of leadership needed to create strong employee retention, attract new talent, and produce a strong ROI for any company that hopes to remain relevant.
—*Lisa McGuire, Personal Brand & Messaging Strategist. Host of Your Passion, Purpose, and Personal Brand Podcast™*

I've had the privilege of seeing Chellie Phillips in action, building and developing a strong, positive, and effective work-place culture. In "**Culture Secrets: Secrets Leaders Use to Build A V.A.L.U.E. Culture**," she builds on her experience by sharing practical and powerful techniques from other leaders in their fields. I highly recommend this book to any leader who wants to build a successful workplace culture.
—*Doug Fitzgerald, Radio Personality, Event Emcee, Best Selling Author, Speaker & CEO, Host of ONESHOT. ONELIFE.™*

"Culture Secrets" is a must-read for anyone looking to set a higher bar for leadership and create a more positive and productive work environment for all.
—*Peter Rabey, CEO of the X4 Group, Host of The Leadership Learns Podcast™*

Chellie captures it. Culture is the essential software defining how good companies take care of their team so they can take care of customers, their community, and business!
—*Harry Hynekamp, VP Guest Experiences, AMB Sports & Entertainment™*

A really interesting and fun way to explore the theory of culture through proven practices, and an absolute honor to contribute to this amongst some distinguished professionals.
—*Daniel Lawrence, Managing Director, Lawrence & Wedlock; CEO @ BotsForThat™*

Dedication

To the bad bosses of the world, thanks for teaching me what not to be. To the great leaders I've encountered, thanks for showing me there's a better way and inspiring me to continue growing so that I can be an agent of positive change.

Foreword

I am sure you have heard the saying that people don't leave bad jobs; they leave bad leaders. This is an absolutely true statement with a caveat. They also leave companies that tolerate poor behavior from their leadership team.

Even if the terrible leader isn't yours directly, the overall company culture will be tainted by just a few bad cultural apples. Leaders have the ability to take a company to its glory, but they can also bring it culturally to its knees. I love how Adam Grant, Organizational Psychologist at Wharton and a #1 NYT bestselling author, phrases it when he addresses culture: *no jerks allowed.*

I've been passionate about culture building since 2016, when I started working on *Panasonic*™ Automotive's Culture Transformation. As a Chief Human Resource Officer (CHRO) with a passion for "people first" best practices, I am relentlessly working to help build a culture to prove that we put people over products. I am also a Global Keynote Speaker, Columbia University Certified Executive Coach, and Culture Consultant who has seen firsthand the benefits of creating an intentional culture.

During my tenure as CHRO, *Panasonic*™ Automotive has become year after year 101 Best and Brightest organization to work for in the United States and a certified *Great Place to Work*™ organization. We have worked together as a company to create a culture where individuals choose to come to work every day because they want to, not because they have to. People that come to work in this kind of culture say that here, it just feels different.

As a member of our local Chamber of Commerce, I had the chance to hear Chellie Phillips, the author of this book, speak at the 2021 Diversity and Inclusion Summit aimed at helping businesses build a better, more inclusive workplace. At that time, her topic was *Igniting the Impact of Your Employees.* Her talk focused on a professional and personal development program she had successfully launched to help increase engagement among the 200-plus employees at her current company. I could tell Chellie was passionate about the people within the company and the culture they were creating. So, when she asked me to share our culture story as part of her book, I was honored. Chellie's understanding of and passion for building human-centered workplace cultures was evident in her presentation. I instantly knew she would bring that spark and persuasive ability to any book she wrote. Her ability to dissect and communicate the key ingredients needed for creating workplace cultures is vital in today's ever-changing business environment. Therefore, I knew supporting her in writing this book was going to make a positive impact on people's daily work life.

I had the opportunity to meet with a number of people who were getting culture right. One thing I learned is sharing the wins and struggles with others who are passionate about the process can help improve the chances the culture shift you want to implement will succeed. That's what makes Chellie's book special. She shares what worked and what didn't from the people making a difference, and she infuses it all together using her skills and expertise.

I have been blessed to have so many amazing Fortune 500

companies, like *Microsoft*™, *GAP*™, and *Hewlett Packard*™, share their best practices with me so I could avoid many mistakes and progress *Panasonic's*™ culture-building process. This is precisely what Chellie is accomplishing with this amazing book; she shares the learnings from industry leaders so you can begin a meaningful impact in your culture company as well.

I have learned a lot about Chellie. As a leader in culture development, she not only walks the walk, but she talks the talk when it comes to building a workplace environment where both employees and businesses thrive. I was excited when she asked me to sit down and collaborate with her for one of her chapters by sharing the story of how, at *Panasonic*™ Automotive, we have what we call our Culture Rebel-ution.

I appreciate that Chellie's book allows me the ability to transfer some of my knowledge to ensure you, today's business leaders, don't make the same mistakes I did. So many people were gracious enough to share their advice and the lessons they learned, so my team and I were able to build an award-winning employee culture inside *Panasonic*™. Receiving real-world advice and experiences is invaluable, and Chellie does a great job compiling not just my ideas and feedback, but many other ideas from trailblazers in the industry. What she shares in this book are the very things every leader (and organization) can use to build a successful culture where both the employees and the company thrives. I know you will enjoy it.

Stephen Childs,
CHRO, *Panasonic*™ Automotive, 2-time HR Executive of the Year, Executive Coach, Global Keynote Speaker

Preface

Culture is what causes things to happen inside an organization—both good and bad.

This book has been 20-plus years in the making. I was studying and learning the basics of building strong cultures before it became a driving force in my professional and personal business. This journey of learning all I could about culture led me to a series of conclusions. I discovered deep down we all want to feel valued. We want to make a significant difference. We want to use our skills and talents. We want happy relationships and to be respected. We want all of these things, not just in our personal lives, but in our work life also.

For 14 years, I worked on a college campus as a volunteer advisor for a national women's sorority. I had the privilege of spending most of my time with the women elected to leadership roles. If you weren't part of a sorority or fraternity in college, you might not know that they are basically run like a business. Some have budgets in the hundred thousands that are managed by 18 to 22-year-olds. There are events to plan, wellness issues to consider, and risk management decisions to be avoided, all while creating an atmosphere of community, inclusion, and collaboration. There is also drama in cohabitating environments where differences of opinion need to be heard. Each member brings their background, values, and beliefs to the table, which requires delicate and tactful considerations. For the group to be cohesive and attract new members each year, they need to build a thriving culture around a core group of values they all agreed upon. Looking back, these things are very similar to what should happen when we build human-centered cultures inside our corporate workspaces.

In my 25-plus years working for electric cooperatives, I've spoken numerous times on national, state, and regional stages about the importance of communicating our value-based system of business and how we need to connect and engage with our current and future members. In doing this work around the importance of culture, I've been recognized and honored with one of the highest awards the *National Rural Electric Cooperative Association*™ bestows, The LaBerge Award for Excellence in Strategic Communication. I tell anyone who will listen, I drank the 'co-op Kool-Aid' years ago and never looked back. I truly believe our business model can't be beaten, and we are poised to attract the most innovative and brightest to work with us as we power the daily lives and businesses of our members. That ability comes because the values we are founded on match those of people entering our workforce.

In my current role as Vice President of Communications and Public Relations for *Coweta-Fayette Electric Membership Corporation*™, I'm blessed to have a CEO who believes in creating a people-centered culture. He has supported my efforts in creating our nationally recognized internal development program, *Vision EMC*, which is now being implemented in other states across the United States. Our innovative program includes elements of professional and personal development, but its main goal is to build a collaborative work environment where employees feel they have a voice and their contribution is valued. The program is in its fifth year, and we've seen the effects on our ability to retain and promote from within as well as breaking down the 'silo mentality,' which is the unwillingness to share information between employees or across departments, and instead facilitate better communication with everyone.

I've led workshops and corporate training events on creating strong, collaborative teams, increasing engagement, and how employees can build their own strong personal brands to be a tool to edify and amplify the employee base, I've been able to test the concepts discussed on these pages and prove they are vital elements in building a people-first culture in the workplace. Using the concepts I share takes away inefficiencies and builds communication lines which are the hallmarks every successful company displays. The feedback I received from the participants in my workshops and training events also helped to solidify my definition of employee engagement and have become the cornerstone for much of this book.

When employees feel engaged, they care about the company, and they do their best work to achieve the company's goals. When employees are engaged, their #1 objective is to contribute to the company's success. Employee engagement is not about employee benefits or bonuses; it's about feeling they are a part of the organization's overall and continued success while also feeling success personally.

After the publication of my first two award-winning books, *When In Doubt, Delete It!* and *Get Noticed, Get Hired*, I began taking notice of employee engagement on a much deeper level. As I began coaching clients, I found they were interested in creating an irresistible personal career brand designed to land them in the interview seat of their ideal career. As they were upleveling their brand, it became apparent many companies were not doing the same to improve their corporate brand to engage the employees they desired. Due to this lack of corporate engagement, my clients were leaving their old positions because they felt undervalued, invisible, and disrespected.

Working with hundreds of clients reinforced how much an engaged workplace culture played into the satisfaction employees felt their careers deserved. What I've learned from them is we all have some basic needs concerning work. We want to feel like the work we do has value and that we are contributing to the success of the company we work for. Today's worker wants to know their employer appreciates the time and effort given, and it's a bonus when our personal values align with those of the company we work with.

We've all encountered different types of leaders in the workplace. There are great leaders who motivate and build up their teams, creating feelings of optimism, confidence, and safety. There's that in-between leader who is constantly throwing out one new initiative after another, making you get that sickly "you've been on a merry-go-round too long" feeling because they have no idea how to coach a team to success, but at least recognize something needs to change. Then, many of us have been on the receiving end of a soul-crushing bad leader who cares about nothing more than themselves and ticking items off a checklist.

How a leader leads is vital to implementing any kind of culture change in the workplace. Culture isn't fluff. It's an investment in the future of both the company and the employees who choose to work there. I believe that leaders have a responsibility to the people who work for them. It's their job to create an environment where both employees and the company thrive. Employees want to show up to work and be inspired, cared for, and a part of something. Leaders have the ability to do just that while creating an atmosphere of trust, innovation, creativity, and belief in the future.

Since you are reading this book, I believe you are the type

of leader who wants to engage with your employees. And, what you have before you is a complete outline on how to set up and execute the first step in the complex task of building a people-first culture in the workplace into small, manageable chunks. I wrote this book so that all leaders, in companies both large and small, could use what I have learned to, in turn, build their own people-centered cultures and develop a workforce that feels valued, encouraged, engaged, and challenged to look for opportunities to make an impactful difference.

As a culture leader within my organization and industry, I know firsthand the power of engagement and how it impacts employees personally. It fosters deeper connections, higher expectations, more accountability, respect for what each team member brings to the table, and a shared vision for the future. These things have become the foundation of the *V.A.L.U.E. Culture* formula I created to connect your most valuable asset - your employees - with the vision and mission of your company. I want you to use what I have learned to motivate today's business leaders to ditch the "but that's the way it's always been done" thinking and look for ways to cultivate innovation and relationship-building in the office so that both the employee and the company feel successful. Companies who reward, prepare, and acknowledge the contributions of their employees while including them in the vision are the ones who will outpace the competition.

I have found that a V.A.L.U.E. Culture is the key to future-proofing the workplace and provides the tools and methods leaders need to build a thriving workplace environment. That is why I've put a roadmap for workplace culture success on these pages for you to access. As you go through each chapter, you will feel the impact this type of culture can have in your workplace. My goal is that you explore every section of this book, make notes, and compare it to the environment you currently have in your workplace. As you identify areas of misalignment, focus on the steps you can take to move more toward a more engaged people-first culture. When you begin to implement improvements, you'll not only experience a positive shift in the atmosphere inside your organization, but your profits will improve as well.

It is my hope that you take action on what you see as possible in your company. We are all seeking to improve ourselves, but to do so in an environment and culture that benefits everyone in all positions is how we can improve not just our companies, but all of humanity.

Introduction

Culture is the fuel that gets things done at work. It's the way people interact and work together. It's the sum of all the beliefs, goals, values, emotions, and intentions people bring with them when they walk through the doors and hit their cubicles, assembly lines, or offices. It's what guides the decisions made in our day-to-day work expectations. It's what makes us outshine our competitors and brings new, innovative talent knocking at the door. Exceptional company culture is what ultimately determines whether a company will be successful or not.

Culture is the heart and guts of a company. It's how individual employees become a team. It's what we care about. It's what we stand for. It's how we communicate. It's how we all end up on the same path, headed to a mutually agreed-upon destination. Company culture is something that customers, clients, investors, suppliers, and even the mailman can feel when they visit an organization. It is the breath and life of the organization and the people within it who make up the team.

However, if the culture has derailed or is non-existent, the organization will never achieve its fullest potential, and the employees will be left wondering if there's more to their career than just collecting a paycheck every other week. Their hearts will not be in it, and soon enough they'll be racing out the door to find new opportunities at a place where the culture is built around the values and aspirations that align with theirs.

The workplace is changing quicker than ever before, and today's employees want to feel they have earned more than just a paycheck. Many employees wrestle with the Monday morning blues knowing they are headed to a workplace where they feel undervalued, disrespected, and stuck without an opportunity to advance or learn. Today's workers want a positive and supportive environment that aligns with their personal values. They want to feel their contribution to the success of the company is recognized and rewarded. Paychecks are only part of why they are there; connection, community, caring, and clarity of the mission all factor in.

There's never been a better time to reimagine workplace culture and the employee experience than right now. Covid-19 triggered a country-wide quitting spree. In 2021, according to the U.S. Bureau of Labor Statistics, over 47 million Americans voluntarily quit their jobs — an unprecedented mass exit from the workforce.[1] *The Great Retirement* has caused 2.6 million more retirements than expected. People are seeking a work-life balance that allows increased flexibility and have decided not to stay in the workplace as long as previous workers have done in the past.

External stress and emotional burnout are also drivers in the decision to take the "early out." [2] They have spilled over into every aspect of life - including home, social encounters, and the workplace. That has led to reduced productivity, less energy, and leaves workers feeling helpless and resentful. A strong culture can help employees separate and balance their professional and personal responsibilities and prevent individual burnout from factoring in an employee's decision to remain in the workforce or not.

As many as fifty-five percent of Generation Z and Millennial workers have stated they plan to switch jobs. They are restless and mobile. They want higher-paying positions and more flexibility. They want respect and to feel appreciated in the workplace. (³)

A whopping fifty-six percent of Gen Z workers said they would quit their jobs if it kept them from enjoying life, and forty percent said they would *rather be unemployed than unhappy working in a job they didn't like.* (⁴)

Glassdoor™ is a worldwide leader in job and company insights and has a mission of building a thriving community for workplace conversations. In their *Mission and Culture Survey*, Glassdoor found that *seventy-seven percent* of adults consider a company's culture before applying. Over 5,000 respondents said a *company's culture was more important than salary* regarding job satisfaction. (⁵)

In April 2022, CNBC™ reported *25 percent of people* who had *left a job* in the *last six months* had done so *because of the company culture.*(⁶) The workplace environment is critical. Almost 60 percent of employees polled said they have left a job or would consider leaving a job if they felt the culture was full of negative office politics. You may want to ask yourself, where does your organization fit into these statistics? How are your employees feeling compared to these industry reports? What is the trend in your office - are employees all in, or are they on their way out?

The newest term and trend emerging is the *Quiet Quitters*. These people show up at work, but they no longer actively put any effort into what they do. They perform only the minimum required to get by. They do not desire to do any extra tasks or learn new things, and don't want additional work. *Gallup™*, an American analytics and advisory company known for public opinion polls and helping leaders improve their employee and customer strategies, says *Quiet Quitters* make up at least fifty percent of today's workforce, if not more. (7)

Workforce concerns are the things nightmares are made of for business leaders because they involve the most valuable asset in the company - the employees - and can involve emotional considerations standard business metrics don't address. Based on the research and interviews for this book, even though many CEOs are struggling with environmental, supply chain, and financial concerns, I learned they still rank *culture in the workplace* in the *top three things* that keep them up at night. They all said culture is *one of their key priorities.*

It's crucial business leaders understand the significant impact workplace culture has on the success of their business because culture building can get lost in the day-to-day shuffle. Culture can flounder because it's not easy to define. If you asked 10 business leaders to define company culture, you're likely to get just as many definitions. And, let's face it, culture fixes get tossed around like the shuttlecock in a badminton game. Many managers try employee pizza parties, logoed apparel, and numerous other forms of recognition, but few ever ask their employees what's missing or what they need. That means they may not even know if there is a culture issue inside the organization. Real, lasting culture change takes more than employee appreciation events and logoed apparel. Real culture includes shared values and goals, an attitude of respect and acceptance, and an accountability feature built around an agreed-upon set of behaviors.

As a business leader, you can articulate current advertising campaigns, unique selling propositions, or what makes your product better than others. But, in today's competitive work environment, you must go much deeper. You have to make sure you are creating a workforce that feels passionately about your core values, embodies your beliefs, and acts out the behaviors that align with your expectations. When your employees feel appreciated, recognized, and rewarded, they go the extra mile to help the company reach its goals.

Thinking of company *culture as the internal brand of your company* is the best way to put it in perspective. A brand is a way a product, company, or individual is perceived based on the experience someone has with it. Internal branding is shifting the focus from how external audiences view your company to a view that focuses on core values and identity as your employees see them. Your culture, or internal brand, becomes what sets you apart from the competition. Your company culture becomes your golden differentiator. In fact, the *internal brand* is your organizational culture, and it's the most important piece you should focus on if your goal is to build a successful company.

Take a moment right now to ask yourself, "What is the internal brand of my company?" Then go a step further and consider the answers you would receive if your employees were asked the same question. Do you know how your employees describe your company when you aren't around? Can you articulate why a potential employee would want to work with you? Do you know what today's workforce craves? Can you attract the highest-level talent from Generation X, Y, and Z? Does your internal brand bring the diversity necessary in today's workplace? If you can answer all these questions, fantastic! If not, the following chapters you are about to read will help you develop a deeper understanding of what elements build a strong company culture. You'll learn how different types of culture impact the organization and why culture isn't a "one size fits all" process. You'll uncover why people-centered cultures are the strongest and most profitable, and you'll receive tools to help you get excited to begin building the unique culture your company needs.

My vision for the workplace is that it becomes a place where people bring their whole *being* to work. Where people *feel* connected to those around them and build strong, *collaborative* relationships. Where failures can be encouraged, even celebrated. It's a place where people feel *valued* and heard. In turn, high-quality work is produced, and both the company and the employee are compensated financially. Imagine if the vision I just painted became the internal brand of your company! Envision the impact it would have on future recruiting or on your ability to retain your current employees. Consider how much a unified, thriving culture would bolster productivity and catapult profits. It would be an absolute game changer in employee satisfaction, performance, higher bottom lines, and improved customer service.

This book shines the light on how entrepreneurs, C-suite executives, and others who want to achieve success can build a people-centered culture and create a business where everyone *wants* to work. It will show how to build a unique culture around a set of core values while building a system that rewards a set of behaviors designed to move the company forward. Each idea in it is designed to help enrich what is currently right with the culture inside the organization and overhaul the areas which need improvement.

If you are an entrepreneur, manager, owner, CEO, or executive, this book will give you the tools to create an engaged workforce that feels valued and rewarded while setting your company up to win in the marketplace. Each chapter outlines how you can turn your employees into your biggest asset in your quest for success. Every tool and suggestion is shared so that you can fully tap into the skills, dedication, and innovative spirit your employees bring to their workspace each day. When you cultivate a culture that keeps your people at the center, you're going to outperform your competitors and become viewed as a partner in your employee's career development path.

I can only imagine you are here because you care about your co-workers and team members, and you have the desire to recognize the value they bring to your organization in a way that aligns with the strategic direction and mission of your company. This book lays out a simple-to-follow plan that will tie your organizational vision with your profit and people-centered goals.

I invite you to implement what I have shared here and then watch as your employees shift their mindset from "got to go to work" to "get to thrive at their job." Once this happens, watch your profits and customer satisfaction levels, as well as your enjoyment in the workplace, soar to new levels of success. They say a great leader is one who not only knows the way but shows the way; building a vibrant, inclusive, people-first culture is a fundamental part of a leader's job description. Allow what you read here to help you achieve the goals and aspirations you have for your company and inspire those who show up to happily become invested and join you on the path to success.

Wishing you great success,
Chellie Phillips

How to Use This Book

Inside these pages, you'll find a playbook for building an intentional culture inside your business. As you move through each section and chapter, you'll be able to accurately identify the current state of the culture inside your workplace. You'll realize the financial and social costs bad culture has on your business's bottom line and its effect on employee morale. You'll be able to quantify and advocate for a culture-building initiative based on productivity and financial increase. Finally, you will see real-life applications of people-centered cultures in today's workplace and use the examples I provide to build your own unique internal culture. The best part is, your plan for a people-first workplace culture is just a few turns of the pages away from becoming a reality.

To make sure you get the most value, I have divided the book into three sections: *Culture Basics, Actions of Culture Builders,* and *Poised for Culture Success.* Each section is designed to help you navigate a distinctive culture change inside your organization.

Section 1, *Culture Basics*, helps you identify where your workplace culture currently stands in your organization and provides a list of ingredients needed to build a people-first workplace culture. It breaks down how a people-centered culture is centered around a core set of values and principles. It shows why you should invest in workplace culture by shining a light on the tangible (increased sales and repeat customers) and intangible (engaged employees) benefits that come from having a strong people-centered workplace. When you have a purpose, passion, and values, you can retain and attract great employees. In this section you'll find a list of questions you can share with your employees to begin the conversation and tools to help you assess where your culture is right now.

Section 2, *Actions of Culture Builders*, shares the fundamentals and key concepts you'll need to build a successful culture of your own. Here you'll see how building a strong V.A.L.U.E. Culture impacts and improves not just the business, but all the people in it. This is where you will roll up your sleeves and ascertain how you can create a winning culture amongst your current team and how to attract new employees that will take your business to the next level.

In addition, this section shows you inside the minds of culture change agents in today's workplace. You'll learn how prominent CEO's create a culture shift as well as navigate roadblocks along the way, and you'll hear from boots-on-the-ground leaders, from varying size companies, on why strong cultures are built on the V.A.L.U.E. Culture foundation.

Throughout that section, you will hear the powerful conversations I had that emphasize while workplace cultures may look different from the outside looking in, successful ones share the traits defined in this book. The wisdom from each of these individuals was so profound that I have shared their exact words, verbatim, in an engaging conversation format that allows you to imagine sharing a conversation with them over a cup of coffee or having them in your office as a valued internal consultant. I believe sharing these interviews will give you access to valuable insights which will have a huge impact on how you can successfully implement a culture change inside the walls of your company.

Section 3, *Poised for Culture Success*, contains three case studies from three very different types of organizations: *Panasonic™* Automotive, a global manufacturing company, Electric Cooperatives of America, not-for-profit electric utilities, and *King of Pops™*, a family-run gourmet popsicle company. Each one of these diverse companies and industries is navigating or has navigated a culture shift and understands the need to attract the next generation of workers. Representatives from each company share candidly about what worked, what didn't, and how they are continuing to build on their successes to reach their corporate and culture goals. Each organization is very different, but they all share the traits found in the V.A.L.U.E. Culture formula and their case studies will benefit you.

Learning and implementing the V.A.L.U.E. Culture concept into your business will be a game changer in your organization because it impacts everything from the pace of business to decision-making, to marketing and sales. To run a successful company today, it's a mistake to think culture doesn't matter. It does. Culture determines whether people want to work for or with you, and that impacts so much more than the bottom line.

At the core of a V.A.L.U.E. Culture, you will find how companies treat their employees is what truly matters. A positive V.A.L.U.E. Culture allows employees to feel like they are part of a *bigger vision* and mission, while their personal values align with the company values. The work environment becomes a place employees feel supported in every aspect of their role and trust there is a long-term place for them. When a workplace culture is built successfully, company and individual employee goals are clear, retention is high, and everyone knows exactly what they need to do to succeed. Team members feel safe enough to speak up and are rewarded for good performance while customers feel a sense of cohesion all around.

To reach your desired culture, you'll need to measure progress and consistently take the pulse of your employees. Therefore, chapter 15 is all about measuring successes and how that can translate into a return on investment (ROI) even the most thrifty of management can't ignore.

If you don't want to wait to read that far, here's a simple way you can get a glimpse at how your culture fares in your workplace right now.

Get out of your office and *watch your parking lot* if you want to see a vivid picture of the culture in your organization. Yes, the parking lot. On Monday morning, how do your employees arrive at work? Do they pull into the parking lot, feel a knot in their stomach, and give themselves a pep talk about how they can make it through the day before waiting until the last minute possible to slowly walk through the doors and settle into their cubicle ready for the work week? Do you see employees socializing and sharing conversations on their way inside? Or, is it so quiet it feels like people are trying to fly under the radar and not be seen?

You can check the parking lot once again when the clock strikes five. Do your employees leave as quickly as possible, jumping in their cars, driving off as fast as they can? Do they leave in groups, lingering in the parking lot, still engaged with each other? Do you hear laughter? What do their faces look like? Do they seem tired, frustrated, or angry?

The parking lot experiment is an oversimplified way to get a quick picture of your company culture, but it can give you a quick snapshot of where you stand and help you identify if you have an issue. This book is going to force you to ask, how does it feel to work in your company, and can you create a better environment for others to succeed in? The answer to these simple questions reveals a lot about your starting point and where you need to go moving forward.

The good news is workplace culture is adaptable and constantly evolving. It's not stagnant, nor does it have to stay the same. You'll have employees who retire, move on to other opportunities, and you'll replace them with new people who have more aligned values and ideas. That means a desire to change the culture in the workplace may not be easy; that's why, in chapter 14, I include how to overcome roadblocks and obstacles you'll encounter along the way. You won't make everyone happy. You'll face people resistant to change. Yet, knowing ahead of time what to look for and preparing for how you will deal with these issues before they occur will move you one step closer to achieving your desired outcome.

Despite what you may have been told, culture doesn't magically appear. Great cultures and their leaders need to be created and cultivated. I've dissected what great leaders bring to the table when creating great cultures and how culture thrives under such guidance. That's the V.A.L.U.E. Culture concept you'll find throughout this book. Each letter represents a trait or action needed to build a strong, thriving culture and outlines exactly what I believe are the key components in creating a culture that fulfills the needs of everyone throughout the company.

V is vision. As a business leader, it's your responsibility to cast your vision so your employees, board, and customers can clearly see how you will meet their needs. The culture you create will be based on the vision that reflects your goals, principles, and dreams.

A is accountability. Accountability doesn't only exist at the top level, in management. You must build a system that moves accountability throughout the organization. Each employee has to have buy-in in the process and recognize their role and the responsibility they have to their teammates to show up and do the things they said they will do. It's the foundation of establishing trust. Accountability is an essential element found in high-performing teams because it leads to better relationships, taking ownership, owning mistakes, and improving job satisfaction.

L is leadership. Leadership is what drives your culture initiative; it is the fuel that moves the vision throughout the organization. Leaders are the people who help create growth, set goals, provide opportunities and give recognition. And it is up to you to make sure people in those key positions have the skills and training necessary to be effective, so the initiative is successfully reached.

U is the uniqueness of each employee. Every person brings their past, present, and future to the workplace. No one knows what they have lived through in the past or are going through currently. Each person has their own set of values and beliefs. Some may be motivated by thoughts of promotion; others are happy collecting a paycheck, walking out the door at the end of the day, and not worrying about work until they arrive again in the morning. Strong, successful cultures consider each individual's experiences and seek input so that a supportive and inclusive workplace is the outcome.

E is engagement. You'll find an engaged workforce when you have a strong culture that has been woven into the fabric of the organization. This engagement leads to higher productivity, less absenteeism, less turnover, and higher job satisfaction. These are the markers any successful, profitable business would be happy to see.

I believe when companies and organizations instill the V.A.L.U.E. Culture concept and get clear on their purpose, they perform better, achieve more, and create a place where workers enjoy coming to work. Therefore, you may be tempted to start implementing each process you encounter on these pages immediately. But, may I please suggest you resist that temptation until you've read completely through each section. That may sound like an odd request, but it's important. If you've never had a culture program in your organization, or you've had numerous attempts at building employee engagement, but they didn't happen consistently, you need to regain the trust of your employee base. You need to roll out a cohesive plan that highlights well-thought-out values and behaviors and reinforces culture is something that will be prioritized and supported by management.

When you take your time implementing a new culture program, you'll gain buy-in and an understanding of how each piece is needed to create a positive culture that permeates throughout your company. That means, by the time you reach section 3, you'll have the tools necessary to build a V.A.L.U.E. Culture that is manageable and sustainable. You'll be equipped with strategies designed, so your culture is successful and co-created from all levels inside your business. Such an approach takes time, and creating an atmosphere of trust inside your employee base is vital so don't rush it.

The most important thing I want you to know is that each workplace culture is as unique as your business structure. Because of that, you can't pick up a culture from another company and decide that it is now yours. Your culture must reflect all that is unique about your business, processes, products, and people. There are no two businesses exactly alike, therefore, my goal for you, after reading this book, is that you will be able to:

- Develop a clear picture of your current work culture and gain a deeper understanding of the vision you want your employees to be a part of.
- Utilize the V.A.L.U.E. Culture framework to help focus

areas of growth and determine the opportunities you have for improvement.

- Create and implement a series of tangible steps designed to create a workplace where both your employees and your company thrives.
- Once you understand each of these points, you too will be able to successfully create a culture movement inside your organization that drives profits and employee satisfaction.

Regardless of any past approaches or attempts at building culture, you now have this book, filled with tools and tactics to build an extraordinary V.A.L.U.E.-filled culture inside your organization. Every chapter is packed with ideas, strategies, and real-world learning so that your business becomes more than a business. Your business will blossom into a place where people can't wait to show up each day and grow into such a powerhouse your competitors are clamoring to learn your secret sauce. And, as you begin to implement what you have learned, you will feel a sense of pride and know that through your leadership, you have created an environment where each person feels part of a team committed to something greater than themselves.

Knowing that you now have in your hands the tool you need to create the culture you desire, Let's dive in and get started!

SECTION 1:

Culture Basics

Customers will never love a company until the
employees love it first.
- SIMON SINEK

As a business leader, it's important you understand how significant the role of culture is for people entering the workforce and those in transition looking for a better place to work. Before a business leader can build a V.A.L.U.E. Culture, they need to fully understand the basic necessities and what goes into a culture that brings positive results to the workplace. They need to think deeply about why they are in business and how they want to impact their employees' and customers' lives. A clear why is the fundamental force behind the corporate vision, which is the key component in creating a workplace culture designed for lasting success.

Having a V.A.L.U.E. Culture environment addresses the needs and wants of people entering the workforce and those in long-term employment with the company. A defined culture goes beyond a mission statement, gimmicks, and quick one-and-done employee appreciation moments. Culture is much more than that. It includes an agreed-upon set of values, accountability, and a dedication to engaging employees, so they feel seen and view themselves as a part of the company's success.

Today's workers want to feel their work matters, and a V.A.L.U.E. Culture reinforces that feeling and gives employees a sense of belonging. It is vital for today's leaders to recognize the importance culture has on the success of their organization because culture is at the core and heart of all businesses; it is the life force that connects the people with the company.

When a culture is built correctly, a business will see positive employee engagement and profitability impacts. There are also several intangible benefits like increased confidence in abilities, a sense of community, willingness to try new processes, and sharing of ideas your organization will receive when culture is curated and implemented correctly.

Often, when I first step into an organization I create an assessment to get a clear picture of where their culture is currently. I see how the culture is working or not working based on everyone's understanding of core values, the engagement level of supervisors and employees, and the quality of cohesive teamwork. This first step becomes vital in guiding the management team toward a shared culture vision that comes from identifying the areas where feelings of job satisfaction can be improved and collaboration is encouraged. By showing how starting with the basics will impact not just engagement, but productivity and profitability, it's not hard to see why investing in workplace culture is a key component for business success.

When you follow the V.A.L.U.E. Culture formula, you encourage open communication and feedback, allowing all voices to be heard, and you create a culture of trust and transparency that fosters collaboration and innovation. That helps to recognize every employee's unique perspective and contribution which leads to a stronger, more engaged workforce, and better business outcomes as well.

As your culture trainer, I revel in providing real-world

guidance that supports your goals. So, I encourage you to follow this V.A.L.U.E. formula and create a workplace culture that recognizes each and every employee. I want to see you succeed and reach the full potential of your business.

Yet, before we can fully dive in and implement big changes, I first want you to understand the core values and purpose of your organization, so that you fully comprehend the importance of building a people-centered workplace culture. Knowing the why behind your culture Rebel-ution will be the difference between a superficial attempt at culture building and a genuine, long-lasting transformation of your workplace. It will help align your organization's values with the needs and desires of your employees and create an environment where they feel valued, and enthusiastic to come to work every day. This will help generate excitement in your employees when you involve them in the process from the start.

As you begin to unpack the basic ingredients needed for a V.A.L.U.E. Culture and read the takeaways from some of today's brightest business leaders, you'll, without a doubt, come away with a list of the foundational ways to begin implementing a more cohesive culture in your workforce.

In the following seven chapters, you will discover the secret ingredients to start building an incredible culture. These are the basic building blocks all successful companies need to create a workplace where both the employees and the company achieve success. Use these chapters to begin assessing your own work environment and look for the ways you can involve your whole team in creating a culture that highlights the uniqueness of your employees, that revolves around an agreed-upon core set of values, and has clearly defined behaviors designed to make both your employees and the company successful.

CHAPTER 1:

Why Invest in Your Culture?

As I sit down to write about workplace culture, I can't help but feel a twinge of nostalgia. You see, I've had my fair share of jobs over the years, some good and some bad, but the ones that truly stand out in my memory are the ones with great workplace culture.

I remember the first time I walked into the office of a company I had just started working for. I was nervous like anyone would be on their first day, but the moment I stepped inside, I felt a wave of warmth and positivity come over me.

The people were friendly, the atmosphere upbeat, and there was a sense of camaraderie that I had never experienced before in a workplace. As I settled in, I realized just how much workplace culture can affect our daily lives. It wasn't just about enjoying going to work every day (which was certainly a nice perk). It was about feeling like I was part of a team, that my contributions were valued, and that I was making a difference.

On the flip side, I remember the feeling of dread that would sink into my stomach as I walked into some of the less-than-ideal workplaces I've been a part of. The negativity, the toxicity, the lack of support or recognition... it all added up and took a toll on my emotional well-being.

That's why I believe that workplace culture isn't just a buzz-word or trendy topic—it's a vital component of our lives. We spend so much of our time at work, and the culture we experience can have a profound impact on our overall happiness and fulfillment.

As we explore the topic of workplace culture together, I invite you to reflect on your own experiences and how they have shaped you.

Most business leaders recognize culture is important. However, views on culture's 'role' in a business's success vary greatly. Some upper management think of it as *soft, feel-good fluff*. Others view culture as a key to high performance and a productivity driver, but few know that a V.A.L.U.E. Culture can build an even stronger organization. Culture isn't dependent on the size of the business. A strong culture can help a small business grow and expand; likewise, even large businesses can see improvement in the metrics used most often to measure, manage, and communicate results.

Building a workplace culture is necessary today and has a definite impact on the profitability of your business. *Why?* Because workplace culture, either positive or negative, impacts your ability to gain repeat customers. Possessing a bad culture in the workplace can destroy a business almost immediately.

Deciding to bring culture into your business and give it a role, is the fundamental first step you can make. It will ensure that your workplace becomes a positive and productive environment for everyone involved. When you intentionally invest in your team and take the time to form the culture you desire, you are creating a shared sense of purpose, values, and goals that can inspire and motivate your employees to do their best work.

David Branderhorst is a serial entrepreneur who left the

constraints of corporate America and has since started multiple businesses over the past decade, growing several of them to a million dollars plus in sales. He's the winner of the coveted 2 Comma Club Award, given by *ClickFunnels™* to select entrepreneurs who generate well over a million dollars through a single marketing funnel. His current focus as a business coach and co-founder of *Design, Launch, Grow™*, is helping new entrepreneurs build successful people-first businesses around their message. I sat down with David to discuss the importance of investing in culture and the outcomes that create in both your people and the bottom line. David was both clear and concise on how culture sets the tone for how a team interacts with each other and the clients and how that works together, so everyone achieves success.

Q. David, is culture a necessary investment for any business owner or leader?

I believe one of the biggest challenges companies face is convincing prospects to become customers. Culture is a key driver in creating a memorable customer experience for all the right reasons. Convincing someone who has never purchased from you to give you a chance can be an expensive and challenging venture.

Q. Companies like Amazon™, Netflix™, and Walmart™ invest heavily in brand awareness and customer acquisition. In fact, it is a common practice for large companies to spend $100 or more in advertising to simply get a customer to purchase a $20 product they might make a profit of $3-4 on. They are losing significant sums of money on each of those transactions; it seems preposterous. Why would they do that?

Once a customer makes a purchase, the odds of them returning and making additional purchases increase dramatically. While these companies may lose on the front end, they make it up on the back end with repeat business. But there's a catch. I tell people that repeat customers only happen if a strong culture exists.

Think about it this way. Let's say you visit a store for the first time. They had a sale on a needed product, so you decided to try it. While you were there, you asked a team member for help, and they were rude and short with you. No one on the team seemed to smile. The store felt disorganized and haphazard. You decide to make your purchase and never return.

Q. Therefore, a customer experiencing a negative culture impacts your ability to gain repeat business?

Exactly! The company lost its repeat business and now must invest additional money to find new customers. As you can tell from the math, it won't be long before the business shuts its doors.

ENGAGEMENT MATTERS

Poor employee engagement leads to loss of sales and customer retention. Did you catch that in David's comments? Think about your company for a moment. Do you struggle to have repeat customers? Do you keep an eye on your website reviews to see what is being shared online about your business? Do your employees go the extra mile to ensure your customers' experience is top-notch, or do they just go through the motions? How your customer feels at your business and after they leave is vital and directly correlates with the culture you create, which impacts your ability to generate profits.

To gauge the level of your employee engagement and set a starting benchmark for improvement, consider how you would answer the following questions:

- Does your team enjoy coming to work?
- Are they just putting in their hours to get a paycheck?
- Are they invested in your mission?
- Do they see serving and helping customers as a joy and look for ways to go the extra mile regarding service?
- Do they look at their daily tasks as annoyances?

Your team's engagement level is the first of the basic V.A.L.U.E. Culture fundamentals and a direct reflection of the impact your organization has on the customer experience in either a positive or negative way.

Knowing the importance of the customer experience, I asked David to share a bit more.

Q. David, how deeply are customer perceptions impacted by the level of employee engagement?

Company culture greatly impacts your customer experience, which falls on the back of your organization's leaders.

If the customer feels respected, valued, and cared for, they will likely become repeat buyers and loyal to your brand. If not, they will leave as soon as someone makes them a better offer. If you invest in your team and help them feel valued and important, the trickle-down effect on your customers and bottom line will be significant.

Monitoring your customer experience and keeping a check on the pulse of your employee engagement level is a necessity in today's business environment. As a leader, you have the ability to influence and help correct culture issues which are impacting your bottom line. That influence is increased when a leader begins to learn more about their team and the emotions, values, and experience they bring to the workplace with them each day. David agreed and feels the difference between good and bad leaders comes with their willingness to connect on a human level with their team members.

Q. How do you think leadership influences workplace culture?

Culture is a top-down creation. It starts with your leaders if you want a positive culture where customers feel valued and keep coming back. A strong leader sees their team as the people they are responsible for serving. The individuals under their charge are the ones who make everything happen.

The leader's job is to ensure they are fully equipped and have everything they need to succeed. Strong leaders also pay attention to what's happening in their employees' lives. If one of them is going through a difficult stretch, they reach out and offer assistance. They truly care about and shepherd their people.

While some of this is just about being a good human being, they also know this creates an engaged workforce. And, an engaged employee looks for ways to create the best, most efficient solution possible. They voluntarily seek out alternatives when they know something could be better. They find ways to save the company money and serve the customer at a higher level. Simply put, they care.

Q. To contrast this, how does a poor leader see their team? Do they see them as people who are there to serve the leadership?

To them, team members are resources they use to get them what they want. They have little empathy for their lives and don't care to know them as individuals. In this scenario, the team members feel unappreciated and unvalued.

They don't see a future for themselves in the organization and are simply there to earn a paycheck. When problems arise, they move past them. They aren't interested in improving the organization because they don't see themselves there for the long term. If they feel undervalued and unappreciated, that directly affects how they engage with your customers. A happy team member creates satisfied customers that come back again and again. An unhappy team member treats customers poorly and leaves them never wanting to return.

Think back to a time when you had a bad experience at a company, with an employee who didn't seem to care about their experience or yours. That interaction may have caused you to immediately look for the nearest exit and vow never to return! We've all had those negative experiences with companies or employees who just didn't seem to care about our needs, our satisfaction, or our experience as a customer or client.

Maybe it was a rude salesperson who made you feel like you were wasting their time, or a customer service representative who was more interested in following a script than actually helping you solve your problem. Or, it could be a company that made promises they couldn't keep, or otherwise didn't deliver on the quality of their product or service.

Whatever the case, these negative experiences stick with us for a long time and can even turn us off from doing business with a particular company or industry altogether. That's why it's important for businesses to prioritize creating positive, engaging, and satisfying environments for their customers. And, one of the first ways you can do that is by actively working on the culture inside your company. Think about how those bad experiences made you feel. How can you take those lessons and incorporate them into the values and behaviors you want your workplace culture to nurture?

EMPLOYEE CLIENT RELATIONSHIPS MATTER

While working with my coaching clients, I've heard dozens of examples of employees making the decision to leave a workplace because leaders held employees accountable for losing a repeat customer, despite failing to equip them with the ability to address customer concerns proactively. Others shared they felt invisible at work. Their supervisor had no clue what was happening in their lives and didn't seem to care as long as a certain quota was met.

I noticed how few of my clients understood where their role felt in the overall mission of the company. There was no sharing of values, no offering of feedback or idea collaboration, and no known plan for progression. All of these things added up to frustration or, worse, complacency. The common theme was, "Does it really matter to anyone if I show up every day?"

It's easy to see how that feeling of invisibility diminishes any desire to go over above in the service provided to customers. That's why building a V.A.L.U.E. Culture around a core set of beliefs and expectations is so valuable, no matter the size of your company. Workplace culture must be woven into the fabric of your business, whether you're a small business or a global manufacturing giant. Having a strong culture gives you a competitive edge. I asked David if his experience led to the same conclusion.

Q. I know that workplace culture is relevant no matter the size of your company, whether you're a Fortune 500 small business or an entrepreneur just getting started. David, what has been your experience?

Most small businesses don't have a multi-million-dollar advertising budget to work with. As a result, they need to find other ways to grow. One of the best ways is through referrals. Let's say there's a new restaurant in your town, and you decide to check it out. Upon opening the door, you are greeted by a festive environment and a smiling face that welcomes you. You are promptly seated at your table and given an ice-cold glass of water without asking.

The waitress explains the menu simply and makes a couple of recommendations. You make your selection and are pleasantly surprised at how good the food tastes. The waitress is attentive to you throughout the evening, and you give her a nice tip and think about the pleasant experience.

The next day you meet up with some of your friends. One of them mentions the restaurant that just opened. You quickly pipe in with a glowing recommendation and tell all of them they should consider going there. By creating a culture where the customer was valued, team members were happy to be at work and do their jobs with excellence, and you just picked up some extra customers without any extra effort.

Q. What would happen if you thought about that situation in reverse?

Have you ever been to a restaurant and had a bad experience? The food tasted bland. You had to waive your arm multiple times to get the waiter to give you any service. When they did come over, it felt like you were an annoyance to them.

When it comes time for your check, the waiter suddenly becomes friendly and starts talking about how hard it has been for them and how they are struggling to get by. You feel a tinge of guilt because you wouldn't leave much of a tip. Instead, you leave a moderate-sized tip and vow never to return. Now, which restaurant do you think will still be there in a year?

Other than bad reviews or lack of referrals, bad culture can negatively impact your organization. Too many times, business owners/leaders focus solely on the bottom line, getting more sales and saving money.

Q. That leads us back to the importance of investing in culture and treating it as a revenue generator. Why is it that some business leaders are still hesitant to commit funds to a culture initiative?

Usually, a business leader's first question is, What is the ROI? In other words, what can I expect to see in revenue if I spend this much money? While this is a sound business practice, too often, the decision-maker becomes too narrow in their focus. They want to see a direct one-to-one connection between the money they spend and the money they make in return.

This narrow focus can cause business leaders to miss the bigger picture and miss the indirect impact their decisions have on the bottom line.

Q. CEOs have a difficult job balancing their investment in Human Capital with other business metrics. After all, without people, you don't have a business. What are business leaders and CEOs missing?

I love what you said there, Human Capital. Leaders fail to acknowledge one fundamental truth: Businesses are made up of human beings. When you treat them like machines, you remove humanity from the process, and the heart goes out of your team. Their creative energy and spirit get removed. In its place is a spirit of obligation and fear.

Q. Yes! Exactly! What usually follows is a string of problems. Can you tell me some of them?

By choosing to ignore culture in your business, you can expect to face the following issues:
- High turnover
- Low engagement
- Poor morale
- Lackluster customer service

It doesn't take a rocket scientist to realize all these things will dramatically impact your bottom line and ability to grow your business. You must understand that running a successful business involves becoming a strong leader. Strong leaders create great teams. Great teams generate happy repeat customers, happy repeat customers generate additional income, feed your bottom line, and make future success possible.

You may want to take a moment and review David's list to identify which ones are true for you. Bringing culture into your business and giving it a role is the first step toward creating a workplace that people want to be part of. It's a decision that can have far-reaching effects on the success of your business and the happiness and well-being of your employees.

EMPLOYEE INVESTMENT

Your employees are your biggest company asset. As such, you need to look at culture building with the same mindset you would if asked to invest in new equipment that would boost your revenue and increase your productivity. Investing in your human capital is necessary for building a V.A.L.U.E. Culture, and will provide you with a tangible return on your investment in them.

Any amount of investment in your human capital will turn into an increase in your customer satisfaction as well. Since employees have direct contact with your customers, the outcome of that interaction directly relates to how they feel about organizational leadership, their ability to make decisions, and if they are empowered to solve problems for customers no matter the size of your company. Their level of satisfaction within your organization will be reflected in your profit/loss statement at the end of the year.

While there may not be a physical line item in your yearly budget labeled culture, the cost is worth it. In fact, you may want to put that phrase, the cost is worth it, on a sticky note on your computer monitor, so you remember to maintain, retain, and scale your culture. Building a strong workplace culture requires a different way of thinking and goes beyond the typical allotment for tangible things.

If you want to invest in human capital, you have to get to know the human. To dig in further and better understand why spending time developing human capital and investing in culture is a key success ingredient for businesses, I interviewed Adam Schwartz, the founder of *The Cooperative Way*™, a consulting firm with the mission *To Help Co-ops Succeed*. He helps cooperatives define their mission, intentionally create organizational purpose, and build a cooperative culture using a 'seven-step' process. *The Cooperative Way*™ is a strategic partner with CDS Consulting Co-op, a shared services cooperative of 35 cooperative consultants. I wanted to use Adam's experience in leading organizations to proactively create, reenergize or maintain high-functioning cultures to emphasize the importance of investing in your employees.

Q. Adam, when it comes to the importance of investing in your employees, how do you learn what makes people tick?

I like asking questions. I like to get to know people and what makes them tick. What are their life experiences? For example, if I'm talking to a leader and find out they have farming in their background, I would ask them, "how did you increase productivity on your farm?" They might say, "Oh, it's simple; I fertilized my soil."

Then I tie that in and connect it to culture building. How? Fertilizing is nurturing the soil to get higher yields. They were cultivating, right? They know if they do that as a preparatory step, it will yield a better result. With *culture*, you can draw the same analogy. You need to do certain things to cultivate how people will feel in the workplace.

Q. Bottom line, you invest your time by asking your employees about their lives—their experiences. That can be a big benefit to the employee as well, right?

Asking them about their experience is connecting. I like to know how they would describe their culture. As they talk about jobs that they've had in the past, they will share about jobs that they've liked and jobs that they didn't.

Now, when they share the story about "why didn't they like the job," that will give you a big clue on how to move the conversation forward with them. As a consultant, I cannot tell anyone to do anything. I have the authority and ability to suggest that they consider something and hopefully lead them on the trail that they will take themselves. One of my favorite quotes from Gandhi is, "You must be the change you wish to see in the world."

As you can see, Adam shares how investing in getting to know your team and employees builds the foundation for you to start a culture shift inside your organization. I'll share more insights from Adam in the chapters to come.

Understanding the relationship between an employee's mindset and attitude, along with how they can impact customer engagement and directly impact the company's ability to produce profits, is a pivotal point in building a workforce culture that leads to a thriving business. It begins with connecting on a human level with the employees you supervise. Follow that by empowering employees with the ability to find solutions for your customers, and you have the first steps of a strong culture build.

One of my clients shared with me that once she began to notice her employees more and learn their stories, she noticed a significant shift in the level of trust in the workplace. Suddenly, her employees seemed more engaged, more interested, and more committed to their work.

It's not a secret that building trust with your employees is crucial to creating a positive and productive work environment. But what many supervisors don't realize is that getting to know your employees on a personal level can be one of the most effective ways to build that trust. When you take the time to learn about your employees' lives outside of work - their interests, hobbies, families, and goals - you're showing them you care about them as people, not just as workers. This can help foster a sense of belonging and connection, and make your employees feel more invested in the success of your company. Furthermore, when you have a better understanding of your employees' personalities, strengths, and challenges, you can tailor your management style to better suit their needs, just like my client did. This leads to better communication, more effective problem-solving, and a more harmonious workplace overall.

As we finalize this chapter, think about your people, and remember, human capital is what you are investing in. Keep your team as your focus, and you will start to see your awareness increase and your culture begin to shift.

Investing both in the individual and the culture will result in outcomes that will leave your competition wondering how you're surging past them. That means, to all the leaders out there, I encourage you to take the time to get to know your employees on a personal level. Learn their stories, show interest in their lives, and create an environment where everyone feels valued and supported. It may take a little extra effort, but the rewards—in the form of increased trust, loyalty, and productivity—are well worth it.

CHAPTER 2:

V.A.L.U.E. Culture: A People-First Mindset

Purpose and culture go hand in hand. Purpose captures *why* a company does *what* it does. Having a purpose when it comes to culture is the most effective way to improve your business outcomes and propel your employee's growth forward. Purpose within the culture is *the glue* that binds employees and leadership together to begin creating a people-first mindset in everyone.

In chapter one, you were introduced to the concept of human capital and thinking about culture as an investment in your business. There's no misunderstanding that you are in business to make money, and how well you do that is defined by the culture you create.

As you read further, you'll clearly see that defining a people-first mindset while building a workplace culture is what keeps people committed and drives profits upward. To reinforce this concept, I want to introduce you to Harry Hynekamp, Vice President of Guest Experiences with *AMB Sports and Entertainment™*. Harry Hynekamp is headquartered in Atlanta, Georgia. I knew I had to interview Harry so that you could see how everything shifts when we define our purpose and focus on a people-first mindset and profits that aren't lost in the process.

Harry is part of the *Arthur M. Blank Family of Businesses* (BFOB)™. In addition to the *Arthur M. Blank Family Foundation*™, the BFOB portfolio includes the *National Football League's Atlanta Falcons*™, *Major League Soccer's Atlanta United*™, the state-of-the-art *Mercedes-Benz*™ Stadium, leading golf retailer *PGA TOUR Superstore*™, and *AMB*™ *West* in Montana which includes numerous stunning for-profit and non-profit ranches.

Harry said, "Passion, purpose, and profits are core elements in creating successful associates, fans, guests, customers, and business relationships." The three P's - passion, purpose, and profits- work in tandem as you build a people-first culture. One does not diminish the importance of another. I am excited for you to discover how Harry explains that when you have these three core elements in your business, you create an atmosphere where employees feel valued and your business becomes financially successful.

Q. Harry, please share about the concept of Passion, Purpose, and Profits.

Well, that's something that has stuck with me ever since the first time I heard Arthur Blank explain it as well as his recommending the reading of Viktor Frankl's famous book *"Man's Search for Meaning."* When Arthur speaks, he often speaks from the perspective of *what's our whole purpose being here on this planet? It's to repair the world.*

And, I agree; that's truly what we're all here to do. It's about passion, purpose, and profits. It's not just about profits. It's about those three things. It's about doing the right things for the right reasons and living with those results.

You know from the name, V.A.L.U.E. Culture is going to be value-based. As you build and strategize about the culture inside your business, it's going to be necessary for you to decide on your set of guiding values as well. One thing that makes this set of values successful is their simplicity, along with their impact. You'll see other examples of that scattered throughout this book as we go forward. But first, let's find out how Harry, along with his team, incorporate servant leadership and philanthropic measures into their core culture.

Q. Harry, will you summarize the core values the Blank Family of Businesses is built on?

Sure, 1) put people first, 2) include everyone, 3) lead by example, 4) listen and respond, 5) innovate continuously, and 6) give back to others. It's this whole *servant mindset.*

It's no accident that in key business meetings, all the businesses are represented, including the Arthur M. Blank Family Foundation. I think that's unique because you have a family foundation that's sitting alongside for-profit businesses. That's the whole connection to passion, purpose, and profits brought to life.

It's also the perspective of what we as associates are all a part of trying to make the world a better place, repair the world, and do the right things for the right reason. It's about ensuring all profitable businesses are also purposeful, right? And, it's inspiring to work for Arthur because he himself has committed to The Giving Pledge.

Q. For clarification, will you share what is the Giving Pledge?

Absolutely. Created by Warren Buffett, Melinda French

Gates, and Bill Gates, the Giving Pledge is a public commitment by the ultra-wealthy to give away the majority of their wealth back to the community. Arthur has publicly pledged ninety-five percent. So, for all of our *for-profit* businesses, it's pretty easy to wake up and go to work each and every day because it's exciting to know the value that we create, the profit that we can generate, from creating great experiences for fans, guests, and customers, gets channeled back to making the world a better place.

This engine of passion, purpose, and profits continues to heal the world. We're all operating in this ecosystem of good. It's why the Blank Family of Businesses operate under the same core values and Arthur Blank's latest book "*Good Company*" is an absolute must-read for anyone looking to build a successful and thriving business that makes a difference and one you can be proud to work for, be a part of.

The *Arthur M. Blank Family Foundation* focused on topics I care about, specifically democracy, youth development, the environment, mental health and well-being, and an enduring commitment to the Westside of Atlanta, the birthplace of civil rights. In terms of their strategic initiatives, all are geared toward making the world a better place. That's how the businesses fit together and align around the philosophy that purpose and profits can go together and repair the world.

Underlying for me are two things, 1) our Core Values and 2) a *servant philosophy* from a leadership perspective. It's taking the traditional hierarchy of an organizational pyramid and structure and basically flipping it completely on its head.

Q. So, it is like an inverted pyramid? Tell me more about that, Harry.

In the inverted pyramid, leaders are here to serve associates, team members, fans, guests, and customers. It's the circle of life for our and any great and meaningful business. If we take care of our team members, if we take care of our associates, and if we take care of each other, then they will take care of our fans, guests, and customers.

It's the experiences our associates create, whether it's in the *PGA Tour Superstore*™, at a sporting event, or at a ranch, whatever it is. That's where we create value for our customers, fans, and guests. That's what gives us the ability to expand our fan base, create loyalty, create advocacy, create the ability to design premium experiences, and drive revenues and profits. It all circles back to making the world a better place.

Arthur will always say, we do nothing of great value alone. The only way we bring value is by working together. That's when we're at our best.

You'll read more from Harry as we continue, but I hope this plants the seed of how passion, purpose, and profits, along with a strong vision, are vital to building a V.A.L.U.E. Culture. These cornerstone themes provide the foundation for each step moving forward. Focusing on these elements will provide a strong connection between leaders and team members. Without that connection between leaders and teams, your culture-building effort will likely fail. Connecting with your team and placing emphasis on the human element comes with an expectation of strong communication. Without communication, the people-first focus of your culture might be lost. When both employees and leaders feel heard and understood, the culture you create will be built on a solid foundation. In fact, listening and communicating is such a key piece to successfully implementing a culture shift that you'll find a whole chapter dedicated to how you can do both effectively in chapter 12.

You may want to reflect on a time in your work history when you felt heard and recognized. Remember how that felt when you finally spoke up about something that was bothering you at work, and instead of being ignored or dismissed, your thoughts and feelings were acknowledged and validated. It was like a weight had been lifted off your shoulders, and you felt seen and appreciated for who you were and what you had to offer. That sense of recognition and support is so important, and it can make all the difference in how we feel about ourselves and our work.

STRENGTH FOUND IN PEOPLE-FIRST CULTURES

The stronger the culture inside your organization is, the more employees understand their job expectations and can see themselves as part of your organization's future. Employees do this when they see your vision and purpose clearly. When the company's purpose or vision ties in with its personal values and purpose, the more engaged they become.

Culture and purpose are heavily linked to your business's brand. It's how both employees and customers begin to talk about your company. Purpose and vision cross generational lines, and since today's workforce contains a mix of at least three generations (Baby Boomers, Gen X, Gen Y, and Gen Z), your internal brand is a way you can create a feeling of community inside the office. No matter the generational mix, today's workforce wants to work with companies with a strong purpose. What employees experience inside the walls of the office is what they share with family and friends outside the office. That connection will be a filter through which the world looks and forms opinions about the organization.

Think about the companies you visit time and time again or

the business you can't wait to do business with. Ask yourself why you have these feelings. What made you aspire to go there, work there, or shop there? I am certain it is because these companies have managed to create a compelling and inspiring brand that resonates with your values and aspirations. They have not only built a great product or service, but they have cultivated a strong culture that celebrates innovation, creativity, and excellence.

Perhaps you were impressed by their mission and vision, or maybe you were drawn to their unique approach to problem-solving. Maybe you were inspired by the way they treat their employees and the investment they make in their growth and development.

Ultimately, what sets these companies apart is their ability to connect with customers and employees on an emotional level. They understand that people are not just looking for a job, they want a good fit. They left a job because they felt replaceable or their new job didn't meet their needs or deliver what they were sold during the interview process.

This feeling of disconnection isn't anything new for today's workers. According to *Gallup*™, over half of the individuals who leave a job leave because no one ever talked to them about their job satisfaction or the future they had inside the company. Since they didn't hear about a future, they decided there wasn't one there for them.

Creating a V.A.L.U.E. Culture inside your organization makes you more likely to succeed in building the workforce you need because it captures the vision and ideas of the leadership team and *generates an atmosphere of value and gratitude* for the employees, inspiring them to want to contribute to the overall success of the organization by meeting and exceeding their day-to-day work requirements and responsibilities.

Building the right workforce involves more than just

checking off a set of skills or having a certain amount of experience. It involves taking the time to make sure the person you place in a position not only has the skill for the job but that they also are a culture fit. To do that, you need to understand what's on the mind of today's job seekers. That prompted me to ask Mark Allred, Director of *Talent Development and Growth for Reveal Global Intelligence*™ and award-winning host of *The Career PROgression Podcast*. At Reveal Global Intelligence, they believe employers should start an internal discussion about hiring with a single question, "Shouldn't recruiting focus on what's most important - the lives of the candidates we seek?" This human-centered approach to recruiting is why I share what Mark and his team have discovered about the wants and needs of today's job seekers. For many employers, he says, factoring in the "outside the office" world of potential candidates is a new approach.

> *Q. Mark, it seems like today's workforce is smart about what they want in their careers and work environment. They want to work hard but want to be appreciated. Is this the same thing you are seeing?*

It's true. Today's workforce is smart about what they want. They don't necessarily believe ping pong tables and bean bag chairs make great culture, even if *Google*™ and *Facebook*™ are posting saying this is how they treat their employees.

I think they're smarter than you think. They see those things, and I think they're intrigued by them, but they aren't necessarily as enchanted by that as some folks would have you believe. It's all fun to think that, but if you have a ping-pong table in an office with a manager who is still overbearing and doesn't pay attention to your needs, it won't make anyone want to stay.

Ping-pong is just a little release for a little while, right?

As Mark so eloquently shares, culture isn't a gimmick, and smart business owners treat it as a valuable investment. Before learning about culture, many business owners find themselves focusing primarily on the mechanics of their business: managing finances, improving operational efficiency, and increasing revenue. While these are all important aspects of running a successful business, they often overlook the crucial role culture plays in shaping the long-term success of their organization. Without a strong culture, businesses may struggle to attract talent, foster innovation and creativity, and build a loyal customer base. Today's worker is hitting the market after being given plenty of time to ponder what's right or missing from the workplace.

After being sent home thanks to the Covid-19 pandemic and watching the *Great Resignation* unfold, companies have been left wondering whether anyone is ready to go back to work. The pandemic fundamentally changed the way people view work and their priorities. To address these changing expectations, companies need to re-evaluate their workplace policies and culture. Mark had great insight on this very topic.

Q. Are people ready to return to work?

Here's an interesting thing I read. This generation is open to being back in the office. There was one young lady who started her career in Covid-19. She had to do it remotely because she couldn't be in the office. The way she described it to me was

(It was) like my career was a video game. I was just sitting at home playing this game. That was my career, and I didn't like it. I wanted to be among people and things.

So not to say that this generation isn't also intrigued by the idea of working at home, but I don't think they're as much as some folks might think.

Q. *Tell me more about what you mean.*

I think they are savvy in understanding what culture truly is. They want to be respected at the end of the day. They want to be heard. They want to have the opportunity to have the freedom to make some mistakes but also be coached and mentored when that happens.

As Mark so wonderfully shared, people need to feel valued, and the culture should reflect that. Feeling valued means better engagement, wherein the mental health of everyone is at a higher level of satisfaction. A strong culture inspires, motivates, and encourages collaboration and teamwork, creating a strong sense of purpose and vision that adds up to a healthier, more productive relationship between an employer and employee. As I have said before, employees are the backbone of a business; the feeling of being valued means higher productivity and a higher likelihood the employee will stay with your organization. The more committed employees are to their work, the more they have a positive impact on your business brand with both prospective clients and future employees.

You'll read more from Mark later in this chapter when we expound on the idea of *meaningful work*. When you build a V.A.L.U.E. Culture, the act of connecting with and listening to your team creates an atmosphere in the workplace where employees feel their daily work effort is appreciated and gives them a sense of fulfillment; this fosters their purpose in the company. You'll see the benefit multiplied throughout your organization when you accomplish this sense of value and purpose. Valued employees work harder, stay with the company longer, and are more committed to helping you fulfill the company's vision. That, in turn, increases employee confidence in themselves and their position within the organization.

Valuing employees is not a new concept. However, the way you go about it is changing. Employees want to be treated as individuals and not just spreadsheet numbers or placeholders in cubicles. It's up to you, as a business leader, to provide opportunities for growth and development, foster open communication, and instill that feeling of value in them. Through people-first culture-building efforts, you're less likely to need the services of a recruiter and more likely to have employees who are keen to be your brand representatives, write and share glowing reviews, and make referrals so you can choose from a pool of potential employees who are primed to share the same ideas and beliefs as your current workforce.

When you grow a V.A.L.U.E. Culture, employees are eighty-seven percent *less* likely to leave for other opportunities. People feel valued by companies that place a high emphasis on development and mission alignment. As a personal branding coach focused on career development and advancement, I've worked with hundreds of individuals who were contemplating leaving their current employer and seeking a new opportunity. In over sixty percent of the onboarding interviews, my clients told me the company had stopped training and educating them. They felt stagnated. They felt ignored. They felt that once they had completed an onboarding process, the company no longer cared if they grew professionally. This held true whether the person was a mid-level employee or moving into a senior leadership role. While those in leadership positions tended to have opportunities to receive some additional training through conference attendance, many said what they received during those events didn't correlate to the skills they wanted or needed to improve to be better at their job.

While purpose is a piece of your culture, it must be something employees see lived by and emulated in each of their supervisors and the CEOs of the company. The employees with more profound roles in the company are examples to everyone else, and this needs to be reflected in day-to-day interactions. Employees aren't the only ones looking and listening to see how companies are fulfilling their purpose and how their core values align with worldly matters. Lenders are checking out what you and your employees are saying. Competitors are also paying close attention to how your company is fulfilling its purpose and how your core values align with worldly matters. In today's business landscape, companies that are seen as ethical, socially responsible, and environmentally conscious are often at a competitive advantage.

Leaders of other companies are also keeping a close eye on how you and your employees are representing your brand, as they know that a strong reputation is crucial for attracting top talent, establishing partnerships, and building trust with customers.

In addition, investors and stakeholders are increasingly looking for companies that not only provide financial returns, but also demonstrate a commitment to creating long-term value for society and the environment. They want to see that companies are taking a responsible approach to governance, risk management, and sustainability.

Therefore, it's important to recognize that the way a company conducts itself in the world has a far-reaching impact beyond just your immediate employees and customers. As companies are being driven to track environmental, social, and governance (ESG) responsibilities, it's more important than ever for employees to see, hear and reflect your values when they share about your company. By being mindful of your purpose and values while working to align them with the concerns of the broader world, you can not only create a more successful and fulfilling organization, but also contribute to a better future for everyone.

Organizations that fail to notice and address what is taking place in their work environment will feel the impact sooner rather than later in the form of higher absenteeism, higher rates of burnout, and increasingly negative impact on your external company brand because employees are sharing their feelings of disgruntlement to anyone who will listen both online and in person. It's alarming to think only half of today's workforce would recommend their company's products or services, and almost *sixty percent* of these workers don't feel satisfied with their jobs.[1]

In a world where company issues and concerns can become a *Twitter*™ storm in a matter of minutes, leaders must take a close look at the internal environment created for workers. In the wake of the Covid-19 pandemic, many employees were disciplined or fired because of their posts regarding issues that fall under the category of workplace safety. Employees had strong feelings about vaccines, work-from-home options, and sick leave policies. Others posted about forced layoffs or terminations. These issues and opinions found their way onto all of the social platforms, were not well received by the public, and for some companies led to more than bad press, as they were forced to pay millions in damages once lawsuits were challenged. For example, one Ohio nurse's *Facebook*™ post sharing her termination due to vaccine choice was shared more than 400,000 times and gathered over 200,000 comments in just four days.[2]

Her ability to share her workplace culture resulted in a massive public outcry of sympathy and a smear on the reputation of the healthcare facility she had been employed with. People from all over reacted with sympathy and support and reached out to express their solidarity with her and denounce the company's decision to lay her off for speaking out.

The incident sparked a larger conversation about the ability of employees to share and express their opinions without fear of retribution or retaliation. It also highlighted the power of social media to hold companies accountable for their actions and amplify the voices of those who may not have a platform otherwise. As a result of public outcry, companies have been forced to assess their policies and acknowledge employee concerns.

By building a people-first, V.A.L.U.E. Culture and including employees in its development, companies decrease the likelihood of employees taking their work concerns to social media platforms since they feel heard, appreciated, valued, and understood. Companies have a responsibility to create workplace cultures that value transparency, honesty, and respect.

PEOPLE-FIRST CULTURES USE THE V.A.L.U.E. FORMULA

I created the V.A.L.U.E. Culture formula because I wanted people to enjoy their work experience and to feel responsible for and embrace the role they play in the success their company achieves. I knew this thought process would mean a different way of thinking about the workforce for many in leadership today. I knew it would require a change in how the role of internal workplace culture was viewed because it's not just a task that can be delegated to the HR department or a single leader. It's not a one-time initiative or a set of policies that can be implemented and forgotten. Instead, building a positive workplace culture requires a fundamental shift in the way that everyone in the organization thinks, acts, and communicates. It requires a commitment to ongoing learning, growth, and improvement and a willingness to be open and receptive to feedback and new ideas. Yet, I also knew, to truly create a V.A.L.U.E. Culture that fosters innovation, creativity, and collaboration, every employee needs to see themselves as a culture champion and take responsibility for creating a positive and respectful work environment. This means recognizing the power of language and the importance of how we communicate with one another, as well as fostering a sense of belonging and inclusion that allows everyone to bring their full selves to work. It requires a willingness to embrace change, learn from mistakes, and continuously strive toward creating an environment that supports the well-being and growth of every employee.

Using the V.A.L.U.E. Culture formula builds a strong workplace because it contains *five critical elements* that, when combined, forge a successful culture where both the business and employees thrive.

The following 5 elements are 'must haves' in any business, and in case you missed the "how to use this book" section where I explained how this formula works together to create a successful internal culture, I'll give you a quick recap here before we move forward.

V.A.L.U.E. Formula
- **V- Vision**
- **A- Accountability**
- **L- Leadership**
- **U- Unique People**
- **E- Engagement**

V is vision. As a business leader, casting a vision that your employees, board, and customers can clearly see is necessary so they can begin to connect their own values and beliefs with those of the company. The vision cast reflects your goals, principles, and dreams and becomes personal to each person who takes ownership.

A is accountability. Accountability is all about creating buy-in at all levels of the organization. Without it, culture is just a mandate and not a belief. Accountability is found in all high-performing teams because it leads to better relationships, taking ownership of mistakes, and improving job satisfaction.

L is leadership. Leadership is what drives your culture initiative. When leaders are engaged with their team, they become the fuel that moves the vision throughout the organization. People in those key positions need to have the skills and training necessary to be effective, so they become the coach encouraging the team to reach success. The current business climate requires you, as a business leader, to adapt and focus on leadership skills such as agility, resilience, empathy, inclusiveness, and interpersonal communication. In other words, great leaders and culture builders must be people-focused

U is Uniqueness of each of your employees. No two people are alike in the workplace. Each person has a different set of life experiences that shape how they view the world, their co-workers, their leaders, and their job. Some may be motivated by thoughts of promotion; others are happy collecting a paycheck and going home at the end of the day and never thinking of work again until the alarm sounds the next morning. Strong, successful cultures consider each individual's experiences and seek input so that a supportive and inclusive workplace is created.

E is engagement. Strong cultures equal an engaged

workforce. High engagement leads to higher productivity, less absenteeism, less turnover, and higher job satisfaction. These are the success markers any business would be happy to see.

Implementing any one of these elements, or ideally, all 5 of them, will shift a culture from where it is now to one of incredible possibility, fulfillment, and human connection. By building a culture of trust where every employee feels valued and respected, you create an environment where people can unleash their true potential. By fostering a culture of learning, where feedback is encouraged, and mistakes are seen as opportunities, you create a workplace where everyone is empowered to take risks and innovate. By cultivating a culture of belonging, everyone feels a sense of community and purpose, which not only improves productivity but also creates a more compassionate workplace. Together these elements create a culture that is not just a source of livelihood but a source of meaning and purpose. It is a place where people thrive, grow, and contribute to something greater than themselves. It is a culture that connects us to our work, to each other, and to our shared humanity.

Culture is an investment in your people that can result in more profits. However, finding a line on the operating and expense report labeled 'culture building' is often missing because companies fail to connect culture with profits. In saying that, it's important to note that there isn't a one-size-fits-all approach to budgeting in culture – what may work for one business may not be true for another. The question you should ask is, *"How can you direct your funds in a way that benefits your teams?"* The answer allows you an opportunity to work closely with your employees and ask them what kinds of tools, strategies, opportunities, and policies need to be put in place to better support them and improve the overall employee experience. Whether the actual budget item falls under an education and training budget, or you devote culture to its own line item, you will need to commit resources to develop a successful culture.

Culture is *not* a one-and-done. You can't simply have an employee meeting and announce you have a new culture. You must do it methodically and strategically while involving leadership and employees throughout the process. Without that commitment, it will not take hold and continue to grow and thrive. Instead, you need to dedicate time throughout the year to reinforce the values your culture is built from. If you fail to keep it top of mind, people begin to forget what matters. As you learn more from the business leaders featured in this book, you'll see many of the companies keep culture at the front of their conversations, using everything from quarterly employee meetings to appreciation events.

Building a V.A.L.U.E. Culture doesn't happen overnight. It's a continual process that you must commit to growing and maintaining. By building a people-first culture around these five key elements—value, accountability, leadership, uniqueness of your employees, and engagement—and by making culture a necessary item included in your budget, you'll begin to see the benefits across your organization in the form of a heightened sense of community, mentoring, better customer service, the willingness to help others, and higher productivity. As you continue to reinforce your purpose and highlight the meaningful work employees do, those benefits will grow exponentially.

PEOPLE-FIRST CULTURES ADDRESS MEANINGFUL WORK

When Forbes magazine released the results of their 2022 CEO survey, *Reset and Reimagine: Surviving and Thriving in a Uniquely Challenging Business Environment*, internal issues concerning attracting and retaining talent and developing the next generation of leaders emerged as areas of focus.[4] The article pointed out that the pandemic has created a challenge in the workplace, and many companies are now struggling to hire the right people. CEOs are placing greater emphasis on developing their existing employees and building a pipeline of future leaders. To address this challenge, CEOs are investing in employee training and development programs to 'upskill' their workforce so that they have the necessary skills for the future. The survey also found companies are focusing on a more diverse workforce while creating a more equitable workplace culture.

As leaders focus on talent concerns, it's important to understand what actually matters to potential employees. Today, *employees want to do more than punch a clock*. They want to feel that their work is meaningful and has a purpose. And, what that looks like in the workplace is open to interpretation. Meaningful can mean many things. In most cases, it's a job that is about more than paying the monthly bills. It means employees are doing something that connects on a personal level with their values or moral compass, and provides a challenge that keeps them interested. Many leaders wrongly believe only employees in industries such as health care, social services, education, or first responders feel they do meaningful work. We know connecting with a purpose boosts engagement. That's why it's such a core part of the V.A.L.U.E. Culture model. Meaningful work—and the engagement it elicits—doesn't come from a single source. Instead, it is a mixture of factors that drive employees to feel like their time and efforts are well spent.

Let's hear more from Mark Allred. After driving consistent market-leading sales results, building strong employee cultures, and maximizing effective business partnerships for 26 years in the wireless industry, Mark pursued and achieved accreditation from the ICF (International Coaching Federation). As an Associate Certified Coach (ACC) he now works with professionals to help them reconnect with their purpose and navigate life transitions while growing personally and professionally. He is the Director of Talent Development and Growth for *Reveal Global Intelligence*™ and oversees all aspects of the *REVEALTalent*™ Community, which provides coaching and career support for career-minded professionals. Mark has some great insight into what meaningful work means.

> *Q. Mark, are employers guilty of trying to paint with too broad a brush with people regarding what meaningful work is?*

I hate to admit it, but I am guilty of this as well. One of the things whenever we're talking with candidates and when I'm coaching these young, new professionals are talking about their career drivers.

Our CEO Marc Hutto has spent over thirty years working with folks about their careers, and he determined five areas that motivate people about their work. One of them is what we're talking about here, the work's meaning. Others are leadership and management, or how you interact with your leader and what kind of inspiration you're getting from them. Another one is the environment. This looks into the work-life balance and working from home, and potentially things such as compensation or benefits. Finally, personal and professional development.

> *Q. Mark, would you say understanding what's important to the individual employee is key?*

When we work with people, we ask, *what's important to you regarding your work? How would you rank those?* It surprises me how different people's responses are. For me, it's always been the meaning of the work.

I'll take less money to do work that I feel is having an impact. I'm making a lot less than I used to as a district manager doing work that I thought was worthless. I love what I do now so much more, and it's the perfect sector. But not everybody is built that way. I remember talking to one of my clients; He said the meaning of the work ranked lower for him because he goes to work to provide for his family. He wants to be well compensated. He wanted ethical work, but it didn't necessarily have to be meaningful.

Why? Because that's what they do with the church. That's what they do with volunteer time. So, they are not expecting work to fill that space. I respect that. I think you must take that question deeper, and it's something that leaders need to think about.

You can't paint with too broad a brush and expect everyone on your team to be in it because of the meaning of the work. The meaning of work ranks very high for many people, but not for everyone. *How do you respect them for what they consider valuable in those circumstances? How do you support them in that way?*

Q. That's really interesting, Mark. I have to agree with you that the thought process should go into career development.

Some people may be happy where they are and don't want to go home with extra stress. They think...*I'm happy doing what I do. I have a paycheck that takes care of it. I don't necessarily care about making that next leap and adding to my responsibilities.* You've got to have those people. There are certain folks you need to get the job done. They are task-oriented. When they leave at five, they don't want to worry about work again until tomorrow.

We get programmed to believe that people need to want that promotion. And, if folks aren't led well, and they are just blindly following, they get into these promotions and find themselves very quickly in careers that they don't want to be in. And, that's one of the reasons why they're leaving. They woke up.

Q. What is the future of the workplace?

By improving that environment, we improve the person's well-being and create a place people want to be and stay. Organizations should strive to build employees or members up instead of breaking them down. It's a way to future-proof the company.

I think it's going to have to be flexible. I think that's going to be a huge word. Covid-19 introduced this whole new factor of, hey, we can make it work working at home. Flexibility. In a way, we've been on this track for years.

In fact, it's becoming uncommon not to have flexibility. You've got mom and dad both working, and there are still kids who need to be schooled. There are things that will need to be done. If we continue to have a mom and dad working, the workforce will require flexibility.

Automation and artificial intelligence are replacing jobs. You're getting to a place where the amount of available work is not what it used to be. We'll have to come to terms with that and reevaluate things we would never have thought we would reevaluate. Before Covid-19, not many organizations were even considering working from home. Now that's changed. The 40-hour workweek will be on the table.

> *Q. How does that look like the "40-hour work week will be on the table?"*

I had a guest on the podcast who owns a company called *My Work*. Factories and big operations rely on them to fill gaps in schedules when people can't or don't show up.

They bring their folks in. They sign up and make themselves available for whatever shifts they want to be available for. It's kind of like Uber for factory workers.

I asked her how that was working. She said it was phenomenal. Her people can build their own schedules. They can say this week, I want to work the third shift. Next week, I want to work a second shift. This week I don't want to do weekends.

They're building their own schedule and putting it out there. The companies have that need. They're plugging them in. It's all done by the app. Who would have thought of something like that a few years ago?

Learning how to be more flexible is important. The other side of that is being relatable. You've just got to understand your workers at a higher level. That's just a part of the world because there are other opportunities. If you don't choose to do that, it's your choice. But you know, other folks may be stealing those people from you then.

The changing demands of today's workforce may be a hard truth for you to hear, but the great news is when you focus on building a V.A.L.U.E. Culture inside your organization, your people won't be looking for other opportunities. The culture you are creating reinforces the value you see in them, and because you have built it with their input, they feel heard and appreciated.

Building flexibility into the V.A.L.U.E. Culture model allows you to consider the uniqueness of your workforce and what drives or motivates them. It encourages professional development opportunities and allows leaders the ability to create successful environments based on each of their teams' needs. More and more people are asking the question, *Does my work matter?* Most can tell you how they contribute, whether in the number of insurance policies they sell or the number of clients they sign up. However, what they are *really* asking is more value-based. They want to feel they are adding value to others. They want to know which of their personal qualities have helped the company. They want policies and procedures that clearly define expectations and feel fair, so everyone is playing from the same set of rules.

It's important to get feedback and gather information on what matters to your employees because people feel valued for different reasons. It's also important that you talk about why the organization matters. Does it make life easier for working moms? Does it make the home safer in times of trouble? Does the service you offer allow someone the ability to regain their mobility after a devastating accident? Or, does it allow a grandmother to take the grandkids on a vacation they will never forget? The conversation with Mark ties back into the company's purpose and is important to define because it combines the value of the organization with a value that matters to the employee. It reminds them why their involvement is important.

As a business leader, you must begin looking at the true culture inside the company and have conversations with all levels of employees. This is critical because culture is a driver in whether companies can hire or retain their workforce. A V.A.L.U.E. Culture ensures you are building a people-first culture designed to keep and grow a highly engaged workforce. It highlights the diversity found inside your office walls and recognizes the skill each person contributes to the success of the organization. Connecting your people and their beliefs with your company's purpose is essential to win the preverbal talent competition of today's workforce.

Now that you understand the important role culture plays in a business's ability to recruit and retain the right talent, it's time to dive deeper into the talent pool and focus on how you can compete effectively in the current employment market. You'll learn where some leaders miss opportunities due to the *"That's the way we've always done it"* mindset. And, where others thrive because they have embraced and implemented these winning tools. In chapter 3, you'll also discover ways to keep your star employees engaged so recruiters can't steal them away.

CHAPTER 3:

Recruiting Revelations

In my professional experience, hiring the right person for the position has been one of the things that kept me up at night. It was easy to move past the candidates who hadn't even bothered to research my company online and learn what I did. But when the talent and skill were equal, it was harder to discern who would be the best fit on the team. At times it boiled down to a gut feeling; I could feel their excitement and willingness to look at things differently. It's not as easy as marking off skills from a checklist. It boiled down to, *is this the person I want to spend eight hours a day with?*

Getting the people right inside your work environment is crucial. For some, the deciding factor is simply a "gut feeling" that they are the right candidate. For others, it involves matching personality traits with a job description. I wanted to learn more about the recruiting process and what it takes to make new recruits an offer they can't refuse. If you are responsible for or have influence over hiring decisions inside your company, hiring using the V.A.L.U.E. Culture formula as a guideline will shift your culture more favorably and retain people who will add to the cultural goals.

I wanted to learn more about this idea of recruiting the optimum individuals to help support human-centered workplace cultures so I called on the expertise of the CEO of *Unbridled Talent and DisruptHR™*, Jennifer McClure. She's a human resource expert with over 18 years of experience. She's been responsible for recruiting for every position, from the janitor to the CEO. Jennifer then worked exclusively in the area of executive searches. After that, her focus shifted to retaining talent. Since 2010, she's owned her own business and has worked as a professional speaker delivering talks about topics related to people-centered strategies in the workplace. Her early years of recruiting focused on how you must successfully recruit talent to your organization and what is required from leadership. Jennifer eloquently shares how she sees the current hiring landscape and how the mindset of potential job seekers has changed, especially since the pandemic.

> *Q. Jennifer, the current landscape companies are dealing with makes it appear talent is scarce and more people are changing jobs. How can a business address this?*

It's difficult now to recruit talent for many reasons. If you do find someone with the skills you want, they want a lot more money than they did in the past. That causes internal equity issues. People have also changed their mindsets. The mindset shift began before the pandemic of 2020, but the last couple of years have accelerated it.

They weren't thinking of twenty-or-thirty-year careers. They were thinking of ten-or fifteen-year careers. But now they're thinking of a year and a half, to two and a half years, and then moving on to what's next.

This shift is causing a lot of leaders at companies to rethink many things in terms of what they thought were reasons people would join their company. Sometimes it's a real wake-up call.

What was important when someone entered the company twenty years ago is not why someone would join today. Now, while there will always be an ebb-and-flow in recruiting, *talent sits in the driver's seat.*

Q. Will it go back to employers being in the driver's seat?

Great question. It will move some. But how people *approach work has changed forever* and will continue to change. I see a lot of employers who are changing, and some are sticking their heads in the sand and saying, "I hope it goes back to the status quo, normal."

Some say, "I don't like this new way of working. I want everybody to think like me; that's not working." Then others say, "We don't understand what we need to do to move into this new phase of business," yet they're trying to learn. And then, of course, some companies and organizations are doing really well.

As you can read from Jennifer's comments, one of the biggest mistakes made in the hiring process is not anticipating the questions you'll receive or being ill-prepared to answer where your company stands. Leaders who refuse to acknowledge the changing wants and needs of potential employees will have a much harder time attracting a workforce that aligns with the people-centered V.A.L.U.E. Culture they are building. Just as businesses change with the addition of technology and updated processes, so have the expectations of the people whom we want to hire.

In most businesses, there needs to be rapport among all employees. If you hire someone who does not fit in with the team's chemistry or your company's culture, you may find yourself taking a step backward rather than forward. Focusing on culture fit and flexibility with your incentives can improve your talent attraction greatly. As job seekers have more negotiation power and needs, you must focus on your people processes if you want to remain competitive and set your company up for future success. A positive culture is on the minds of potential employees, and they have higher expectations from the companies they are considering job offers from. Savvy employees are inclined to turn down offers from companies that fail to impress or address work-life balance concerns.

Q. Jennifer, is the shift to potential employees being more in control during job negotiations and interviews happening because culture is something people are really paying attention to now?

Yes. Based on the research, this shift was happening before the pandemic. So before 2020, *culture* was becoming the *number one reason* people would consider joining *or leaving an organization.*

I think the challenge is defining what culture is and what it means to whom. A company says our culture is that we value honesty and integrity, and blah, blah, blah. That's what's on the lobby plaque and the cards they give out to employees. But the *culture is what people feel in their experience with work.*

If you have ten or ten thousand employees, ultimately, that means you've got a lot of different perspectives on what the culture is. The challenge is still to set a company's overarching values. You know, to understand who we are, why we work, and how we work. It is also to understand that each individual leader and their team will have a mini culture within the culture.

Q. How do you ensure those are connected to what you want them to be?

It's not unusual for organizations to have multiple variations of their cultures throughout. Different departments function differently, some much better than others, because of the freedom of information sharing, the level of communication they have, and how well team members know each other personally.

While you may have slight variations in your company culture throughout the organization, your core values should tie the entire organization together. Your core values are what bind the employees inside the company and allow everyone to make decisions from the same starting point. Core values are those fundamental beliefs and principles that guide the behavior, actions, and decisions of every member of the organization. They define the company's identity, purpose, and culture and serve as a compass for employees to navigate through their work and interaction with others. When you are hiring, it's important to make these values clear so you can pick a qualified candidate whose beliefs match those you have set as cornerstones in the workplace.

Think of core values like this. If you put a group of employees together, culture is established fairly quickly—in that everyone agrees on the way things should be done in the office. Why? Because clearly defined core values allow groups of people to collectively agree on the importance of how they each operate and the expectations others have. If there is no set of common beliefs, then everyone creates their own code of conduct. A lack of core values can show up as employees being resistant to change, exhibiting unethical behavior, forming cliques, or just having general disagreements. These can impact potential new employees.

You'll struggle in your efforts to recruit or attract new talent if you aren't clear on your core values. People will be forced to make their own cultural interpretations if they aren't provided with clear context. When your company clearly outlines the core values, it makes it easier to attract like-minded people who fit in with the company culture; this leads to greater productivity, longevity in the company, and cohesiveness amongst all departments. According to Forbes magazine, employers would be better off trading 90 percent talent for just 10 percent character.[1]

From her many years of experience, Jennifer agreed that not only do core values build a more cohesive culture, but successfully communicating those values helps you stand out in a competitive job market with your potential employees.

Q. Jennifer, do you think communicating core values is necessary for companies to be competitive in today's hiring market?

Values are something you have to walk the walk and talk the talk. You can say a lot of things. But if your leaders aren't living it out in their organizations, you will have a problem. For example, if you tell your employees you value work-life balance and want them to be whole people inside and outside of work, but then you have a leader whose actions don't match, it devalues what employees hear.

If you have a leader sending employees emails in the evening, calling people on the weekends to work, and expecting people to respond to them at any given time, then that's not walking in the values, and people feel that.

Q. Does this show up when people talk about diversity, inclusion, and belonging as part of the culture?

Yes, but then you look at the picture of their leaders on the website, and they're all the same. They don't have anyone in leadership positions with diversity, or they only have one. There's also no involvement in the community or any diverse organizations.

Their values are not really lived out. I think people see that and are much more attuned to it now, especially diversity, equity, and inclusion. Many companies will say it's part of their culture or values, but they haven't taken the time to think about how to implement this into their system.

Q. Are you saying culture doesn't stop and start at the top?

That's right. It can't just be discussed at the top levels. The culture is the whole organization. If only those at the top levels of the business are talking about *what* culture is, and you're just creating a statement to put on a piece of paper, it's not a *lived* culture.

My definition of culture has always been the employees' experience working for the company and what they tell other people about their experiences. Any company that thinks they're going *to go away on a retreat with their leadership team* and do their mission, vision, values, and *establish their culture, is missing the boat* because that's not ever going to be what the *culture is or will be.*

As I coach clients, I am amazed at how many employees, especially Millennials, left their job within the first year of employment because they did not feel it was a good fit. That fit revolves around the culture inside the organization. It rarely had to do with the tasks assigned. It had more to do with little opportunity for advancement, poor leadership, and a lack of engagement and purpose in their work. Millennials specifically wanted a position that allowed work-life balance and supported their personal and professional goals. Additionally, Millennials tend to seek out companies that align with their values and have a positive impact on society. To retain Millennial employees, you must provide meaningful opportunities for development, offer a flexible and supportive work environment, *and* create a culture that values employee well-being while providing purpose-driven work.

When I coach Gen Xers who are making a job change, they are looking for a variety of things, including new challenges and opportunities, work-life balance, a positive work culture, and a sense of purpose in their work. They also seek higher compensation and better benefits. Gen X members value autonomy, flexibility, and opportunities to use their skills and experience to make a meaningful impact. They may also be interested in companies that align with their personal values and beliefs. To attract and retain this generation of workers, companies must provide opportunities for professional development and growth and create a culture that values employee well-being and balance.

When you consider the high cost of turnover and recruiting, it's clear that a company's core values should be included as part of the conversation in every interview. Culture itself can feel vague and hard to describe; however, core values are clear and have a concise description. An interviewee can imagine how they are part of business operations when the core values are clearly outlined. Sharing these values defines how a company supports its employees and customers, how employees work together and collaborate, and the type of employee the leader desires for their team. One of the first things recruiters and career development professionals, like me, coach job seekers on is determining what their potential employers' culture is currently and whether it appears to be an environment in which they would thrive.

I asked Jennifer how she would prepare a client to accurately discern the true culture inside an organization they were considering working in.

Q. What do you suggest job seekers do in an interview to learn more about an organization's internal culture?

I suggest that the interviewee asks about leadership styles inside the organization. It's important to understand whether a company offers flexibility in the work schedule or if they expect employees to be working from 8:00 AM to 5:00 PM.

They need to ask about the work environment—knowing how much freedom and communication employees have would also be helpful. Finally, I suggest research. In general, the larger the company, there will be interviews with the CEO where they are discussing their values and vision for the company.

Q. Jennifer, what about looking at sites like Glassdoor™ and Indeed™ to learn more about the job? What can those places do in terms of future recruitment?

Job seekers want to hear from current and former employers about what it's like to work for a particular company. Some discount the information as sour grapes from disgruntled employees. While there is some of that, there is also some good information to gain, especially if you supplement it with other research.

These sites are helpful. They can also be a great eye-opener for leadership in an organization.

Q. Share more about what you mean by that.

One of my first clients hired me because he had a high turnover rate. He said, "This is a great workplace, and we pay good money." He went off with all these things. The reality was it was almost a billion-dollar company that he owned and started in his garage. I had to tell him, "It is a great place for you. You know you have all the freedom in the world, the autonomy, you make all the decisions, etc."

After learning more about the company and talking to people there, I found out it wasn't great further down the organization. I shared one thing I had done before meeting with him the first time. I looked up their reviews on *Glassdoor*™ and *Indeed*™ work forums.

The first thing he said to me was that they were just disgruntled employees. I said, "Maybe, but if I see 300 reviews, and the majority of them mentioned you expect them to be on call 24/7, that they have to have their cell phone on at all times and be available to clients, you know, this is a problem."

I also looked on *LinkedIn*™ and did some underground research, and I could see on those forums that they all said the same things consistently. When you looked at the totality of the results you got a much clearer picture of what was happening inside the company. I think you have to look at it and see if there are clues. If you read thirty reviews on *Glassdoor*™ for a company and one of them says something negative, it's not that big of a deal, but if half of them point out a problem, then that's something you can explore further and try to find more information about.

It's not just job seekers who should be gathering data. However, there seems to be a disconnect between employees and employers regarding another great tool: employee surveys. As I've worked with clients, I've repeatedly heard that no one fills out their survey truthfully. This happens because they fear retribution for anything they say that could appear to be negative. Many have also lost faith that their leadership will use the information as productive feedback and implement change. To succeed at recruiting talent that aligns with your company values, you need to develop a clear picture of what's happening inside the walls of your company. I've devoted a later chapter on *how* and *why* you should measure employee engagement, and I will walk you through ways you can measure the impact your culture change is having on your workforce. At this point, for this discussion on talent, it's important to understand the role your current employees have in the recruitment process. You need to know how they are describing your culture because they are the ones sharing on websites and blogs that specifically report on and rate companies for everyone to read. And those sites are the places today's potential employees go to begin their research on your company.

Finding information on the cultural situation inside your company goes beyond forms and surveys. Ask your internal human resource professionals what positions they are struggling to recruit or retain. Look at the information they have collected from exit interviews. *Do you see trends developing?* As a business leader, it's important to develop open lines of communication with your HR team and remain receptive to the feedback you receive. This team can help you identify if you're moving toward a problem, so you have time to correct issues before it impacts your bottom line. These problems show up in the form of sick time abuse, brand damage, loss of productivity, lack of innovation, and difficulty retaining great employees.

Jennifer had more to share on the value of utilizing the

information already contained inside your HR department as you look to identify culture issues that need addressing.

Q. Jennifer, what internal data should business leaders gather to improve their recruiting ability?

Let's say you're sitting in HR. You've done some exit exams, and you're starting to see a trend that things are shifting in a way that you might not think is the best for the organization. As an HR professional, how can you start those conversations with your upper leadership and upper management? How can you start moving them toward looking at your culture? Key indicators you have a problem could be an uptick in turnover or people taking early retirement. Having a more challenging time recruiting for certain positions is also a sign something is off. If you don't have metrics already in place tracking these things, it will be harder for you to determine when your culture is about to derail. To start these internal conversations, you must collect the right data. You've got to figure out what data you can use to tell that story rather than just anecdotes or one-off stories. If you're starting to see a turnover trend, dive deep. *Is the turnover in one area? Is it one manager or across the organization?*

Hopefully, you're doing exit interviews. What are people saying? What are the themes that are coming up? Get enough data to make a case to your leaders that there's something here that we need to address and change. You can learn a lot from what exiting employees are saying and what *they're not saying*. Business leaders must have enough of a data set in order to make decisions. You can't just go in and say, I'm hearing this. Everyone will say, "Oh, that's just one person." If it's starting to concern you, what data can you gather to show that it is more than just your 'spidey sense' telling you this is a problem?

Q. Data helps you get to the root of the problem. In real life, you may have to dig deep to get the real picture because the initial thought isn't the real problem. I asked Jennifer if she had a real-world example she could share that illustrates this point.

I was hired to fix the turnover issue for a one-hundred-year-old company. I started by talking to the CEO and other executives. Their HR management software was old and didn't give much information. I spent two weeks and many sleepless nights diving into their old mainframe system to get turnover data.

I went back as far as I could to get the reasons for termination just in the system. What I came up with was the turnover rate for the whole organization was 1.5%. Excluding retirees and deaths, when you look at that, you're like, *everybody's telling me turnover is a problem*. But the numbers didn't show it.

I needed to dig deeper. When I did, I realized the issue was with those employees in second-shift manufacturing, and I learned it was because the company was hiring young kids. After all, it was a $7-an-hour job.

They were throwing them into the worst shift possible for the least amount of money. It's not rocket science. There were seven or eight jobs where employees did one task repeatedly; taking sheets of cards off a pallet and loading them onto another pallet, loading sheets into the machine, or stacking boxes. So, they were hired, and they would be the box stacker or the sheet loader. They were bored out of their minds because they were doing this one task all day and not making much money.

Most people mistakenly think money is the fix. But let's look at this another way. I met with the operations vice president, sat down, and discussed the current situation. There were seven jobs, all paying the same thing. Why not have these people at least rotate? They get some variety. They get the opportunity to learn new tasks and new jobs.

The easiest person to recruit is the employee you already have. Retention of employees is one benefit of building a V.A.L.U.E. Culture. It's less expensive to keep employees than it is to replace, train, and bring new employees up to speed. Using training and professional development plans that reinforce your core values is a surefire way to help solidify your internal culture. When you put forth a dedicated effort to actively develop your employees, it demonstrates your company's commitment to them and reassures them they are a valued part of the success equation. It's disheartening when I listen to multiple clients who are highly qualified but feel stuck and unchallenged because they aren't being offered development opportunities. In my own professional life, and I imagine yours as well, it's the projects or promotions that cause us to stretch and improve the skills that we find the most joy in when we successfully accomplish our goals.

In case you doubt the role development plays in an employee's satisfaction with their work experience, consider this comment from my former client, Rebecca.

"I went to work for another company that did the exact same thing as my former employer. The pay wasn't that different, and the benefits were basically the same. I chose them because I knew several people who worked there, and they constantly talked about how their supervisor asked what their interests were and where they saw themselves in the company in five years. They worked together on a plan that allowed them to gain experience in areas that would allow them to progress on their career path. They even paid for

them to get classes outside of the work environment if they could tie the benefits of the training to their current or future position."

We all know that growth matters. It allows individuals to achieve the best possible version of themselves. Personally, I've learned from my clients, growth opportunities provide employees with a boost in motivation, counteract boredom, advance their skill set, and help them master the art of goal-setting. While none of these things were a promotion, the impact they had on my clients was just as powerful. Each of them felt valued and more confident in their position and in the company. Part of developing a V.A.L.U.E. Culture is creating an atmosphere where employees feel they have a path to success. Having a professional development plan for all of your team members is a critical aspect of your company if you want them to stay engaged and keep advancing.

Q. I asked Jennifer if she agreed. She did, but today's employees are more concerned with growth than climbing the next rung of the corporate ladder.

Professional development has always been important. Many companies still think about career development as putting an employee in their high-potential program and saying, here are the classes you'll attend and the certifications that you get. What people are thinking about in terms of career development now is, *will I grow?*

If you want to retain good employees, growth is vital. Employees no longer want to know how long it will take them to move to the next rung on the ladder. Instead, it's about the ability to learn.

For example, an employee doesn't need to come in as the marketing assistant and have you tell them how long it will take you to become the VP of marketing. Instead, they want to know what they are going to learn. They want to have a plan for that.

They want to be able to say, "I'm going to learn how to do market data analysis. I'm going to learn how to do advertising, or I'm going to learn how to do budgeting." It's more about growth. It's about saying, "I'm going to grow my skills." If I take a job or leave it for another job, it is because they've offered me an opportunity to grow somehow.

> ### Q. Should there be conversations around new hires and retaining existing employees?

Great question. When you're hiring people in your organization, and certainly for your existing employees that you want to retain, you should be having regular conversations with them about where they want to grow.

I have long advocated for people not to do exit interviews but *retention interviews*—especially with your top talent. Sit down with them, be with them, and talk with them.

I was an executive recruiter, and I know how this works. As a recruiter, even if someone initially told me they liked their job, when I gave them a chance to tell me something they wished was different or could change, they usually had something. Then I could turn that around and use it to get them to consider my opportunity.

Part of the culture discussion must begin by listening to your employees and offering growth opportunities. For everyone, that's not necessarily a title change or salary change. I mean, everybody likes to make more money. But it's about *I want to learn more; I want to do more.*

Q. Jennifer, what can business leaders do to get the pulse of and understand the culture inside their organization in regard to hiring?

There are three things I would look at to understand if your culture is where it is or where you want it to be. First, know what new hires say about you. It is important to check in at the 30, 60, and 90-day marks after an employee has joined your organization. It is critical.

You want to know if their experience has matched what you offered. What was their actual experience? Was there anything that they were surprised about? Was there anything they were delighted about? What was missing? Is there something they thought they would get that they didn't or haven't gotten to do?

Secondly, know why people are leaving the organization. And, finally, know, from a recruiting perspective, are there people that we're not able to recruit because there's something that you don't offer or that they found out that they won't receive but another organization will give to them?

When you grow a V.A.L.U.E. Culture, employees are eighty-seven percent less likely to leave for other opportunities. They feel valued at companies that place a high emphasis on development and mission alignment. You're also likely to see a jump in how your brand is perceived externally.

People listen when employees share stories about a supervisor investing in their growth versus their bad boss who micromanages a department. And, if you have good employees, the people who are their connections and friends generally exhibit the same traits you saw in your employee. This makes hiring much easier and even more valuable in tight economic times. The most recent numbers confirm that hiring and retaining takes, on average, six to nine months of the former employees' salary to bring a new hire up to speed. That number accounts for time and expenses advertising the position, interviewing, onboarding, training, and getting someone back to the productivity level the person who left exhibited.

It is essential for business leaders to understand the new landscape of talent attraction and the unique needs and priorities of the different generations in today's workplace. With the rise of technology and remote work, companies must be more agile and adaptable to remain competitive in attracting and retaining top talent. They must also recognize that the different generations in their workforce bring diverse perspectives, values, and expectations that require a more customized approach to engagement, communication, and leadership. By understanding and embracing these differences, business leaders can build a more inclusive, innovative, and high-performing workplace culture that attracts and retains the best talent built from all generations. Ultimately, this will not only benefit employees, but also the company's bottom line and long-term success.

Let's get into some deep water with chapter four. It's time for a deep dive and starts to learn the benefits of a V.A.L.U.E. Culture (vision, accountability, leadership, uniqueness, engagement) and what they can do for your organization.

CHAPTER 4:

Benefits of a V.A.L.U.E. Culture

As a business leader myself, I know that as part of the managerial team, you face a multitude of challenges that impact competitiveness and productivity, including talent management, keeping up with rapidly changing technology that disrupts current processes, market volatility, and ensuring employees have a healthy work-life balance, so they don't burnout. By creating a V.A.L.U.E. Culture (V—Vision, A—Accountability, L—Leadership, U—Unique People, E—Engagement), you can address and improve the outcomes for your employees because a strong culture increases trust. I believe trust is one of the most important outcomes in culture building because I've had bosses I didn't trust, or feel like they valued my contribution to the company's success. I've also had bosses I'd go over and above to help succeed because they made me feel my contribution mattered. I trusted them with my thoughts, ideas, and professional development plan and knew they were trustworthy when they shared their work experiences and really listened to my goals. That made me want to go the extra mile to help meet customer needs and learn new skills, and I felt confident in my position, which resulted in a feeling of validation and accomplishment which carried over into my personal and home life.

Workplace culture can foster employee engagement leading to higher productivity and job satisfaction. Culture can help retain talent by creating an environment that supports growth, development, and trust. Trust creates a culture that promotes better, more effective communications. Trust allows for a more welcoming and respectful work environment. A culture built on a trust foundation also enhances your customer experience and empowers employees to deliver exceptional customer service while positively impacting your company's reputation.

Let's look at seven key issues a V.A.L.U.E. Culture can positively impact when trust is instilled in the workforce and becomes an important focus by the management team.

COMMUNICATION BENEFITS

Do your team members communicate well with one another? Do they have a clear idea of what is expected of them? Do they feel both heard and listened to? If employees know the vision of the company and it has been explained well, they feel they can have an impact and act on it. There's an old saying that goes, "he who has the information has the power." Good leaders want to be trusted and therefore share information and disperse it out effectively to everyone.

To start a culture change, you must model and reinforce trust and foster open communication. This is done first and foremost by leading by example. When you demonstrate the importance of open communication by actively listening to employee feedback and being transparent in decision-making processes, you are encouraging open dialogue between all levels in the workplace. Leaders should acknowledge and reward employees who demonstrate open communication, which encourages others to follow suit. Communication is a key component to successfully establishing trust and implementing a culture change in the workplace.

In chapter 12, I share additional listening techniques you can use in your workplace to start modeling this behavior and improve communication.

EMPOWERMENT BENEFITS

Ask yourself, are your employees empowered to get results and are they held accountable for those results and encouraged to achieve more? The right culture gives employees the ability to impact customer experience positively. How? As their job satisfaction increases, employees are often more motivated and engaged in their work which leads to a better overall customer experience. They exhibit better problem-solving skills, are more likely to take ownership of customer issues, and find creative solutions which add to customer satisfaction and loyalty. Employees who feel a sense of trust demonstrate a higher level of attention to detail which leads to a higher level of service. They communicate clearly and more effectively in customer interactions. Most importantly, feeling trusted leads to increased innovation. When employees feel free to bring new ideas to the table, processes are improved, and customers have a better experience. Overall, an empowered employee has the potential to make a significant impact on customer experience, satisfaction, and loyalty, and ultimately this contributes to the organization's competitiveness in the market.

PERSONAL DEVELOPMENT BENEFITS

Opportunities for advancement that are clearly outlined

for employees create a feeling of trust, motivation, and purpose in their work. When employees understand what they need to do to advance their careers, they feel more engaged and committed to their efforts. They feel more motivated and focused during challenging times. It's important to discuss these clear opportunities with your employees so they can see their advancement path. Ultimately they will look to you, their leader, to share this information. If employees feel they receive the training, support, or tools they need to develop, they feel their employer is willing to invest in them, they are more likely to stay with the company long-term. Therefore, I encourage you to make it known that you and your organization support them on their career journeys and that if they want to advance, there are opportunities to work with mentors and coaches to build their skills. A strong workplace culture, with a clear success path, builds trust and benefits an employee's personal development in several ways:

- **A sense of purpose:** A strong culture with a clear purpose and mission can provide employees with a sense of direction and meaning in their work, leading to increased job satisfaction and motivation.
- **Supportive environment:** A V.A.L.U.E. Culture can create a supportive environment for employees, fostering a sense of belonging and encouraging collaboration and teamwork.
- **Improved mental health:** A healthy workplace culture leads to reduced stress levels and improved mental health, leading to increased productivity and overall well-being.
- **Encouragement for creativity and innovation:** A culture that values innovation and encourages employees to bring their ideas to the table can lead to personal growth and a sense of confidence.

- **Recognition and rewards:** A V.A.L.U.E. Culture recognizes and rewards employees for their hard work and contributions, which boosts employee morale and motivation, leading to increased job satisfaction and personal fulfillment.

Imagine your business thriving and your employees feeling invested-in because you've built a culture centered on trust. When you integrate a V.A.L.U.E. Culture into your business you provide a supportive and empowering environment for employees leading to personal growth, personal development, and overall well-being.

MISALIGNMENT SOLUTION BENEFITS

A V.A.L.U.E. Culture encourages everyone to focus on what is important. Often the words, core values, and actions of the company don't match. Many times employees hear management saying they are focused on one thing but see actions that make them believe otherwise. If there is a vast misalignment in the office, it can lead to a loss of trust and credibility among employees, customers, and other stakeholders. To fix this issue, which can lead to discourse in the office, try these steps:

- **Conduct an internal review.** The first step is to understand the root cause of the disconnect between the words (core values) and actions. This can be done through focus groups, internal surveys, or one-on-one interviews with employees.
- **Align the company values with the actions.** Once the root cause is identified, you must take steps to align the values and principles with actions. This may involve revising policies, procedures, and processes to ensure

consistency and accountability.
- **Communicate the change.** It is important to communicate the changes being made to employees to build transparency and trust.
- **Lead by example.** As a leader, you must lead by example and demonstrate the company's commitment to aligning words and actions. This includes holding each person accountable for their own actions and behaviors.
- **Monitor and evaluate.** You should regularly monitor and evaluate how the changes are impacting performance and ensure that the changes made are having the desired effect. If not, make further changes as necessary.

Many times when companies consult with me about improving their culture I start working with them on these 5 things. Analyzing each one of these steps is a perfect place for you to begin to see where your culture currently resides.

Addressing misalignment with values in the workplace is a critical problem leaders need to address if they want to build trust and credibility. When employees perceive that their leaders do not act in accordance with the organization's stated values, it can result in a range of negative consequences, including decreased job satisfaction, lower productivity, and higher turnover rates.

However, when leaders take steps to address misalignment with values, they demonstrate their commitment to creating a positive work environment that aligns with the organization's mission and values. This can lead to a more engaged and motivated workforce, increase employee retention, and improve overall organizational performance.

Therefore, it is crucial leaders take a proactive approach to identifying any misalignment with organizational values in the workplace. By doing so, they can foster a culture of trust, accountability, and transparency, which will benefit the organization as a whole. Addressing misalignment with values isn't just the right thing to do; it is essential to building a successful organization.

V.A.L.U.E. CULTURE BENEFITS YOU THROUGH OVERCOMING ENTITLEMENT

Do employees feel bonuses or celebrations are expected and no longer view them as a reward? Does your employee base feel the only qualifications for promotion are the number of years they have on the job? Overcoming an employee's sense of entitlement can be challenging and if left unchecked can spread and impact the performance of others, but a strategic and defined culture shift can help you see movement in the right direction. A V.A.L.U.E. Culture fosters a sense of accountability by encouraging employees to take responsibility for their actions and hold them accountable for their performance. This can be done by holding regular performance reviews and feedback sessions. A strong workplace culture builds collaboration and teamwork, discouraging a sense of entitlement since employees work together to achieve a common goal. It can also reflect that you recognize hidden gems inside the workforce that provide excellent work and increased value.

PERFORMANCE BENEFITS

Often, companies without a V.A.L.U.E. Culture have little consequences for poor performers. Many times other employees feel forced to pick up their slack. Sometimes problem employees are promoted to become some other department's problem.

Not addressing poor performance can do significant damage to employee trust, morale, and engagement. The right culture will confront performance issues and reward those who go the extra mile, and weed out those that do not.

Defining culture helps address poor performance by setting clear expectations. A culture that clearly communicates job expectations, responsibilities, and performance standards can help employees understand what is expected of them and improve their performance. Poor performance can then be improved through feedback. A culture that values regular interaction and supportive coaching can help employees identify areas for improvement and make necessary changes to their performance.

With feedback comes the need for encouragement and support, which a nurturing and empowering workplace can offer. This support and encouragement can help them overcome performance challenges and enhance their skills. Coaching provided by a team leader also opens the door to professional development opportunities. A culture that values growth and development provides employees with access to mentors and advancement, which helps them stay engaged and motivated in their work.

By creating a V.A.L.U.E. Culture in the workplace that values growth, collaboration, and accountability, a company can help employees overcome challenges and improve their performance over time.

WORK-LIFE BALANCE BENEFITS

Are employees given lip service that *family matters*, or do they really feel that within the company, family needs are respected? Are employees *expected* to work on holidays? Are special occasions that are important to the individual honored or even celebrated? Are employees asked to remain in contact when they are on vacation or out on medical leave? Do emails go out at all hours, not respecting personal time? A V.A.L.U.E. Culture provides a balance between work and personal time while allowing for appropriate relationships at work. It's a culture that values and helps employees feel supported and empowered to take the time they need (and have earned) to attend to personal or family obligations.

How does work-life balance look in your workplace? Balance can come from offering flexible work arrangements or offering employees education on how to manage their work and personal responsibilities more effectively. It promotes healthy behaviors such as exercise and mindfulness practices. It discourages overworking and prioritizes fair workloads, and helps employees avoid burnout. A workplace culture that acknowledges work-life balance offers benefits and wellness programs or family-friendly policies that help employees achieve these goals.

As a leader in your organization, you can encourage these ideas by modeling healthy habits and prioritizing your work-life balance to set a positive example for the individuals you supervise. Know that your team is watching you, so how you show up is how they will show up. If you align your values, they will do the same.

The above seven reasons are both tangible and intangible benefits you can gain when you build a V.A.L.U.E. Culture in your organization. You can see how these benefits boost morale and engagement, which positively impacts your bottom line by reducing absenteeism, less dependence on your healthcare plan, increasing productivity, and happier employees who create happier customers that do repeat business. As you begin to build your V.A.L.U.E. Culture and instill these principles, you will experience increased productivity because creating value builds engaged and motivated employees who want to perform at the highest level for you.

DISENGAGED WORKERS COST MORE

Of course, for every front, there is a back; for every up, there is a down. That means I would be remiss if I did not take the time to share the counter-benefits and consequences of what a workplace filled with disengaged workers costs you.

Did you know that overall, more than fifty percent of workers today say they are actively *disengaged* at work to some degree.([1]) That number is even higher, fifty-nine percent, for females in the workplace. Focusing on employee development can help you outperform the employees and assemble golf carts, ATVs, side-by-sides, and wave runners. Bob has been combining his financial and manufacturing knowledge with tactical execution to achieve long-term gains in performance, productivity, and profitability for *Yamaha*™ for over three years. He's a Certified *Lean Green Belt* and experienced in developing and leading teams to operational excellence.

Q. Bob, why should business leaders try to invest in their employees? What are the internal opportunities that they could offer?

I believe the key is *investing in your employees. Yamaha*™ does a lot of promotion from within. I think part of the reason is that we already know that person is a good fit or they show the spirit, the culture that we appreciate.

There are a lot of benefits from that. Instead of always going outside, developing from within helps keep that constant continuity of culture. It also shows people you're willing to invest in them and help them reach the next level. That's part of the reason why we have such great tenure with a lot of people.

Q. Providing internal opportunities also helps you retain those great employees. If they start to "get bored" with their current tasks and are in danger of looking for new opportunities, what can you do?

If employees start to get bored with something, they will make changes. So why don't we provide that *something for them*? Let's provide an opportunity that will be more interesting or more exciting. Then we will work to see how we can help the employee get there.

For example, if the employee needs to go to school for it, we'll pay their tuition. If they need specific classes or technical skills, we'll encourage them and pay for that too.

Then we allow the employee to put it to use. We have very structured development programs to help people get from an assembly operator to a team lead, to a supervisor, to a manager.

In fact, one of our division managers, one level below the vice president, or would be like a director in another organization, started as a third-shift supervisor twenty-five years ago.

There are a lot of examples of that. In fact, it's always interesting to hear people's stories and all the different roles that they've been in. Many have worked at *Yamaha*™ for fifteen years, but there are eight different positions they've rotated through in those fifteen years.

It's always interesting to see where they have been in the organization. What have they done? Sometimes it's widely varied. You would never guess their path to get to where they are today.

Q. The internal opportunities that you provide are really worth it to your employees. They are motivated by many different factors, but it's not just the carrot you are holding out in front of them; the culture you have created allows them to feel valued.

We've been trying hard over the last couple of years to share some of those stories to encourage people to take advantage of our programs. You may not realize that your unit manager started off as an assembly operator.

Hearing that story can be empowering. You realize, suddenly, *the sky's the limit*. You know you don't have to go somewhere else to do it. We see in the professional world frequently that many people assume you must make a move to get to the next level. So, we're trying to ensure that we're not acting like that. We give those opportunities internally so our people don't seek them elsewhere.

What did you learn from Bob about the benefits of internal opportunities? Can you look at your organization and consider the growth you are offering to your employees? Are you able to assess your organization and consider the internal opportunities available to your employees? Remember, opportunities don't always have to be wrapped up as a promotion; they can be in the form of new challenges, learning experiences, or the chance to work on meaningful projects. While promotions are often viewed as the ultimate form of career advancement, employees can also benefit from opportunities to develop their skills and take on new responsibilities without necessarily moving up the corporate ladder. These opportunities can be just as valuable, providing employees with a sense of growth and progress in their careers.

In one of my latest training sessions, I asked a group of

mid-level managers to make a list showing a variety of opportunities that could be created in their companies that would provide a sense of growth for employees that didn't include a promotion. Here's what they came up with:

- Cross-functional training and development programs
- Leadership development programs
- Mentorship and coaching opportunities
- Job rotations or stretch assignments
- Workshops, conferences, and seminars
- Internal training opportunities for new skills or certifications
- Employee self-guided plans such as LinkedIn™ Learning

Just one of these suggestions could be the thing that tips the scale toward higher engagement for your company. Investing in employee growth opportunities is not just a matter of improving your company's bottom line, it's a powerful statement about what your company values and stands for. I encourage you to hold a meeting and start brainstorming or identifying internal opportunities you could offer inside your company. Think of something that really benefits the organization as well as the employee and write it down for you to flesh out in a later chapter.

When it is your turn to assemble your team and ask for ideas or feedback, remember to encourage open communication. You want to create a safe supportive environment in which your team members feel comfortable sharing. Actively listen to their suggestions and focus on the strengths they want to build. Then prioritize a list and develop a plan that allows your team to see you are invested in accomplishing these objectives. Assign responsibilities for the implementation. Then, don't forget to follow-up and provide updates on the actions you and the rest of your management team are making. These updates will create a deeper trust between you and your team members.

Remember the seven benefits your company reaps when your employees stay engaged? Communication, empowerment, personal development, misalignment ends, entitlement, poor performance stops, and work-life balance is achieved. As you create your plan for a people-centered culture, adding a professional development arm not only will help you with future staffing needs, but also increase the productivity of your current team members. It also ensures your team knows that employee development isn't just a buzzword for you. It's a foundational pillar that will drive your organization forward and ensure the success of both your company and employees as a whole.

In our next chapter, I want to break down the V.A.L.U.E. Culture in such an easy way that you'll remember it like all the plays and passes, with all the fun and excitement of your favorite Super Bowl™ event.

CHAPTER 5:

What Type of Culture Do You Have?

There are many types of workplace cultures. Understanding the basic types provides helpful insight into which culture will work best for you and your company. As you read through the list of eight types of culture, ask yourself, *Would I want this culture for my company? Does this culture reflect our values? Would I want to work in a workplace like this?*

As I researched and learned about the different culture models, I immediately associated them with the different places I've worked. As you work through the list, think about your past work experience and see if you can match them up with any of these culture types.

Now, don't forget your culture doesn't have to conform to one of these basic systems you see in the following list. You are free to develop your own culture. One that reflects your unique employee base and the vision you cast as a leader. I encourage you to think big and imagine your ideal workplace culture. When you build a culture that embraces the personality, vision, and values of the organization it's more inclusive of your workforce and stands a much better chance of succeeding.

Consider these eight types of workplace cultures:

1. **Outcome-oriented.** Results are what matter, and results are rewarded. This type of culture is often found in sales-driven companies.

2. **Innovative.** Creativity and new ideas are the order of the day. It's about figuring out what the marketplace needs and being the first to deliver it.

3. **Lottery.** The people near the top have it made. The hours are decent, and the pay is exceptional. Everyone below the top level is overworked and underpaid. The carrot held as a reward for a great job makes the style work. Everyone is willing to drive themselves incredibly hard to attain one of those rare, coveted positions.

4. **Casual.** Wear what you want within reason. The hours are flexible, so work when you choose, as long as you do your job.

5. **People-oriented.** The value of the employee is above all else. These companies often sacrifice profits to pay their employees above the normal rate. The company policies focus on fairness, and the work environment tends to be casual regarding hours and family obligations. These companies have better retention than others.

6. **Aggressive.** The majority of the team is focused on out-performing competitors. This type of culture can cause employees to become competitive and aggressive. The battle cry is, *We will destroy our competitors one way or the other*.

7. **Stable.** Designed to follow a status quo and commonly found in many large, well-established companies. There are rules, so follow them. A stable culture has a very hierarchical structure and can be very bureaucratic.

8. **Detail-oriented.** Often found in the hospitality, medical, and transportation industry, where the emphasis is on

all the little things. It's all about the details each and every day.

The above list is just a sampling of some of the types of traditional culture models you could choose for your company. While you might recognize and appreciate some elements from each of these different culture types already in your workplace, as you build the vision for your company's culture, consider the best culture model before you decide which one to fully implement. I encourage you to *choose* to build a V.A.L.U.E. Culture that combines the best pieces from several of the types described and then amps up the impact within your business so everyone benefits.

A positive V.A.L.U.E. Culture is *results-oriented* but *not* at the expense of people or innovative productivity driving ideas. It is *stable* and *detail-oriented* while it is also *people and outcome-oriented*. A thriving culture will include a multitude of facets. It's up to great leaders, like yourself, to add the most effective ingredients.

Building a beneficial V.A.L.U.E. Culture starts with developing *leadership* that requires a *vision*, includes *accountability*, and celebrates the unique skills and abilities that each person brings to the table. When combined, it builds an engaged workforce that will leave your competition asking what's the secret sauce you're feeding your employees to get such amazing results.

WHAT'S YOUR CHANGE BAROMETER?

Before you start implementing new ideas, you need to evaluate your organization's readiness to change. Evaluating readiness to change helps determine if the leadership team and the employees' mindset are in a position to make the necessary changes and if the timing is right. Establishing an evaluation period gives you time to ensure you have buy-in from leadership because if they are not committed to making necessary changes to support the new culture build, it will fail. Culture-building programs require resources, including time, money, and personnel. Evaluating the readiness of the organization helps to determine if the necessary resources are available and if they are being allocated in a way that supports the changes needed. Therefore everyone needs to be on board.

Leaders need to understand employees often feel like their workplace changes too much or changes in a way that does not benefit them directly. It is helpful to ask them questions; they may worry that a new culture will negatively impact their job security, working conditions, or relationships with colleagues. It's important for leaders to acknowledge these concerns and communicate transparently about the reason for another change. In some cases, resistance to culture change may be rooted in the fear of the unknown or a reluctance to step outside of one's comfort zone. Leaders can help employees overcome these barriers by determining their level of resistance to change before embarking on a new program. Think back over the last 12, 18, or 24 months and ask yourself:

- Does my leadership team jump on every new practice they hear about at the latest conference they attended?
- Does every employee meeting mean there's a new policy, a new program, a new product, a new management initiative, or a new process?
- Do new initiatives only serve upper management?

If change has been a constant inside your walls, you will need to proceed slowly because change requires employee engagement and buy-in. Evaluating the readiness of employees will help you to identify potential resistance and understand the motivation and expectations of the workforce. Think about the number of projects that are truly successful at your company that have initiated some kind of change. Most workplace changes are released under the guise of keeping up with the competition or becoming more profitable. The key to managing change is focus.

Know that there is a limit to everyone's *change capacity*. A smaller number of changes can have larger impacts. Yet, you also need to gauge the emotional status of your employees. Are they burnt out with all the new initiatives? If your employees are running on empty, be prepared to have real, honest conversations about what's happened in the past and why this change is one to believe in and get behind.

A culture build should align with the organization's business goals and strategies. Evaluating the readiness of the organization helps ensure the culture build program is aligned with these goals and supports the vision for long-term success. If you haven't completed an evaluation of your organization's readiness for change, you should consider waiting to roll out a culture program until you've done the research on your organization and completed this book.

A V.A.L.U.E. CULTURE EMBRACES FAILURE

When I first started my career with a daily newspaper, I wasn't writing articles. I worked in layout, graphic design, and ad creation. During a particularly aggressive election period, there was a highly contested race for Sheriff. Newspapers love elections because there is a never-ending supply of content for articles and a huge uptick in ad sales. I was tasked with putting together a *vote for me* ad for one of the candidates running for Sheriff. He had been a deputy for many years and wanted to include wording reminding people of his long years of service. We were under a deadline to get the paper out. The ad was hastily put together, and several pages of copy were rearranged to make it fit, and it was sent to press. The next morning when I arrived at the office, my editor was fuming when I entered the building. In our haste to squeeze an additional ad into the paper, the ad ran with a spelling error. Instead of talking about the many years of 'public' service the candidate had, it exposed his years of 'pubic' service. Let's just say my editor was not happy, nor was the ad manager because it meant running a free 'corrected' ad. The only person who wasn't upset was the candidate, who later told me that one ad had generated more interest than any other.

My failure taught me several valuable lessons. Don't rely on spell check! Have multiple sets of eyes read through your work. And have a sense of humor. I remember all those lessons today because we learn from our failures. When you're trying something new or are in a new role, not everything works. *Creating an environment of safety and trust is a must.* That carries over into the daily workflow. You want innovative employees, but you won't get forward-thinking employees willing to step out if they fear what happens if an idea doesn't work out as planned.

Holding both employees and leadership accountable is key when it comes to creating an environment of trust which is necessary for a thriving culture. Without that, there's no ownership. Having no accountability hinders teamwork. With accountability, everyone is united, working toward a goal. When a team is united, failures become a learning process for everyone to grow from, leading to greater success. Accountability is key for creating an effective, trusting team environment and cultivating a successful organization. Without it, employees will not be held responsible for their actions or lack thereof, leading to ineffective processes and a lack of ownership. A unified team is capable of learning from mistakes, which in turn leads to greater success.

CULTURE CHANGE GENERATES EXCITEMENT AND ENGAGEMENT

Now is the time for you to build excitement from the multi-faceted approach you take during your V.A.L.U.E. Culture roll-out. When you communicate the vision clearly, employees will see how the change benefits them and feel the excitement coming from the change. You can continue to build on that excitement by encouraging employees to participate by contributing ideas and getting involved in the initiatives. This will help you drive the change throughout all departments. When you take time to celebrate and highlight successes along the way, it helps to continue building momentum and generate ongoing excitement. The sense of community you build promotes teamwork, collaboration, and a sense of purpose and fulfillment among employees. You see the benefit of reduced turnover and building loyalty by providing an employee-focused culture and setting up structures that foster career development opportunities.

Engaged employees have increased loyalty. When you build a V.A.L.U.E. Culture, you can create a highly engaged workforce who wants to be there and will stay long-term. To meet that goal, here are some terrific, proven ways you can implement to create a successful structure:

- Increasing employee visibility inside the establishment
- Building mentor/sponsor relationships
- Communicating effectively
- Fostering collaboration

- Overcoming obstacles
- Recognizing an individual's unique skills and strengths
- Providing a path for internal growth opportunities
- Building strong personal brands
- Building networks that grow careers

Imagine a workplace where employees love to come every day. Yes, there will still be the occasional bad day, but those days won't create the feeling that permeates the organization. Instead, a successful structure will create a place where employees are respected, trusted, and supported every step of the way. A healthy organizational culture is one where everyone takes responsibility and works together collaboratively to achieve common goals. Recognizing individual successes and failures alike fosters a safe environment for growth and meaningful relationships between coworkers. Therefore, with the proper infrastructure in place, including adequate accountability and support, an enjoyable workplace can be created.

I've worked with many companies, assisting them in implementing culture changes, and it's undeniable the effect an excited workforce brings. Excited employees are more motivated and engaged, leading to higher levels of performance. Employees experience higher satisfaction and morale levels which leads to reduced absenteeism and turnover. Excited employees are more likely to bring new ideas and approaches to their work. They drive innovation and growth. Your customers will experience improved interactions, and you'll see increased customer loyalty and positive brand improvement. When employees are excited about their work, they are more likely to collaborate and work together effectively, resulting in better, stronger relationships. And one final fringe benefit is you'll find employees are excited to share the feeling with their friends, which improves your ability to recruit new employees in the future since your company will be known as a great place to work.

One of the ways you can keep the excitement train moving down the track is to identify what your employees want from their careers and build these opportunities into your culture program. Some options are great for multi-generational workplaces because all of your employees benefit from its availability. For example, everyone from Millennial to your Boomer *employees are interested in career development.* This is a staple ingredient in any successful culture program. When employees feel leaders are interested in their development, they feel a renewed excitement and passion for their jobs. On the flip side, companies that ignore development and keep going with the status quo, risk turnover, poor customer interactions, and low morale. To ensure successful career growth, companies should provide employees with regular feedback, training, and development opportunities that are tailored to their individual needs and aspirations. This helps foster employee engagement, growth, and satisfaction in the workplace. Investing in career development is an essential step for any organization that wishes to create a culture of success and loyalty.

Building a strong culture invigorates employees and rewards those who take steps to engage actively. Great leaders often turn their team members into problem solvers. *Who better identifies ways to save money and create better customer experiences than the internal team?* Many great advancements unfold when a team can utilize failures and learn from them. It requires the leader to open themselves up to ideas and embrace change, which means leaders are the first to shift their thoughts and move from past mistakes into potential solutions. As examples of resilience and growth, they make ways for the rest of the team to do the same, helping create an environment where failure is seen as a learning opportunity. When employees see that their leaders support them in taking risks and learning from mistakes, this helps foster a positive working environment that encourages creativity, exploration, and personal growth. Both the leader and the employee have a shared responsibility for tuning into the individual needs of each team member and fostering an atmosphere of trust and collaboration. With these tools in place, teams can strive to achieve success better together than they ever could have apart.

Encouraging a growth mindset creates not only a safe environment for learning, experimentation, and continuous improvement, but builds on the excitement your employees feel because it signals you value their thoughts and ideas. As their leader, support your team members to take calculated risks and embrace failure as a learning opportunity. Then, allow that to be reflected throughout the team dynamics and see how that creates an open dialogue where all voices can be heard, and everyone is encouraged to contribute.

To keep that energy, leaders need to exhibit a growth mindset, too. I've seen bad cultures in the workplace, and those are generally accompanied by leaders who are close-minded or not open to change, instead choosing to continue forward with a *that's the way it's always been done* mindset in spite of needed change. However, I have also seen companies with a positive-minded leader that has led to the creation of a collaborative, engaged, and profitable workplace environment where people clamor to work in. A growth mindset encourages leaders to continuously look beyond setbacks or challenges while seeking out new knowledge, skills, and experiences that help both themselves and the company improve.

In my experience, a growth mindset means leaders are more

open to change and better equipped to adapt to new challenges *and new* opportunities. Employees will feel, and feed off, your excitement over the positive changes. These types of leaders encourage experimentation and support innovative thinking, which drives progress inside an organization. They don't let setbacks derail the movement. They embrace the vision and see the possibilities. Growth-minded leaders aren't worried about it being perfect before they start because they know *consistency is better than perfect any day*. And most importantly, they continue to build on the excitement their employees are experiencing and inspire their team to embrace the culture changes and live the values the company has instilled.

SMALL GESTURES LEAD TO BIG CULTURE IMPACTS

It is incredible how the small stuff, or what seems like a small gesture of sharing can change the culture all around us. Building a V.A.L.U.E. Culture *begins with the small step of appreciating your co-workers and employees by getting to know them personally*.

Remembering special occasions like birthdays and work anniversaries is important to show you value them personally. Communicating in person and making time to be one-on-one with each member of our team is a vital community builder. The personal touch makes a much deeper impression than any email or interoffice memo.

As a leader, commit to engaging those employees who tend to be less visible or social. Every person has their own preference for how they like to be thanked. Some enjoy public praise, while others prefer a quiet word of thanks. Knowing how a person *likes to receive recognition* is also an important part of the leadership process. How you like recognition may not be how your team likes it. Knowing how people enjoy being praised, and validating those differences will bring you closer to each individual on their unique terms. Once you've implemented those personal one-on-one actions, you can make a broader impact in other ways.

A well-liked idea is to go public with your gratitude by setting up a 'brag board' and posting your appreciation there. Try opening your staff meetings with an invitation for team members to thank someone for a recent contribution. Share publicly on social media the great work coming from your team. Handwrite a thank you card. Create an atmosphere where recognition, both large and small, becomes the norm, not the exception.

When employees see leaders sharing and supporting others, it encourages them to model the same behavior. Recognizing the impact members of your team have on a program's success is powerful. You can reap culture rewards for just recognizing someone's willingness to go the extra mile to assist someone else.

Small gestures of acknowledgment and appreciation create a culture that values employees' efforts and encourages them to go the extra mile. From offering recognition for accomplishments in the form of rewards or public accolades to simply saying thank you for your hard work, these small tokens can have a huge impact on employee morale. Implementing a culture of peer-to-peer encouragement and support can create an environment where team members feel comfortable recognizing each other for their efforts and inspiring others to do their best. Recognizing team members for accomplishments can generate excitement in the workforce by showing that hard work and dedication are valued by the organization. Additionally, rewards, such as bonuses and flexible scheduling, can give employees an extra boost of motivation to continue going above and beyond their job duties. Making employees feel appreciated creates a sense of loyalty and strengthens the relationship between employer and employee. Ultimately, this leads to higher engagement levels and a positive overall environment for everyone in the workplace.

Knowing the type of culture you have and the type of culture you wish to create is the first step in recognizing the changes you have the power to make. Nothing truly impactful can happen if you first don't see what you have to work with, what you envision going forward, and what type of culture will work best in your environment. As we move on, you will begin to discover the necessary steps in building a people-first workplace culture.

V.A.L.U.E. CULTURES CULTIVATE GRATITUDE

I believe being grateful puts the human touch back into the workplace, and that is a cornerstone to building a V.A.L.U.E. Culture. Studies have shown employee appreciation, and recognition programs increase team spirit, morale, and productivity. Therefore, it is vital that the workplace fosters an environment for gratitude to flourish. Gratitude can coexist with ambition and competition and be successfully included as part of your employee appreciation and recognition efforts. Gratitude is both a top motivator for employees' job satisfaction and a key driver of engagement. Employees sighted gratitude as one of the top five factors in being motivated at work and nearly two-thirds prefer verbal thanks over any other reward or recognition they receive. It may be surprising, but gratitude has become an essential ingredient in creating meaningful connections between leaders and their teams.

In the spirit of creating gratitude amongst your team, it is important to ask yourself, do you feel comfortable expressing thankfulness in front of your colleagues? Do you actively seek out opportunities to thank and recognize people when they do something well? Is there a protocol for thanking others or do you have the habit of thanking them spontaneously and publicly? Practicing gratitude at work may feel risky, but the results are worth it. It boosts morale, strengthens interpersonal relationships, and reinforces a culture of respect. I've witnessed the results of being grateful as part of a training session a group of managers took part in. During our time together, I asked them to write down a short sentence on why they were grateful to be working where they did and then share it with the group. As you probably expect, I received answers like, "They provided great benefits" and "They were well-known or respected in the community." Then I took the exercise a step further and asked them to write down reasons why they were grateful for each member of their team. For some, the exercise was challenging, and they came up with single ideas like that person is dependable, competent, and great at managing the details. For others, their coaching style of leadership showed through. Their answers included their positive attitude, their ability to de-escalate complaints, and their ability to empathize with other co-workers and help them through rough times, all things that were more team related than single-focused.

Finally, I asked the participants to write down why they were grateful for the person sitting to their right. That took the exercise to the next level as people became personally invested in the authentic gratitude they wanted to share. Having them do this part of the gratitude activity is where the real shift took place. As they shared why they valued their co-worker, the people in the room began to connect to one another on an emotional level. They felt gratitude for more than their skills. They valued the relationships they built and grew a willingness to help each other reach their personal and professional goals. The recognition of one another's efforts and qualities reinforced why gratitude needs to be shared in the moment, face to face. Saying positive things in person to one another is a powerful way to express the value team members bring to the entire office community.

As a leader, regardless of your position, there are things you can personally do to feel and practice gratitude. Take the time to think about your team and where showing gratitude would support them. Envision how the team might react when they receive recognition for their hard work or when they're thanked for their efforts—from the biggest achievement to the smallest gestures—and consider how showing gratitude would inspire them both today and in the future. Showing appreciation has been found to be an invaluable asset in cultivating teams that are engaged and committed, which is why it must become an integral part of a leader's responsibility.

When it comes to gratitude, I want you to meet an incredible person, Kevin Monroe, the founder of *I'm Grateful For You* and owner of *X-Factor Consulting*™. Kevin understands the power of gratitude within the workplace and how it can impact the V.A.L.U.E. Culture. He was willing to share great insight on how building gratitude into your culture can improve the feelings of value and acceptance your employees' experience at work.

Q. Kevin, please share the concept of gratitude in the workplace.

Gratitude isn't an option anymore. It's *vitally important in the workplace.* Both from the employer and the employee. Employees can feel unseen, unheard, and undervalued; however, gratitude is a tool that can be used to build connections.

I see gratitude as an essential skill. Now that we are almost three years into the pandemic and have faced the Great Resignation, *gratitude is key to building connections* more quickly than anything else. It's an essential skill for life and work.

Q. How do you define gratitude?

My favorite definition of gratitude comes from Pat Blackstaffe in her book *It's Not All Strawberries and Cream, But There's Some Wonderful Moments.* Her definition is an *appreciation for all that we have, all that we are, and thankfulness for our ability to show love and kindness to others.* One of the reasons I use that definition is that I grew up in the South, and was taught gratitude as part of good manners—to say please, and thank you.

But, when I started having gratitude practices, it seemed like it was all about gratitude for people and things. *I'm thankful for my wife, our children, my home, my job, and those kinds of things.*

Now, what if we expand gratitude to be all that we are? This is where gratitude gets powerful in the workplace. We're not just saying 'thank you' for the work you did. But *saying thank you for the worker you are and the skills, talents, and abilities you give to our company. Thank you, for investing in our company every day.* There's an appreciation for bringing your authentic self to work.

Q. Incredible. Can you share an example of a business leader who understood the concept?

I've got the perfect example. Bob Chapman, CEO of *Barry-Wehmiller Companies, Inc.*, said for years, *we paid people for their hands when they would have given us their heads and their hearts if we only knew how to ask.*

Gratitude is not just saying thank you for a task. When we

say, I appreciate you or I'm grateful for your skills. I'm grateful for your effort in going the extra mile or staying longer to care about our customers and clients. Gratitude needs to move from transactional to transformational in the workplace.

Q. How do you do this in a way that comes across as genuine and not just as words coming out of your mouth?

We launched a card campaign called *I'm Grateful For You*. As we were launching, I realized *simple plus sincere equals significant*.

We made it simple. We have two versions of a card. One is just business card size, and it says *I'm grateful for you* and the back is blank, where people can just write a note. The other is a note-size card.

If you recognize somebody for some achievement or they're getting an award, write a longer note. I promise you, no one who gets a card throws it away. The card becomes a keeper.

I've got a CEO in California who gave a card to a friend, and her friend then gave it to her son. The CEO said her friend told her the son said, "I'm putting it on my refrigerator and never taking it down." Three weeks later, her son called her and said, "You know what, I saw that card today. And, I thought of you. I'm grateful for you. That card's never coming off my refrigerator."

People keep these things. The message is very simple; I'm grateful for you. But, if I add some sincerity into that expression and communication, it becomes significant.

Q. How do you ensure that gratitude comes across as sincere and not shallow?

I'd like to say it never happens, but occasionally it does. I've worked for leaders that if their company were working on gratitude, it would look something like this. I'd go in on Monday morning to the team meeting, and attached to the meeting agenda would be one of these cards. Item one on the agenda would be gratitude.

The leader would say, "Hey, everybody, look at your agenda. Attached to the agenda is a card. I'm grateful to you. You *know*, I'm grateful to you. Okay, let's go on to what's next." And, that would be a gimmick. Shallow is a gimmick.

Q. Kevin, share more about how recognition and gratitude amplify each other.

Here's what experienced leaders and HR professionals tell me. *We've invested in a recognition system, and nobody uses it. It seems formal and slow.* The problem with standard types of recognition is the length of time involved. When you have somebody submit something, and it's weeks or months after the event happened before somebody's being recognized for something, it loses its meaning or importance.

The person being recognized is like, yeah, I kind of remember that. But what if, to quote Ken Blanchard, *we catch people doing something right?* And when you catch somebody doing something, right, what if that is the moment you stop them and say, "You know what? What you just did was amazing."

If you're in a call center and you're listening, some companies require their leaders to monitor those calls once a month. You could potentially hear one of your employees dealing with an irate customer exceptionally well.

In that moment, you should go over and praise your employee, making sure you are being specific. You say something like, "Hey, Michelle, I heard how you handled that situation with an irate customer, and wow, the empathy and compassion you showed were amazing. You diffused a very negative and volatile situation with kindness and compassion, and that's why I'm so glad you're representing our company."

Now, what's Michelle doing when she goes home at night? She's absolutely sharing what happened at work today. She's going to tell her friends, and she is going to tell her family.

Q. Kevin, is it powerful to give recognition in the moment?

When you catch someone doing something right, or when you see people living out the values you want representing your company, you recognize them, and you say, "Wow. You just honored your commitment to a customer; you kept your word, you kept our word, and as a company, we value that."

It's these little things that are expressions of gratitude. But they make the most impact when they are specific and sincere.

The real magic of a gratitude practice *happens because you are helping people be seen for who they are and what they bring to the work, not* just in the tasks they do but in what they invest in themselves and the way they are living out the core values your company believes are important. I know from my experience that showing gratitude in the workplace will help drive your employee engagement off the charts. *Why?* Because people *feel* appreciated. People *feel* valued. People *feel* respected. Those feelings go a long way to bolster your culture-building efforts.

As you think of how you can create more gratitude in your office, enjoy more of Kevin as he shares examples from a hotel manager to a school-system leader on how you can implement gratitude into your office. These successful tools are easy to replicate in any industry setting. Kevin also has some great advice on how you can convince upper management and your board of the value of investing in a culture initiative that includes an element of gratitude.

Q. Kevin, I know you feel gratitude, and culture change can come from small beginnings. Would you elaborate?

Suppose you aren't a senior leader in your company or have difficulty convincing a board to allocate funds for a culture initiative. You can start impacting organizational culture even from your cubicle.

Have you ever heard of Chip and Dan Heath? They have written several books, and one of them is called *Made to Stick*. (2) They talk about being a bright spot. They share how you, as one person, with just your cube, office, or team can help build culture and become a bright spot.

Other people will begin wondering *What's happening with that person?* They have higher results. They have more camaraderie. They have a lower turnover. Wow, how do I get to work with that person? You become a bright spot. Much of that happens just by expressing gratitude.

Q. Kevin, is incorporating gratefulness an intentional action?

Absolutely! I sign my emails with some kind of gratitude:
- "In gratitude"
- "Gratefully"
- "With gratitude," etc.

But it's not part of a standard signature. Why? I want to type it every time.

I want to actually pause for that moment and say, "I am grateful for this person. I am grateful for this conversation or this opportunity."

It's not just part of the default signature. I purposely want to add it in. Imagine if people started using these words. I'm not trying to put words in people's mouths. But whether you say with gratitude, or gratefully or I'm grateful for you, whatever your preference, people will notice when you start signing all of your emails like that. People will notice that positive perspective.

Q. Does gratitude change how we see the workplace?

What gratitude does is it changes how we see the world. Gratitude is a perspective and sense-making skill we need. DeWitt Jones, a photographer from *National Geographic*™, talks about it. His whole message is what's right with the world.[3]

If we go looking for what's right with the world, what's good in the situation, or what is there to be grateful for, it changes how we see things. We don't see the world as it is; we see it as we are.

You may have those negative Neds and negative Nellies that no matter what happens, there's always something negative about why. They have a negative outlook on life. Likewise, if we're looking for the good or we're looking to find something to be grateful for in the situation, we will find it. And that desire will direct where we go and what we find. And it creates that kind of positivity. And people want to be around those people. People want to work in a workgroup that's led by somebody positive and uplifting, and encouraging.

Q. Kevin, what do you think about the workplace community? Is gratitude becoming increasingly important to today's workers?

Gratitude is becoming increasingly important to today's workers. Employees thrive when they feel like they are part of a strong team. According to a McKinsey report,(⁴) *next to not feeling valued, not feeling a sense of belonging is the reason people leave their job.*

If you want to be grateful, no one can stop you. They can't come out and say stop being so cheerful. They may criticize you; however, it's a personal choice. Nobody can stop you. And, what if you started just infusing a little here and there? Imagine the impact.

Engagement is a direct benefit of a value culture.

Q. That brings me to another question. Kevin, do you have an example of how one person practicing gratitude impacts the workplace?

Oh, yes. The teacher's name is Heidi. It was at a time during an election cycle when it got really toxic and negative. She said the teaching lounge had once been a place of refuge, but it had become a place she didn't want to go. There was so much negativity and toxicity, and she wanted to do something about it.

Heidi didn't ask permission from anyone. She took a poster board, went in on the first day of a month, and wrote, what are you grateful for? She stuck it up (on the wall), and she wrote something on the note. Maybe one or two other people did it that first day.

The next day, she returned with a new poster board with the same question, what are you grateful for today? She repeated the process every day for a month. By the beginning of the second week, there were lots of people writing on the poster board. She said by the beginning of the third week, the atmosphere in the teachers' lounge had changed.

She didn't ask permission. It wasn't a company-sponsored initiative. She just put up a poster board every day, asking,

"What are you grateful for?"

Q. Technology is taking a front seat in the way we communicate in the workplace. There is less and less face-to-face interaction. I asked Kevin to share some ways business leaders can use technology to help spread gratitude.

Two years ago, when we first started doing gratitude challenges, we were just using email. At that time, Melissa Boggs, Co-CEO of *Scrum Alliance*™, started posting whatever the prompt of the day was in our email on their company Slack channel.

Just like with Heidi, it didn't take off overnight, but some people started responding. About three months later, Melissa told me other people started sharing the prompt. And, then all of a sudden, several times a week, somebody just does a shout-out, "Hey, what are you grateful for now?" Or, "what's the best thing that happened to you today?"

And these things just ripple throughout the company. Anybody has the power to post on a Slack channel. Anybody can post others' posts; what's their favorite inspirational or motivational quote of the day? *Domino's*, a Latino family services organization in New Mexico, starts with a mindfulness moment in every meeting.

I've been part of several of their meetings. Different people bring mindfulness moments each time. It's a point they read or a daily devotion or inspirational piece. The beautiful thing is they just take two minutes at the start of a meeting and have one of these uplifting, encouraging moments. It changes the tone. It's so simple.

Q. As we see these changes happen, I wonder how we can measure the effectiveness of gratitude?

While there isn't a line on the balance sheet for culture initiatives, implementing these changes can have a real impact on the profitability and productivity of a company. First of all, ask what measurements are important to your company? Every company is measuring something. So, what is it that you're measuring?

Be curious how positivity and gratitude will impact that measurement. If it's employee engagement, you will watch that number go up. If you're concerned about turnover, you will watch turnover go down. I have some statistics.

Seventy percent of employees would *feel better* about themselves if their *boss* were *more grateful*. Eighty-one percent would work harder. This information is from *Glassdoor™*. When we start with gratitude and embrace positivity, I think it will move any number in the right direction. A friend shared with me *fifty-nine percent of people have never had a boss who truly appreciates their work.* That's six out of ten people who feel they have always been undervalued. What they're saying is they feel taken for granted.

Q. Kevin, it brings up a powerful point. What other measures can we take to see the culture change?

Let's look at discretionary effort, which really means going the extra mile, going above and beyond, and doing more than required. Discretionary effort shoots through the roof when people feel appreciated.

One of my favorite studies shows that three groups of people are impacted when appreciation or gratitude is expressed. The person expressing the gratitude and the person to whom the gratitude is expressed is a given. But there is a third group, and think about this group in the workplace. It's the people that see a leader or a peer appreciating someone else in the company. Anybody that sees that has a positive response to it.

They are more likely to say yes to a project or go the extra mile when they feel that effort.

Q. That is a great example of how positive change can start with a small movement!

It is! I've seen people just go in and write it on the whiteboard in a big common conference area, and people just come in and start responding. And, it just spreads. It's the simple things that cost no money. Now, you can do formal programs, which could be good for you, but you can also start with nothing and one person.

Heidi made a difference in that school. Because she was fed up with it, she became the one person who made a difference.

What if we started our team meetings with what we have to celebrate this week rather than what went wrong? What happens with so many team meetings is people come in and discuss that last customer encounter they had or the colleague that wasn't doing what they were supposed to do, and it becomes a gripe session from the beginning.

What if, instead, somebody said, "Hey, let me tell you what just happened? It was the most amazing thing." What was the most amazing thing that happened to you? What was the best client encounter you have had so far?

It changes the atmosphere. It's a simple question. You can ask that question in so many different ways. It's not just what you are grateful for. It is also, *what was the best part of your day? What went really well?* It just ripples, and the ripple effect is amazing. That is a great example of how positive change can start with a small movement!

Q. I can see how all of that is true. Can you share how gratitude is a great rebuilder of connections?

Yes. I can share a story about Nick. He's the general manager of *Hilton Garden Inn™* at Albany Medical Center in Albany, New York. The hotel is connected to the hospital. Many people stay in the hotel and have family or go into the hospital themselves for surgery. Nick has so many stories, but the pandemic wiped their team and business out.

Nick has been rebuilding, and he rebuilt with gratitude and expressing gratitude. He just watches it permeate the team and the facility. He sees it transform some challenging guest encounters and witnesses the change in people.

He called me a couple of weeks ago to tell me about a guy that was just *so in his face.* He was so mad about the situation. They were playing a *Little League™* baseball tournament, and his son got hit in the head. He was rushed to the hospital by helicopter. He and his wife were rushing in the car, trying to get there.

They're all upset and don't know what's going on or what's going to happen, and there is a lot of emotion. But Nick handled it with gratitude and understanding. The next day, the guy looked him up and apologized. He said, "Man, you know I overreacted." Nick's open understanding and kindness diffused a negative situation.

Q. Kevin, what does the opposite of these gratitude actions look like? What is the ripple effect?

Well, the sad truth is the impact of those negative encounters is hard to overcome. The negative impact seems to permeate the culture like crazy.

Studies show it takes at least five positive encounters to offset a negative experience.(6) And, these bad experiences are more likely to be shared faster than positive ones.

Q. I have heard you mention the ripple effect, what is that?

What if instead of negative, you're the person that's creating positive ripples?

My friend Jenny calls it building the gratitude reservoir. What if all of these times you're expressing gratitude, you're just filling up the reservoir? Think about it like in the electricity business. A storm hits, and people suddenly work outrageous overtime to restore community power.

Suppose those employees feel appreciated and recognized for all that they do when those storms hit. In that case, employees are proud to be out there representing the company and going above and beyond to restore power.

They know they are a vital service to our community. But if employees feel neglected, overlooked, and ignored, they're not out there with any joy. In those moments, they're begrudging. They have to do it.

We all see people we can tell love what they do. And, they get to be a hero by helping others. When we appreciate them for that, it fills their tank and inspires them to do more.

I am so grateful to Kevin for sharing so much about gratitude and how using it in everyday business, with both customers and the team raises the connection and compassion we all need in business. If you read any of the great business books and follow most of the top CEOs, many of them list gratitude as the key component in creating a successful workplace culture. Gratitude is not simply a 'nice to have' but an absolute essential in today's business world. There have been numerous studies conducted on the positive impact of gratitude within organizations, and it has been found that gratitude leads to improved satisfaction levels among employees. When employees feel appreciated for their efforts and valuable contributions, there is a greater sense of involvement leading to higher engagement rates.

Gratitude also helps create a more unified environment, fostering relationships between colleagues and managers. By implementing programs that deliver public praise, rewards, or incentives for high-performance achievements, businesses can provide an atmosphere where everyone feels valued and respected. Acknowledging team members, both individually and collectively, sends a powerful message from leaders that each individual plays an important role in achieving organizational goals. Fostering a culture of gratitude will ultimately lead to increased morale, teamwork, and loyalty towards one's work - which are all essential components in any company's success.

BAKE, BUILD, AND BRING GRATITUDE INTO EVERYTHING

Incorporating gratitude into the culture and workplace is an essential component of creating a positive and thriving work environment. Gratitude builds strong relationships among employees, enhances job satisfaction, and fosters a sense of belonging and fulfillment. By expressing appreciation and recognition for the hard work and contributions of others, employees feel valued and respected, which in turn leads to higher levels of engagement, motivation, and loyalty.

Cultivating a culture of gratitude also helps to promote a sense of positivity and optimism, even during challenging times, which can improve overall well-being and reduce stress. The overall practice of gratitude can have a profound impact on individuals and the organization as a whole, creating a more supportive, collaborative, and successful workplace.

Adding gratitude to your culture program costs nothing, yet the rewards will be great. In my professional experience, I've worked in an organization where employees didn't feel valued, where they watched poor performance be rewarded, and where a simple thank you wasn't heard. The small act of letting someone know their actions were valuable and mattered creates a major-league kind of impact.

The most meaningful way to show gratitude to coworkers is to lend a hand when you see them struggling to meet a deadline or finish a project. Volunteer to cover a task so they can focus on the big project at hand. Acknowledge when they go out of their way or exceed expectations, and reach out simply because you appreciate their hard work and dedication. These actions practiced consistently will generate an air of gratitude that will permeate throughout your company, creating a unified culture where everyone feels valued, respected, and appreciated. Building a culture filled with gratitude is a culture to be proud of!

Since you now understand the benefits and have a firm foundation of the value of adding gratitude to your workplace, here's a simple process you can use to create a gratitude and recognition foundation with your team.

- **Start with yourself:** before you can effectively promote gratitude and recognition among your team, it's important to cultivate these practices within yourself. Take time each day to reflect on what you're grateful for, and actively look for opportunities to express appreciation to those around you.

- **Communicate the importance of gratitude and recognition:** Schedule a team meeting and communicate the importance you place on gratitude and recognition. Share research or anecdotes highlighting the positive impact these practices have on employee morale, productivity, and retention.
- **Encourage peer-to-peer recognition:** Rather than relying solely on top-down managers, encourage your team members to express gratitude and recognize each other. Consider implementing a recognition program that allows employees to nominate their colleagues for recognition or create a space for public shoutouts and personal thank yous.
- **Lead by example:** As a leader, your behavior sets the tone for the rest of your team. Make a point to regularly express gratitude and recognize the efforts taking place by your team. Make sure your gratitude is done in a way that feels genuine and sincere.
- **Integrate gratitude and recognition into team processes:** Incorporate gratitude and recognition into your routines, such as regular check-ins or team meetings. This can help ensure the practice becomes a natural part of the team's interactions.
- **Regularly assess and adjust:** Regularly assess how your team is responding to your efforts to promote gratitude and recognition and adjust your approach as necessary. Get feedback from your employees on what's working and what can be improved. Be willing to make changes based on what feedback you hear.

By following a few easy and simple steps, you can begin cultivating a culture of gratitude and recognition that has a significant positive impact on your team's morale and productivity. If you do just one thing from this entire book, this should be it: Make sure to thank people for even the smallest accomplishments and recognize them for everything they do. And if you're not sure where to start, this is the best way to begin: make a list of the small but noteworthy things your team does every day and show your appreciation for each one. The power of appreciation should never be underestimated; take the time to express it when it's due and watch as it works its magic!

CHAPTER 6:

Where Do I Start?

I hope I have adequately and eloquently sold you on the importance of creating a V.A.L.U.E. Culture in your workplace, and you're ready to dive into making massive organizational shifts. I want you to feel the excitement building like someone getting ready to open gifts on Christmas and know that once you make this shift, you'll see a significant increase in employee engagement and overall satisfaction. By prioritizing culture and investing in a positive work environment, you'll create a sense of purpose and belonging among your team members. Once that happens, get ready to experience the benefits of a strong workplace culture—from increased creativity and innovation to stronger relationships with customers and clients. With the right mindset and a commitment to making positive change, you can create a workplace people are excited to be a part of, and you are proud to represent.

So, let's start building...

As you begin to design your culture plan, let's start by defining the DNA of your culture. This will allow you to establish all the value strands and characteristics that need to be forged together to make your unique V.A.L.U.E. Culture thrive. This beginning point will reveal to you what your workforce intrinsically needs and the best way to start sharing your ideas.

When working with my client's management team, I ask them to get everyone in a room together because they need to clarify the company's *purpose, vision, and values* before they move forward. They need to agree on a set of expected employee behaviors that are based on those values. They need to generate buy-in from all levels of management on the behaviors they will model for employees, so those are the ones duplicated in day-to-day work.

Let's break these vital steps down further by starting with defining your company's purpose.

CULTURE STARTS WITH PURPOSE.

Culture starts with a purpose. Ask yourself, *why is my company in business to begin with?* Your answer should give you a great direction. *Purpose serves as your DNA marker.* It becomes the framework to build your unique culture around. Purpose is all about the "why" your company is in business. It should reflect the company's values, culture, and goals. It serves as a guide for both decision-making and action-taking. When you know the company's purpose, you are able to align company objectives with the expectations of stakeholders, including customers, employees, and investors. A clear purpose serves as a guide for setting priorities, establishing strategic priorities, measuring progress, and creating a workplace that people get excited about being a part of. Ultimately, it should capture the essence of what the company does and why it matters. A great purpose doesn't have to be complicated. In fact, the best is simple and easy to remember.

Later in the book, you'll hear from the *WD-40™ Company* CEO Garry Ridge and what he has to say about the importance of purpose. (Here is a hint! *WD-40™*, a company that usually brings to mind a product that loosens screws or stops squeaks, has an entirely different purpose statement. Their purpose is simple, to create memories—but more on that later).

To establish a powerful purpose statement, use words that reflect your company values, goals, and brand. Think about the problem your business solves for your customers and the value it provides to them. Think about who you are impacting and the impact your business has on the community it is a part of.

What makes your company different from your competitors?

What is the long-term vision for your company?

How do you want the direction of the company to inspire the team?

The resulting purpose statement should be concise, clear, and inspiring. Start by boiling your answer down into *two simple sentences or less*. Make sure in those two sentences to reflect the unique business identity and values. The reason why I recommend two sentences or less is that it needs to be simple and easy to remember - not only for you, but for your employees also.

A concise and powerful purpose helps to unite every person in the workplace, giving employees a sense of direction and a common goal. When everyone understands and believes in the company's mission, they are more motivated to contribute to its success. This stimulates a culture of people-centeredness, inspiring collaboration, communication, and innovation.

Here's where you'll want to grab a pen and piece of paper, use any note-taking app on your phone or take advantage of the blank lines below. Use whatever it takes for you to capture your ideas or gather your thoughts on a clear and concise purpose statement.

Now that you have a purpose statement you like and feel defines the essence of the company, use it to inspire and motivate your team to take action. The purpose statement should be reflected in every aspect of the business, from how customers are treated, to job expectations and employee training. By incorporating the values within your statement into daily operations, everyone in the workplace will understand their role in achieving the organizers' goals.

In addition to operational integration, there are other ways that you can utilize your purpose statement to build a strong workplace culture. Regular meetings with employees and team-building events can help to foster an understanding of the company's vision among all members of the team. These opportunities provide invaluable insights into how each individual contributes to driving progress for the organization as well as give them a sense of pride in being part of something greater than themselves.

MISSION DRIVES THE PLAN

A company mission is a statement that clearly defines a company's goals and values and serves as a guiding principle to help align staff toward a unified purpose. It shows potential customers, employees, and stakeholders what the company stands for and gives them insight into its culture. A great company mission also outlines how things are measured and monitored, so leaders can track progress toward their stated goals. However, it's important to note that mission statements aren't always indicative of the *culture* within an organization. The two may live in harmony, but what you say your team wants to accomplish should not replace open dialogue with employees—understanding their needs should come first. The best way to create an empowering workplace culture is to actively listen to your team's feedback and use this as the basis for creating a human-centered vision that incorporates both the employee's desires while also adhering to business objectives.

With thoughtful planning, mission statements can be used as powerful tools to help business leaders create inspiring cultures that support collaboration, growth, and innovation. Cultivating a thriving culture works in parallel with a great mission statement—it's about actively supporting the employees who will bring that mission to life. Executives should strive not only to define their team's mission and objectives but also to get out in front and lead by example within the culture.

A company's mission statement should be seen as an organic living document that evolves alongside its organization. Business leaders must strive to continuously review their mission and use it as a springboard for understanding how their team works best—whether through progress reports, surveys, or other forms of employee feedback. It is with this kind of insight that leadership can craft a dynamic workplace culture that will stay strong as everyone works to achieve the mission cohesively

As a leader, you must use the mission statement to cultivate a company culture that speaks to the values of the organization. By understanding and adhering to the company's core mission, you can create an atmosphere that drives employees to succeed and encourages growth within the team. Additionally, fostering healthy communication between executives and staff on how to accomplish the mission is essential for continued organizational development; it allows everyone to gain valuable insight into how the team will achieve the overall mission, which creates a thriving, dynamic culture.

"WHY" CREATES THE REASON

If your mission statement is the who, what, how, and when, your purpose is the *why* behind your mission statement. Articulating why your company exists in the world is extremely important. For example, how are you adding value to your customers' and employees' lives, and *why* is that important? The *why* allows your employees to connect on a personal level with how their job matters, not only to the company but to the customers they serve. When employees understand and connect with their company's *why* they can see how their job fits into the bigger picture and how it contributes to the company's overall goals. This can help them to feel more fulfilled and engaged in their work. For example, consider a company that is focused on environmental sustainability and whose purpose is to reduce its environmental impact. In that case, employees who work in areas like production, logistics, or purchasing can feel personally connected to the company's mission and motivated to make changes that will reduce waste, emissions, or other negative impacts. If a company's values include giving back to the community, employees who work in areas like customer service or marketing can feel connected to this mission by understanding how their work impacts customers or supports the company's philanthropic efforts. They can feel a sense of purpose and pride in working for a company that is making a positive impact. The *why* helps align all the employees around a common goal, creating a sense of purpose and meaning in their work. If a company has a clear *why* it means they have a clear purpose. This purpose goes beyond simply making a profit and is centered around creating value for their customers, employees, and society as a whole. It helps a company differentiate itself from its competitors. This is especially important in industries where products and services are similar.

Knowing the *why* behind the purpose helps a company make strategic decisions about allocating resources and pursuing growth opportunities. By focusing on its purpose, a company can prioritize investments that will have the greatest impact on both its employee base and its overall directive. A meaningful why gives greater traction to a well-defined purpose; they equally go hand in hand.

Having a clear *why* benefits the company in several ways. If you are eager to define your company's why, let's start with some questions that will help you.

- What inspires your business ideas?
- What is your founding story? What is interesting or

different about your company story? What had to be overcome to even open or create the business?

- What problem does your business solve for your customers?
- How has your business changed over the years?
- Why does your business exist?
- Does your business support a philanthropic cause? Why did you choose a particular charity?
- What do you believe in personally and professionally as the leader?

With those questions in mind, you can clearly define your workplace DNA because knowing your purpose is your *why*. Your answer will internally and externally, build a clear purpose that you can then use to determine the core values and behaviors you want employees to exhibit that reflect your corporate values. All of these key components create the framework—the DNA of what the company is aiming to offer—and become the fabric and the foundation of the culture you aspire to build.

THE WHY DRIVES THE MESSAGE HOME

If you haven't watched Simon Sinek's 2009 TEDx™ Talk, "How great leaders inspire action,"[1] I encourage you to do so. With over 61 million views at the time this book was published, Simon introduces a wonderful concept called *The Golden Circle*, and shows you how to create a successful three-layered business story.

Sinek says, "Almost every business knows *what* they do, some know *how* they do it, and even fewer know *why* they do it.!" To emphasize that thought, many companies know their *what*, some will know their *how*, but very little knows their *why*. Remember, the *why* is the DNA you need to establish in your business.

Knowing your why helps you and your team design a workplace culture reflective of the things both you, as a business leader, and they, as employees, are concerned about. This book has the many secret strategies Simon didn't share in that speech to make your unique culture a reality, and you will only reach your cultural nirvana by making sure to do the work.

That means rolling up your sleeves and going back to the questions above. Read over them again and think about each one specifically. After you've thought through your answers, have the rest of your leadership team or those you supervise do the same. Then compare notes and find if there are areas of difference. Share the answers and work towards one cohesive purpose you can share with the whole organization.

As a business leader, you need to shift from talking about what you do to creating an emotional connection with *why* you do it. That *why* doesn't only attract customers; it builds a connection with employees and future employees. When you identify the company's why and its true purpose, you grow loyalty and engagement on both fronts. Not only will your employees have buy-in when they understand their role in achieving the purpose, but the overall success will improve as well.

To be effective in implementing the *why*, you must determine how you will measure it. How will you determine if the plan is working? What do you want and need to improve? How will you know if your employees know their *why*? Does the team understand the future goals and how their work will contribute to the cause? It is important to ask these questions and communicate the why with your employees. Your company *why* will help align them with the organization's mission.

Working toward a common why raises morale, increases trust inside your workforce, and strengthens the workforce toward culture-building inside the company. Understanding the *why* helps employees see how their individual contributions fit into the big picture. The value they bring to the company will result in a stronger sense of ownership and connection for them. In turn, this can foster deeper loyalty and commitment among the team members as they strive to meet their collective objectives, resulting in greater productivity and success for all. Each one of these concepts is a key component in building a strong workplace culture. We'll discuss more in section two, Actions of Culture Builders.

The final step in creating purpose, mission, and *why* is to bring front-line employees into the discussion. Share your agreed-upon list with them. Without their buy-in, a culture can not grow. Brainstorm ideas together. Ask for feedback as the plan develops. Allow them to help shape the final look of the plan. If you provide a feedback opportunity for your team to offer their input, you'll increase engagement right from the beginning.

CULTURE EVOLVES ENDLESSLY

A corporate culture isn't ever static, especially at the beginning. As the leaders, you must *establish opportunities to strengthen and evolve your culture*. One way of providing culture-building opportunities is through feedback. While you can and should encourage random feedback, having an established process where employees understand how they can give feedback will be most effective.

Feedback is the lifeline of a company and the first indicator if your culture is reflecting your purpose, mission, and *why*.

All good companies want feedback because it is the first indicator of how effective the culture initiatives are, and whether employees are living up to the expectations of the purpose statement. Feedback allows management to quickly identify shortcomings that may be preventing their organization from achieving its objectives, as well as areas where more resources or focus should be allocated. Additionally, if the goal is to create a positive culture, then it's essential that employers take action based on employee feedback to ensure they are fostering an environment where everyone can succeed.

Try these suggestions to create an environment where everyone can feel valued, appreciated, and able to give constructive feedback.

Questions to Ask Employees to Strengthen Your Workplace Culture:

1. **What improvements or changes would you like to see in our company culture?** Every employee has at least one idea about how improvements could be made. Many ideas won't be feasible, but you're sure to get some good suggestions if you simply ask.

2. **What is your biggest gripe or pet peeve about the current culture?** If you're hearing the same couple of complaints from multiple employees, you have a great opportunity to make everyone happy with a few alterations.
   - Fixing something that annoys everyone is more powerful than adding something everyone likes.

3. **What do I need to do to be a better leader?** You'll have to dig to get honest answers, as many employees are reluctant to criticize their boss. But, the feedback you get is some of the best information you'll receive. It's not easy to see our own shortcomings, but using a

positive/leadership mindset will help you be more open to constructive feedback. Learning from mistakes and being open to criticism allows you to identify areas of improvement and become a better leader. Also, create an environment where honest feedback is encouraged, lauded, and not criticized or punished. Doing so will give your employees the confidence to be candid without fear of reprisal.

- *The use of anonymous suggestions might be beneficial.* You could require all employees to submit a monthly form with replies to all of these questions.

4. **What have you been doing to grow yourself as an employee?** Asking individuals what they have learned will open the door for more open sharing and encourages employees to strengthen their talents and develop new ones. Encouraging and recognizing growth do great things for the culture of a company. By asking questions of genuine interest regarding their future, you create inspired action in your employees.

5. **What is the one thing you would change about our product or service?** Your employees are bound to have good ideas for improving your products and services. Many heads are better than one, so use the team you have to find improvements you might not have even been aware of were needed. This also reinforces the value they contribute to the success of the organization.

The culture-building process is a time of *asking questions, not telling answers*. You are creating and growing feedback within your ecosystem. Leaders can influence change and foster the acceptance of cultural changes across the board when they encourage and welcome honest constructive criticism.

Put a plan in place to get monthly feedback from your employees regarding your products, services, culture, and management. Don't just ask for feedback; require it. *Feedback not only gives you a ton of valuable information, but your interest in the company improves the tone of your workplace culture.* You're simultaneously *showing that you value communication and regular improvement.* That allows employees to know you value their opinions and feedback.

Once everyone has agreed on a plan of action, you must document the goals and distribute them throughout the office. Everyone is then responsible and invested in reaching those outcomes. Your goal document should be visible and referred to often. Displaying it for all to see will ensure that everyone is held accountable for their part in reaching the goal.

Discovering your *why* is key to building a workplace culture that reflects your company's wants and needs. Knowing your purpose and the specific objectives, strategies, and tactics needed to achieve them will set the foundation for a high-performance culture and successful achievement of goals.

Now get to work, and give me some hustle. Think about your mission. Make a list of employees you want to involve in the visioning process. Make a list of the ideas and processes that need revamping to strengthen your business, and pick a start date.

CHAPTER 7:

Where is Your Culture Currently?

When I work with corporate clients, one of the first things we do together is a self-analysis of the current culture. The analysis forces leaders to examine organizational values, supervisor-employee interactions, management relationships, job satisfaction, and teamwork. It's important to ensure everyone shares an agreed-upon starting point when embarking on a culture-building program. Then they can move forward with an intentional plan of action to achieve a V.A.L.U.E. Culture. It's no accident that companies with the highest-rated company cultures are among the most successful. In fact, in chapter 16, I'll share more from my foreword writer, Stephen Childs', story of *Panasonic*™ *Automotives Culture Rebel-ution*. Their work culture has led to the company being recognized as a certified *Great Places to Work Organization* and one of the *101 Best and Brightest Organizations* for multiple years. Hearing from Stephen will help you see how taking the time to get your unique culture right creates an environment that draws high-quality talent and doesn't need gimmicks to be successful.

Until then, let's continue working on establishing your newly-defined culture. If your company started as a one-person show, grew exponentially, or is dominating in its market sector, I encourage you to prioritize culture. *However the company grows, its culture plays an increasingly important role in its future success.* The sooner you decide on and establish a company culture; the better off you'll be. Don't make the mistake of waiting and neglecting the need to consistently monitor and improve your company's culture to match changes in mission, technology, industry trends, and customer needs. Think of culture as the shared beliefs, standards, values, and procedures of a company and its employees.

The company's goals, structure, customers, strategy, and communication create the culture. *To determine the basic culture of any company is quite simple when you ask yourself a few poignant questions*:

- Who gets promoted?
- Who gets fired?
- Who is stuck in their position for life?
- What types of behavior are rewarded?
- What behavior is punished?
- What's important to the company?
- Who fits in?
- Who doesn't fit in?
- How would you describe our company's purpose in a few words?

Just like the parking lot observation from chapter 1, these short, quick questions can give you a very quick way to assess the current state of the culture within your organization and where to focus as you begin building for a future filled with engagement and productivity.

YOUR V.A.L.U.E. CULTURE REQUIRES SEVERAL THINGS

As you begin to build your own V.A.L.U.E. Culture use the list below as a gauge for measuring your progress and ensuring that all five of the principles are powerful drivers in your organization: *Vision, Accountability, Leadership, Unique contribution of employees and Engagement.* With each principle comes corresponding behaviors and workplace norms that contribute to the company's culture and overall success.

Use the following points to determine how you can...

- Encourage everyone to have a shared vision
- Establish clear lines of accountability
- Identify and cultivate leaders who will bring out the best in all employees
- Nurture positive engagement between employees and with customers
- Value each individual's unique contributions

As you move through these checkpoints, you'll be able to see how your culture is progressing, if it is accomplishing your vision or if there are areas you need to keep having internal discussions around.

1. **Clear core values.** One thing all successful workplace cultures share is a set of core values that are perfectly clear to all employees. What will your company's core values be? There are a variety of things you can emphasize.
   a. Innovation and creativity
   b. Balance and Contribution
   c. Assertiveness or Authenticity
   d. Results

    e. Casual/ Strictly professional

    f. Teamwork

    g. Relationships

2. **Respect.** Respect is an important part of workplace culture. Respect between peers and all positions in between, from the C-Suite level to the interns must be apparent. Equal respect should be the goal. Employees who feel disrespected quickly become disgruntled. The quality and quantity of their work suffer. Define who in your company is feeling disrespected and ways you can mitigate it.

3. **Communication. Open communication within the company fosters greater success.** Open communication means that co-workers and the various leadership positions throughout the organization have regular communication across all levels. Company-wide meetings can be very effective if logistically possible. Decide how you can improve communication.

4. **Inclusivity.** The significant separation between the upper- and lower-level employees has often been a source of friction. What can you do to establish a corporate culture that includes all employees, regardless of gender, skin color, age, race, or religion? Treating employees inclusively means that each individual is given the respect, trust, and opportunity to contribute uniquely. The importance of diversity and inclusion should be reflected in the core values and culture and throughout the organization, from recruiting and hiring to everyday interactions with colleagues.

5. **The culture matches the business and the employees.** Different cultures are suitable for different industries. It's okay to be innovative and push the envelope. However,

remember the culture you are building must support your
business type, clients, and employees of the workplace.

    a. Banking is a traditionally conservative business.
Making a casual culture of jeans and golf shirts might
be off-putting to some.

    b. A tech company would struggle to find the right
employees if its culture were overly conservative.
Can you imagine a tech startup that doesn't value
creativity and innovation?

    c. Out-of-the-office workers might appreciate flexible
hours and calling in every day from home, whereas
employees with young families might appreciate
structured work hours to plan daycare and family
time.

    d. Companies known for their commitment to sustain-
ability and social responsibility could have a culture
built around their deep sense of purpose and commitment to positively impacting the world. Leaders
who don't empower employees to take action on environmental and social issues, or provide employees
with time off to volunteer and get involved in the
community might experience a backlash.

6. **Everyone needs to be held to the same standards.** In
many companies, people look the other way when an
executive fails to abide by the culture or rules of the company, building dissent and anger. How you carry yourself
and the way you show up should be the same as how
you expect others to behave - with vision, accountability,
demonstrating leadership, recognizing the value of the
contribution of co-workers, and creating engagement.
Doing your part to create a V.A.L.U.E. Culture helps foster
a sense of trust and understanding throughout your

organization as everyone respects each person's contributions and views them all as collective assets for success.

7. **Employee recognition.** Positive work cultures recognize employees for their accomplishments above and beyond the norm. Recognition can take the form of monetary awards, additional days off, lunch with the CEO, or even just mention in an email or company newsletter. Regardless of the size of your company, find a way to recognize an employee when they do something exceptional.

8. **Keep the employee's goals in mind.** Finding ways to help your employees progress in life is important. *Your dream may not be their dream.* Every manager should know his employees' goals, whether to learn a new software program, move into a sales job, become an executive, one day write a book, sail the English Channel, or climb Mount Kilimanjaro. Strong company cultures support employees in pursuing their goals and dreams, even if they are sometimes outside the company. Knowing how their work supports their dreams and how your interest in their pursuits builds their sense of value creates an atmosphere of community inside and outside the walls of your organization.

9. **Employee feedback.** Ask for and use employee feedback. You can't be everywhere at once and don't know the best way to perform every job in your company. Your employees know things, and it would be wise to extract the information from them. Encourage your employees to provide regular feedback on all aspects of the company.

10. **Transparency.** Being transparent goes back to communication. You need to be as transparent as possible. The old mentality of *You don't need to know anything beyond what you need to know to do your job*, is obsolete. *Keep employees*

in the loop and be respectful. They *will be appreciative and value that* you have shared information with them.

11. **Consistency.** Consistency means it applies to all employees, even you. It also means it holds true at all times. You won't have a stable culture if you're willing to throw out your values during a personal crisis or selfish need. Culture needs to come before everything else. Otherwise, you are sending the message that it's just 'smoke and mirrors' and isn't grounded in truth.

Take the time to give each of these items some thought as you begin to craft your own culture. Think about how you would implement these items one at a time, in an order that suits the team and supports where the company is headed. Ask yourself, *How can you include each of these currently, and in the future, to best serve you, your employees, and your customers?*

Building a V.A.L.U.E. Culture with these principles can turn any environment into a place of cohesion, connection, and constant cash flow. When you show an employee you are willing to invest in them, their future, and the company's collective culture, you're giving them the knowledge that their opinions, skills, and potential are valued. This appreciation of their presence is essential for a team to work together effectively towards its shared goals.

When you create these strong emotions, you inspire hope for a better future and turn on a signal in your employee's minds that you are preparing them for the next step or opportunity. They'll start looking elsewhere without a sense of hope or the feeling their dreams aren't recognized. You must make them see themselves as part of your organization's future vision by emotionally giving them a place they want to come to work at every day.

BUILDING A V.A.L.U.E. CULTURE IS AN INVESTMENT IN YOUR COMPANY

Running a business requires many kinds of investment. You invest money in advertising, technology, security, product development, and more. Employees also invest in the company with their time, energy, and talents.

As a leader, the time is now to invest in them as well. After all, the average employee works 81,396 hours in their lifetime. Think about that for a moment. If nineteen percent of employees say they are miserable at work, how tragic is that?

I believe you must regularly share how you are investing in your employees. I encourage you to hold regular meetings, either in team settings or one-on-one, to discuss opportunities for development and growth. I also encourage you to communicate successes related to your culture programs or growth initiatives, such as new training programs or promotions. Doing so will help show your employees you are actively working to invest in them and that real action is taking place.

Celebrating employee achievements with the rest of the company lets others know you are proud of the contributions that are being made. I can't stress the importance of communication in your culture program's success enough. By investing in your employees, you gain loyalty, and they are more interested and involved in their work. You create a culture where people show up differently. You engineer a shift that creates enthusiasm, excitement, and high engagement.

Since I've coached career changers and led culture-building training events, I'm convinced that when employees feel valued, not only is their productivity positively impacted, but their attitude about work changes also. I ask clients to remember the day they received the call offering them the job they had been waiting on. I remind them to think about the excitement they felt at that moment. They couldn't wait for their first day. I want every day with your employees to have that first-day feeling. When a team member feels invested in and has a path to success, their customer interactions improve, their co-worker relationships are more collaborative, and they feel increased satisfaction.

I've been on the opposite side of going to jobs I despise because I felt devalued and unimportant. I've sat in a parking lot with a pit in my stomach, trying to convince myself to go inside and spend another day grinding at the office. Dread is not a great feeling. I knew my manager wasn't invested in my success or providing me with support and guidance, so I never felt like I had a clear path ahead of me. When I experienced those feelings of dread day after day, I didn't feel motivated or inspired, making it difficult to stay engaged with my duties. To top it off, there was no appreciation for my hard work, leaving me without any sense of connection or loyalty to the company.

A strong V.A.L.U.E. Culture means employees see themselves as integral to the organization's mission, values, and vision. They understand and enjoy their role. They feel a strong collaboration among the teams. They take ownership and feel empowered to solve problems, share information, and respond to more than just their own needs.

During an employment interview, you've probably asked, "Why do you want to work with us?" The interviewee probably gave you an answer based on a mission statement they found on your company website that was written years ago.

Stop and think. If they were to look around, would they see those same values in action presently? Or would they struggle to find examples around the office that matched the publicized vision and mission? Would they wonder if they were interviewed at the same organization or if your company is truly authentic?

QUESTIONS TO ASK YOURSELF TO BUILD THE MOST SUCCESSFUL WORKPLACE CULTURE:

1. **What are my employees like?** Think about your typical employee. Are they a 20-something liberal techie? Or are they an Ivy League™ MBA with a trust fund?
   a. Certain cultures suit certain types of employees. Design a culture that supports the characteristics of your employees.
2. **What are my customers and clients like?** Who are your clients and customers? Doctors? Investment bankers? Children? People who just want their car washed?
   a. Do your customers and clients come to your workplace? What would you want them to see?
   b. An investment banker might not be impressed by seeing everyone wearing shorts and playing frisbee on the front lawn on *Casual Friday*.
   c. Consider the people and businesses you serve.
3. **What are my values?** What are your personal values? If you value family and balanced life, then a take-no-prisoners aggressive workplace environment will be at odds with your personal values.
4. **What should we keep?** Don't think you need to trash everything your current company or organization has in place now. Look closely at what is working. Keeping the best parts of what has worked in the past is okay. History is important. Just make sure you can weave it into the future view of your company.
5. **What type of workplace culture would I enjoy?** It's your company, and you'll be there all day and many nights.

What type of environment would you find pleasant? *You can't choose the culture of the company you work for, but you can choose your own company's culture.* Choose something you and your employees will enjoy.

6. **What type of workplace culture is needed for success?** Of course, you can't just worry about making yourself happy. You want everyone else to be successful, also. The key is to find something that checks all the boxes for more than just you.

Establish a culture that meets your values but is also one you enjoy. Your culture should also have a high level of potential for success and address the needs of your employees and customers. Building a culture encompassing all of these areas can be challenging, but like any great creation, it is all about vision and creating buy-in and alignment from all people involved. Take your time and get your culture right.

THE CORE OF CORE VALUES

I encourage many of my coaching clients to make sure they have a clear understanding of a company's core values before they accept an offer to work there. I believe these are critical to making an informed decision about their career, finding job satisfaction, and working in a positive and supportive work environment. I believe we are all more likely to feel fulfilled and satisfied in our jobs when our personal values align with the company's core values.

A business's core values are at the center of everything it does. Their values are reflected in the company's decision-making, hiring, firing, outside partnerships, raises, advancements, marketing, research and development, and so much more. I believe core values should be the constant underlying factor in every business decision. No matter what happens in the marketplace, the decisions you make for your business are always based on your core values. *Core values aren't dependent on any particular company or product.* They are based on the fundamental vision and mission for the company.

I encourage you to think about the core values your company is actively demonstrating and how you can create a stronger, more motivated, and successful organization by clearly reviewing the current set of core values you hold or defining new values not yet in place.

Examples of core values include:

- **Trust and accountability**—A company guarantees that it will provide for customers and employees when they need it.
- **Commitment to quality**—A business puts its high-quality standards for its products or services above all else.
- **Innovation**—These companies are known for their ability to keep coming up with new and revolutionary products.
- **Building community**—A business that revolves around the idea of creating a positive, supportive community for its customers and employees.

I am constantly reminding the business leaders who I work with about the impact core values can have on the success and culture of their organization. Often new leaders and junior managers tend to skip this step only to find that when they do, employee morale is low and issues such as lack of trust and cooperation arise. Taking time to think through what your organization stands for and how these values will be translated into actions helps create a stronger team environment, leading to better performance. Developing core values also shows employees that their contributions are valued and appreciated. This can lead to higher engagement levels, which will have a positive effect on productivity, customer satisfaction and profits.

Throughout my research, I have discovered there are three keys to maintaining what I call *the core values of a workplace culture*. (Yes, I'm about to reveal some more secrets you can trust. This book is filled with so many because I want you to take what I have shared and build a culture that is reflective of not only your purpose, but of the values which are important to you. Of course, sharing them is just one part of the process, the real work happens when you maintain and continue them.) You must go beyond just listing your core values, you need to give them life. This involves coming up with strategies and pathways that ensure everyone understands and applies the core values consistently. Communication is key, as will allow you to make sure everyone is on the same page and can hold each other accountable for living up to the agreed-upon standards. Additionally, making sure that employees have the resources they need to succeed in their roles, while also leading by example, will help bring the organization's shared values to life and create a thriving workplace culture.

Here are three keys to maintaining core values.
- **Unity**—Core values are well-defined, and everyone understands them.
- **Belief**—Everyone inside the company believes the values.
- **Adherence**—A leader is not just giving lip service to the values. The values are actually in play every day.

Most companies spend a great deal of time focusing on the technical aspect of marketing, business operations, and product development, but many neglect defining their core values. Core values are not slogans or buzzwords. They are the north star for the company and the litmus test for all major directions and decisions within the company. To maintain the integrity of a core value it should be simple and clear. It should be doable and obtainable. It must be actionable and measurable. They should be the guiding principle for all decision-making and problem-solving.

Core values help differentiate your company from competitors by highlighting what sets you apart in terms of culture, mission, and approach. They not only help you attract great employees, but values also draw in customers looking for a company that aligns with their internal values.

Do you already have core values in your business? What do they look like? Are they consistent with your product or service? Have you communicated them to your employees? Can they use these values in dealings with vendors and clients? *Your core values are how your culture is defined.*

I hope that your mind is formulating what core values will be most useful and appreciated by you, your team, and your organization. I trust that you will take the time to discover which core values are best in your unique circumstances, so that they can be embraced and celebrated company-wide. By doing this, you will create a powerful and positive culture that everyone can be proud of. Connecting your employees with your company's core values and purpose is a game changer. An engaged workforce impacts not only the morale positively but also the company's profit margins and bonus opportunities.

By embracing core values and valuing the learnings that come through implementing them, you build a culture created on a foundation of trust and accountability. Core values are exactly that, the core of an organization's mission, purpose, and culture. They guide decisions, dictate behavior, and ultimately define how the organization is viewed by both employees and external stakeholders. A strong set of core values helps ensure all members of the team understand what is expected of them and are able to align their efforts with those principles. Furthermore, when a company has a strong sense of its core values, it makes it easier for new employees to acclimate to the company's culture quickly while also instilling a sense of loyalty among existing staff.

With the V.A.L.U.E. Culture foundation in place, leaders and companies can celebrate their progress and be on their way to creating a successful workplace culture. By demonstrating a commitment to vision, accountability, leadership, the uniqueness of your employees, and engagement, you can be confident that you are taking the steps necessary to cultivate an environment of trust and collaboration among employees. Ultimately, this translates into improved employee morale and engagement - two crucial elements for long-term success in any business endeavor. This model provides a comprehensive framework for understanding why it is important to prioritize culture development and how this can be implemented in an effective and efficient manner, but there's nothing like hearing from boots-on-the-ground leaders, from varying size companies, who are willing to share their success stories of how strong cultures are built on the V.A.L.U.E. Culture foundation.

SECTION 2:

Actions of Culture Builders

I believe experience is the best teacher. There's no way to over-estimate the impact learning from others can have on how quickly we can see a shift in our organizational culture when we hear about the successes and failures others have encountered in their quest to build human-centered cultures in the work-place. Working with numerous companies in various industries has taught me that it is not about cloning or copying what others have done. It is about benefiting from the lessons and wisdom gained from the mistakes encountered along the way.

Etsy™ Inc. is an American eCommerce company that gives a home to creators of handmade or vintage items and craft sup-plies. You can find everything from jewelry, bags, and clothing to furniture, toys, and art. At *Etsy*™ they believe culture isn't just a small part of what has made them successful; it's the key. They say, "A strong culture can overcome almost any set of poor decisions, but the best tech or the best decision-making cannot save a weak culture."

The first section of *Culture Secrets* helped you identify the current state of your company culture and walked you through critical elements you need to consider as you begin identifying workplace improvement areas. Now, it's time to focus on the 5 key elements of the V.A.L.U.E. Culture model one at a time.

Breaking down and understanding each of these values specifically will help ensure that they are appropriately integrated into the company's culture, goals, and overall performance. This detailed approach to building a better workplace culture can help companies achieve true alignment between employees' daily work and their greater mission - ensuring that everyone is operating towards the same common purpose.

For you to fully understand the impact each of these elements provide, I've brought together some of the most respected names in the business so you can learn first hand how the components of successful V.A.L.U.E. Cultures look in action in the real world, and who better to learn from than these culture leaders:

> **Garry Ridge**, is the **Chairman Emeritus of** *WD-40™ Company™* (NASDAQ WDFC), headquartered in San Diego, California. Ridge has been with *WD-40™* Company since 1987 in various management positions, including executive vice president, chief operating officer, and vice president of international. He has worked directly with *WD-40™ Company* in more than 50 countries. A native of Australia, Ridge has served as national vice president of the Australian Marketing Institute and the Australian Automotive Aftermarket Association. Garry is an adjunct professor at the University of San Diego. He teaches leadership development, talent management & succession planning in the Master of Science in Executive Leadership program. He's the founder of *The Learning Moment*, a business consulting and services firm designed to help create cultures where teams can deliver their best and go home happy.

Richard Sheridan is the **CEO and Chief Storyteller at** *Menlo Innovations*™, a software and IT consulting firm that has earned numerous awards and press coverage for its innovative and positive workplace culture. *Menlo Innovations*™ has won the Alfred P. Sloan Award for Business Excellence in Workplace Flexibility for six years straight and five revenue awards from Inc. magazine. He frequently speaks at business conferences and to major corporations such as *Mercedes-Benz*™, *Nike*™, and *3M*™. He's the author of *Chief Joy Officer* and *Joy, Inc.* He lives in Ann Arbor, Michigan.

Bob Brown is the Vice President of Finance and Operations Support for the Newnan, GA *Yamaha*™ facility located in Newnan, GA, about 45 minutes south of Atlanta. The manufacturing facility sits on 280 acres and is 1.4 million square feet under the roof. They have 2,200 employees and assemble four main product lines: golf carts, ATVs, side-by-sides, and wave runners. The plant is about to celebrate 35 years of operation in 2023. Their goal is to create a lifetime of exciting and memorable experiences for their customers and employees.

Adam Schwartz is the **founder of** *The Cooperative Way*™, a consulting firm with the mission "To Help Co-ops Succeed." He helps co-ops define their mission, so employees and members remember it. He is in Washington, DC.

Daniel Lawrence co-founded *Bots For That*™, a UK-based company calling London, England home. Their purpose is to solve problems for companies by doing work better for people, profit, and the planet by automating work through hosted, fully managed Bots-as-a-Service.

Harry Hynekamp is the **Vice President of Guest Experiences for** *AMB Sports and Entertainment™*. It's part of the *Arthur M. Blank Family of Businesses* (BFOB). In addition to the Arthur M. Blank Family Foundation, the BFOB portfolio includes the *National Football League's Atlanta Falcons™*, *Major League Soccer's Atlanta United™*, the state-of-the-art *Mercedes-Benz™* Stadium, the *PGA TOUR Superstore™*, and *AMB West™* in Montana which includes numerous stunning for-profit and nonprofit ranches.

Each of these business leaders has been part of implementing and maintaining successful cultures in their companies. They represent a wide range of industries covering everything from technology to entertainment. The culture's inside their respective companies all follow the cornerstones found in a V.A.L.U.E. Culture. These leaders understand a great culture starts with a vision that inspires change employees want to embrace. They realize successful cultures are cultivated through accountability and strong leaders who live the message and can share values that build belief. The V.A.L.U.E. Culture inside each of these companies considers the uniqueness of their varied workforce and utilizes their talents and skills.

As you read what they have learned, you'll see common threads tying these cultures together, yet they still capture the individual companies' spirit, vision, and essence. I believe these stories will inspire you as you build your vision and define the core values your company will be known for. Just as employee development can benefit from a strong mentorship program, I look at these leaders as mentors in culture building. I believe their real-world experience in creating and cultivating culture will be a great benefit to you as you begin to roll out your own people-first V.A.L.U.E. Culture.

I frequently hear this monologue when I run training programs. Employees don't feel they can think creatively or innovatively after being told multiple times, *that's not how we do it in our company.* This "old school, somewhat backward" way of thinking makes it very difficult for organizations to adapt to new challenges and opportunities, and can result in slower response times in a rapidly changing business environment. One participant told me, *"It's not worth it. I quit making suggestions after a couple of years. I was told during my evaluations I needed to stay in my lane. Just make my quota, and everything will be fine."* How discouraging is that? What benefits does the company miss out on by not listening to the ideas?

I've heard countless employees say they have ideas that could streamline processes or even reduce costs, but their direct supervisor isn't interested in listening. Feeling unheard eventually leads to employees who settle for status quo performance because they've been trained that there's no need to think out of the box or approach management with ideas because they will be ignored by supervisors or those higher up. The problems caused by employees feeling ignored can be corrected when the company vision is matched with individual employee goals; when employees can see their work directly impacts the company's success.

Organizational breakthroughs *won't happen* without *personal breakthroughs taking place first.* For Rich Sheridan, author of *Joy, Inc.* and *Chief Joy Officer* and co-founder of the tech leader, *Menlo Innovations*™, that vision took time to develop. I asked him several questions about vision and what business leaders can do to create one. His expertise is built on real-world successes and failures. His cultural success didn't happen overnight. I want you to get the essence of his journey, and how that experience helped him build a workplace culture that today, thousands visit and observe so they can take the lessons home and emulate them in their own organizations. Focus on how his vision evolved, and think about how your vision is changing or has changed.

> *Q. Rich, will you share the background of your career journey? I think it's important to see how one experience builds on the next.*

For me, finding organizational breakthroughs was a journey. As I rose up the management ranks, every time I moved up the career ladder, I thought, here's my chance. I can get things right. I don't have to do all the same stupid things my boss did.

Then I'd get up to that perch, and everything looked different from there. Suddenly, everything looked a little more difficult. Suddenly, everything was more complicated than I thought it was. Maybe I had even a little bit of empathy for the person I was calling stupid last week now that I'm up at the same level and having a different perspective.

> *Q. It really is a different ballgame when you are the player. Would you call yourself an eternal optimist, and with that attitude, did you feel there had to be a better way of organizing things?*

Boy, that's an understatement. I had to read and learn what others did to have success. I was drawn to authors and books. The books I was drawn to were Peter Drucker's books on management[1], Peter Senge's book, *The Fifth Discipline: The Art & Practice of The Learning Organization*[2], Tom Peter's book *Compact Guide to Excellence*[3], and all the excellent books that he wrote along the way.

Many of those books would tell about other companies with amazing results. You could start to see the pattern of it's about the people, the teamwork, the collaboration between those people.

Q. What a great list of books for any leaders to reference. I have also shared a suggested reading list at the end of the book so you can continue your culture-building exploration. Rich, how did you figure out culture before culture was cool?

Well, that is funny. When I started my exploration, the idea of *culture* did not even cross my mind. I don't know if the word culture was used back in the 80s and 90s. I yearned to create an atmosphere of camaraderie, human energy, and collaboration with the people who worked for me.

I'd had moments when that happened. They were magical. The question I kept having was, how do you get to that point and keep it there?

In 1997, I got promoted to a big leadership position. I was now a VP of R&D for a public company. My first stupid instinct at that time was just to work harder. Just try harder. Just do more. You know, be more of a hero than you were last year.

All I found out was I just got tired. Then around 1999, after a couple of years as VP, I ran as hard as I could, trying heroically to move this organization forward. If anything went wrong in the part of the company I was working for, it was on my plate.

I was never inclined to say, "if we only had better people, I could get that." I would say things like, "Wait! You're the leader; you should be able to do this." Then a moment happened and clicked.

Q. Rich, what was your big a-ha moment?

My big moment came when I did three things: I read a book, saw a video, and met a guy. The guy (James Goebel) is now my co-founder here at *Menlo Innovations*™. I brought him in as a consultant. The book was about differently organized soccer teams. But, the video is really what captured me.

It was on an industrial design firm in California called IDEO, and Nightline had done this 30-minute segment on their team. (4) It was a fictitious project of redesigning the standard wire basket shopping cart in just five days. You can still watch this video.

What's interesting is that I was not sure I realized that what I watched was a *culture*. But what I saw was what I wanted. I saw this teamwork, this collaboration, the diversity of the thinkers, the energy, the innovation, the new creativity, creative ideas, and everything. I wanted that. My heart was just aching for that compared to what I've had for the previous almost twenty years of my career.

Q. Rich, twenty years is a long time to wait for an opportunity or to know what you want.

I describe the first twenty years of my career as my trough of disillusionment. It wasn't horrible every day. It was just that when things seemed to be clicking, and everything was working, I couldn't sustain it. Maybe it's partly my personality. Maybe it was my mood of the day, or the right combination of people, or the right combination of projects.

I kept thinking there's got to be a better way to make this all work together, Like all the time and without my heroic effort. I couldn't step away for a week's vacation and not come back without it broken in pieces on the floor.

What happened? How did you guys let this happen? So, James Goebel, who is now my co-founder, was a consultant. We realized we were reading a lot of the same books. I brought him to help me do some technical things with my team, but he kept throwing out these really weird ideas, and I kept saying, "Yes."

Then we watched the video (IDEO redesigning the shopping cart) together, and he saw what I saw. He wanted to help me move my team in that direction. Over two years, we did it. We created this amazingly energized team that was sustainable, and it didn't require my heroic efforts. It was working. It was a process. It was teamwork. It was a collaboration. It was trust. It was amazing, and then it was all taken away.

Q. Rich, that is a great lesson to learn. What happened next?

When I thought I had the key in 2001, a circumstance beyond my control happened—the internet bubble burst, and the culture I wanted disappeared instantly. However, I learned a valuable lesson.

In an instant, I lost my job, but they couldn't take away what I had learned in those two years. What I learned was *you can be intentional about your culture.*

Q. That is so true. You get to keep what you learn.

Yes. One way to do that is to set very clear expectations for the people who work for you. Those clear expectations aren't the typical bang-your-fists on-the-table type expectations. Our expectations included:
- How will you guys behave with each other as peers?
- What will your relationships be like?
- What are our expectations for how you treat another human being?

One of the things I learned along the way through that, and I wasn't able to articulate this until just the last few years, is that if you're going to create an intentional culture. I'll just use my phrase—intentionally joyful culture—you must take a deep, hard look at every traditional step of human resources and rework every one of those steps.

For instance, recruiting, interviewing, selecting, onboarding, promoting, giving feedback, and maybe even firing; if you don't look at all those components and rework them to align with your cultural intentions, you'll never accomplish the goal. Your people processes must match your cultural intention.

Q. Rich, your company has become a model for thousands of people each year. When they visit, what do they see?

It's true. There are three to four thousand visitors a year from all over the world coming to *Menlo Innovations*™ to see our unique system.

People come to see how everything happens. Maybe one of the strangest things we do here is to put two people with one computer. They work in pairs. Everybody here works in pairs. We switch the pairs every five business days. So, if you and I pair together for five days, we wouldn't pair together next week.

We might come back together again later, but we're going to keep almost like square dancing. We're going to work together all day long at a computer together. So, you can imagine that's a very different way of working, especially for software professionals.

We usually put programmers in what I call sensory deprivation chambers. They have headphones on. We turn the lights down low and be quiet because they're thinking deep thoughts. Here, it's a noisy environment. People are collaborating all day long. They talk to each other continuously.

Q. Rich, you've said all of your people processes needed to be changed. Can you explain the interview process and how it's changed since you became human-focused?

We felt the standard interview wasn't working. I described it this way. Interviews are where two people sit across the table and lie to each other for a couple of hours. That was my standard.

Then it's time to make some big decisions for both of us. I decided whether to bring you on my team. You decide to quit wherever you are and come here and work. And it's all based on fiction, right? Then we both hope it works out, and often it doesn't.

Absolutely, human-focused is the way we do it now. We don't ask any questions during the interview. We make it an audition. We pair two candidates with one another and have them work together. We set very clear expectations from the moment of first contact; your job is to help the person sitting next to you get a second interview, and by the way, they're competing for the same position you are.

Imagine your brains are like twisting in the wind, like, what? "No, I want the second interview. Why should I help this person succeed?" We're teaching our culture from the moment of first contact. Our expectations are clear, and we believe the rational and reasonable expectation is you are here to help another human being succeed.

And it starts right here in the interview. If you can demonstrate good kindergarten skills, play well with others, and support another human being, you will get invited in for the second interview.

Q. Your culture is incredibly unique. Your vision for cultural success inside your organization doesn't have to resemble any other one out there, but it does take focus and mindset to create one that lasts.

Absolutely! When I wrote *Joy, Inc.*, people came here from all over the world to see what we did differently. I believe they're coming to see what it takes to create an intentionally joyful culture. It's the people processes. It's the actual work processes here. It's not an onerous fear-based management system over-loading everything. It's an overtime-free culture.

We don't like when people go on vacation to keep working. We expect them to cut themselves electronically off from the business and just enjoy time with their family or wherever they're doing. It's a very different approach, but all with this focused mindset on what it would take if you wanted to create that kind of culture and enjoy the results that kind of culture produces.

Rich shared so many valuable nuggets of gold in his inter-view. One, great cultures take time and include experimentation. Two, culture doesn't happen by accident, culture must be inten-tional, and as unique to you as your business formula is to your company. And three, you must include a rethinking of your people processes from the very beginning point—the initial interview.

Everything Rich shared is why I filled this book with so many questions for you to consider as you build your own V.A.L.U.E. Culture inside your organization. I want you to use those questions to break down and re-evaluate your business like Rich did to find your ideal success.

Of course, the learning and ideas continue. I thought now

would be the perfect opportunity to share more insights from Bob Brown. Remember, he is from *Yamaha*™, and they have facilities all over the world. I asked him if he was surprised when he saw variations in cultures from facility to facility.

And he responded with, "Well, we're a part of a much larger, global company. You know *Yamaha*™ doesn't just make motor products; there are also music products. So, there's a company culture for sure. But we're large enough on-site to have our own local culture."

Multiple cultures can exist within a single company, especially in today's globalized business world. It's not uncommon for a company to have employees with diverse cultural backgrounds, each with their own beliefs, values, and norms. Diversity can bring a variety of experiences and perspectives into the workplace.

Different divisions, just like Bob shared, can exhibit different cultures also. These differences can happen for several reasons, including differences in products and services offered, variations in company history and legacy, and different management styles. For example, a company's research and development division might have a culture that values innovation and creativity, while the finance division might have a culture that prioritizes stability and risk management. These differences in culture can have a significant impact on the way a division operates, and the types of employees attracted to each division.

Leadership needs to be aware of these differences and work towards creating a cohesive culture that takes into account the needs and values of all divisions. By developing a shared list of core values and vision you can unite an organization.

Company culture is influenced by a variety of factors, including national cultural norms and values, legal and regulatory requirements, and the unique history and legacy of the company.

There's also a difference in culture based on the business model. A start-up can be very different from a traditional company model. Start-ups are often characterized by a fast-paced, high-risk environment and a focus on innovation and growth. Their unique structure can lead to a culture that values risk-taking, agility, and a willingness to challenge the status quo.

In contrast, traditional companies may have a more established culture that prioritizes stability, efficiency, and a hierarchical management structure. These companies may place a greater emphasis on following established procedures.

Many start-ups are also focused on creating a positive, inclusive culture that values its employees, while many traditional companies are actively working to promote a culture of innovation and agility.

Since the culture of a company is shaped by the values, beliefs, and practices of the leadership, I thought it would be interesting to look at culture from a more global perspective. In order to investigate culture across the globe, I reached out to Daniel Lawrence. He co-founded *Bots For That*™, located in London, England. He agrees great cultures take time and that building one will not happen immediately or at the beginning. Building a strong culture is all about patience and timing. Daniel's perspective also comes as the founder of a start-up. He shares some unique nuances regarding mindset and culture building, which employees and potential employees are challenged with when they choose to be part of a start-up organization.

Just like the idea of a watched pot never boils, meaning the liquid will bubble when it's good and ready; keep that heat on—don't quit!

Q. Daniel, how did culture evolve for you?

We didn't take the typical management approach where you sort of write a manual, and then you go off and see, does this work?

We spent a couple of years fumbling around, making mistakes, and finding out what worked and didn't. Companies are our clients and have their own culture, but we can't bend to every single one. We've learned what works for us and what things lead to successful outcomes, and which things don't.

When you boil it down, after looking back, we focused on the reasons good clients were good and why bad clients were bad. We dug in a little bit and understood why. We looked across the environment. We looked at finance. We looked at customers. It came down to those simple things: environment, finances, and customers.

It's very simple core values. Now we've embedded that in as well. That's sort of what we thought we were doing anyway. Now it's just making it tangible so that everyone knows it. That's the hard part. Everyone knows it and holds each other accountable. If we do something that doesn't honor those, we have to call each other out.

Q. Daniel, what is it like being part of a startup that requires a different mindset?

People think they want to join a startup, but the realities are that they are far different from what people look for in their employment. People see psychological comfort in a regular salary, annual pay increases, structured working time, and the next five levels above you. It's fairly static. It's fairly rigid. It's fairly comfortable. It's not that way in a startup.

People think a startup sounds like a wonderful idea. They think I can get lots of experience. But the reality is, it's a little bit different. I think culturally that requires a different mindset. It's something we do when we advertise jobs.

When we first meet a candidate, we don't talk about competency and skills; we don't talk about a compensation package; we talk about culture because we don't want to have a misfit. We will probably exclude 80% of our candidates on the first call. We give them examples of our culture and our values, which are synonymous.

Q. What is the recipe for a successful culture?

Our acronym for our value-based system is *RECIPE*. There's a link for that because we build Bot recipes. For example, one of our pre-built Bot activities takes information out of your Salesforce system and creates an invoice in your accounting system. So, we have these pre-built recipe Bots.

We also devised an acronym tied to that to give us some consistency and fun. Our value acronym is the recipe, which is

- *Respect,*
- *Excellence,*
- *Customer Integrity,*
- *Performance, and*
- *Execution.*

Q. Core values don't have to be complicated. How do you use those values as a basis for your hiring selections?

When we first speak to a candidate, we go through core values because this is what we really value above all else. We give them examples of the kind of person who wouldn't fit our culture. We just have a very open and honest exchange on that. Much of the time, people go, yeah, you know what?

I thought this was what I wanted, but those two things there, that one there and that one, that's not me. I'm not going to fit in. Most people exclude themselves at that point, which is good because it saves us wasting time down the road.

But the one or two that get through are the ones that are going all the way to the end, generally speaking, and they're the right ones. We're right for them, and they're right for us. It tends to last longer.

Q. Daniel, is the culture you developed with the acronym RECIPE solidified after examining what made them successful and happy?

I'm quite a logical, rational thinker. As much as I would like to be something different, that's basically what I am. I'm a logical, rational planner. So, what I tend to do is rationally look at a situation, and I start to categorize, sub-categorize and structure it in a way that I can understand it and then present it back to others. Since that's how I operate, that's what we did.

When I sat down and asked let's look at what's worked over the last few years? What's led to really pleasant happy moments? What's led to having clients we love working with and ones that we haven't? And why?

Examining where we've succeeded and where we failed that's really where I always start with it. Then things naturally bucketed themselves into customer, finance, numbers, and culture. From that, we ended up with our recipe structure because it was those simple factors that underpin what makes us successful and what makes us happy.

Q. Daniel, does all of this have to do with casting the vision right from the beginning? How essential is the vision?

We must approach *vision* from the very start. The other reason we have those guiding values is that there isn't a big, high, tall structure when you're a startup. Much of our communication must be horizontal and quick to be effective.

If you're relying on getting a decision from someone above you, it will not work.. So horizontal, quick, rapid, fail fast, move on, learn, get on with the next one is the kind of the approach that we take. Because of that, you've got to have a basis to fall back on, and it's that fabric—our values that we use. We know that execution is paramount, and we've got to deliver.

If we know that good enough isn't good enough, you can always fall back on those guiding principles to decide what to do. The vision helps the whole company know it, and since we all know CEOs can't be everywhere, and I shouldn't be everywhere, vision allows people to keep working because they have a focus and a framework to work toward. We all make mistakes, but it gives you something to go by. It's better than having nothing at all.

Daniel does a great job showing how different types of businesses have to adapt to different cultures and structures. Knowing your culture values from the get-go gives you, and your employees, a strong position to use as a basis for decision-making and keep everyone oriented in the same direction.

As I move back into my interview with Rich Sheridan, let me stress the importance of casting your vision in a way your employees and teammates find relatable. While it's important you know and understand your vision, that vision is not going to work for you until you put it in front of your employees. One of the best ways you can communicate is through using stories. Stories allow people to connect with the ideas and context your vision holds. People remember and can share those stories. The recall of a story is much greater than that of a list of items. If we are designing people-centered cultures, doesn't it make sense the manner in which we share our ideas and plans also connect on an emotional level? I asked Rich specifically about stories and visions and how he used them to further the culture shift at *Menlo Innovations*™.

Q. Rich, I have to ask, what is the secret to creating a Vision?

Simple, a vision is like creating a story. You are creating a version of the future you want others to be able to relate to and connect with emotionally. A story gives your current employees something to share and your newer hires something to grab onto and aspire to help move forward.

Think about stories from your childhood. Many were filled with values and designed to move you toward some action while entertaining you. They were easy to remember and easy to share. The story you create should reinforce the values and change you want to be reflected in the workplace.

Q. Rich, that makes the concept of vision very tangible—like something we can really sink our teeth into.

One of the lines in my book is that culture eats strategy for breakfast, the famous Peter Drucker line. *My belief is storytelling sets the table for that meal.* The story is what connects heart to mind, body to spirit, and concept to reality. Stories make it real.

In life, it doesn't matter what you said; it matters how it *made me feel*. And quite frankly, a boring PowerPoint with graphs, bars, spreadsheets, and numbers we want to improve, like revenue by 3.2%, is uninspiring.

People shrug their shoulders and think I'm not sure how I'm involved in that. They can't imagine or connect the dots between what the boss just talked about with these charts and graphs and their goals for the year and how that should impact me personally. When you can translate that into a story of a vision for the future, an inspiring vision, it just connects.

Q. Rich, who else has inspired you to combine storytelling with vision?

Ari Weinzweig, the CEO of *Zingerman's*™ in Ann Arbor, MI. It's a famous food empire here. Ari says to pick a day in the future and describe it in drippy detail.

For us at *Menlo Innovations*™, it's February 11, 2027. We're having a party. All our friends are there. All our employees are there. We're celebrating (Thomas) Edison's hundred and eightieth birthday together.

We have this vision written, a story about what happened that day. Who's there? Why are they there? What changes have we had in their lives? What impact did we have in our community, both directly with our customers or indirectly with the people who once worked here?

When you do that kind of future storytelling, that visioning process, people can start to put themselves in that picture. Can they imagine where I am in that story? What contribution am I proud of that I made?

The stories we tell from the past should be stories of both triumph and defeat. We need to curate both stories to remind ourselves why we are here. How did we get here? What was the difficult journey that got us here? Where did we have to overcome a big obstacle because that's an important thing to remember.

Q. Rich, what happens when you are getting exhausted? What helps you?

My co-founder, James Goebel, has this beautiful metaphor for those moments. He says, "When you're climbing the mountain, it's hard, and you get up to a certain little sub-peak, but there are still miles to go. Stop. Turn around. Look down. Revel in the vision and the scenery. Revel in how much work you expended to get here. Reflect on how far you've come. Then turn around and start climbing again. Those are the stories from the past." Because at that moment, you recount the success that got us to where we are today. The difficulty of the journey along the way bonds people together. That shared sacrifice is what binds us together. We did this together. I think that's where storytelling plays a key role.

Q. Rich, how did the role of stories become even more clear to you?

Much of it happened after hosting many of our site tours to *Menlo Innovations*™ to see how our processes worked. What we do on the tours when they're here is tell stories.

I would often lead the tours, so I'd walk people around the room, telling stories. I used to think the stories I was telling were for our guests, for the visitors, because that's why they were coming.

But, then I noticed something. Not only were the visitors listening, but my team was listening. I thought, *What are they doing?* They hear the same stories over and over and over again. Then, I realized the stories were holding me accountable.

I would never want anybody from my team to come up to me after a tour and say, "Hey, Rich, that company you were describing on tour sounds amazing. Where is it?" So, you'd better be telling the truth because otherwise, they'll all be like its BS. There are so many facets of storytelling, but ultimately, it is the most human part of us where we all want to believe that we are like, logical, sensible, and rational creatures.

We're anything but that. We are emotional. We are irrational. We are driven by our feelings far more than our logic. That's just a simple truth about humans. So, if as leaders, we're trying to get people to move with us; there's no better way to do that than with the story.

Creating a cohesive V.A.L.U.E. Culture allows employees to help *shape the story*. They do this by living the core company values through their behaviors, actions, and attitudes. When employees talk about the company culture with others, both inside and outside the organization, it helps reinforce the culture and spread the story. Feedback opportunities give employees buy-in to the mission. Offering employees the chance to participate in cultural initiatives, such as volunteer work or community service projects, helps to further define and reinforce culture also.

The way you connect your core values and continue to deepen that human connection is by embracing the power of storytelling.

I'm going to go back to Harry Hynekamp of *AMB Sports and Entertainment*™, an Arthur M. Blank-owned company to uncover more about storytelling and engagement.

Q. Harry, I understand that stories can also be powerful tools that allow employees to see the value they bring. Take us to the stars with this. Blow our minds.

We run a recognition program for our team members called *Heroes of Hospitality*. It's from here where many of our values in action stories will come from. They are usually from a fan, guest, or customer, and are pretty amazing.

It takes something for someone to set aside some time and send in a hand-written note. That means we impacted them, right? I know some people may roll their eyes when they hear the word 'story'. They might think of storytelling as fluff, but stories are just facts delivered with context, passion, and emotions.

At the end of the day, we are all just human beings. And as human beings, all we are is a collection of memories. Really strong emotions usually accompany memories. Good ones or bad ones, reside within us. And they can stay with us for a long time. So, value in action stories are important to us, we share our stories at every event.

Q. We are a collection of memories, stories. I love that! Harry, tell us about huddles and leadership briefings.

Whether it's a briefing or a huddle, the Core Values and usually a core value of the day is always shared. We're constantly reminding ourselves about them. But not only what the core value states but giving examples of each of them in action.

We have a *Values In Action* program that recognizes team members for living our Core Values. We also have something called the *Heroes of Hospitality wall*. It's inside the stadium. Most organizations have their employee recognition wall in the back office on an old pegboard.

Ours is sitting front and center, right outside the Gullwing

Suite, which is home to the owner's suite, for all of our fans, guests, and customers to see and experience. We have a ceremony once a quarter where we induct new team members into our Heroes of Hospitality. Again, we hold these examples and stories in extremely high regard.

At leadership briefing and team member huddles, there is always a value in action story about how someone positively impacted a fan, guest, or customer. There's a quote over our *Heroes of Hospitality Wall*; it's from Arthur Blank; it's something along the lines of people will come to *Mercedes- Benz*™ Stadium and they'll see the amazing architecture, they'll see the halo board and experience all the amazing technology, but they're going to forget all about that. The last thing they will remember is *how they were treated*—how we made them feel.

So sharing stories is really important to define what excellence looks like or demystify what excellence looks like. They make it understandable that that's something I can do. And translate it in a way that demonstrates we are recognizing folks for going above and beyond. Because let's be honest, we all need an "atta boy" and an "atta girl". We all do. I don't care if you're the CEO of the biggest company in the world, you still report to a board. You, as a human, still want to feel valued, appreciated, and recognized. Values in action stories help us do that every day.

> ***Q. I agree with you, Harry. We all want to be appreciated and recognized.***

We sure do. Everyone likes to be appreciated and recognized. I think we all know how that impacts people. For most, it's literally like *rocket fuel*. And here's a secret, it costs nothing!

In fact, I believe we breathe life into people by appreciating and recognizing them. You can change an entire day. For us, it's not just about feeling good. It's about demonstrating our core values. Because at the end of the day, once you recognize someone, it's another way of putting people first. Because you recognize someone, you are listening and responding because you either saw something, heard something, or someone's sharing information about you.

You are including everyone because you're sharing that single story with everyone for everyone's benefit. You're trying to demonstrate that associates are leading by example. Because here you're holding it up high in terms of what that story's impact is and what it means.

You're trying to demonstrate this is how you can innovate and create great experiences. It took just that little effort. The power of storytelling is huge; huge for us in terms of many different aspects: including coaching, developing, recognizing, appreciating, and learning from one another.

Perhaps the knowledge comes from my background in public relations and journalism, but one thing I'm certain of is the powerful component stories play in our ability to connect people and to remember key elements. Stories work because they share something of the originating idea or personality of the leader. They share why customers need them. Let's look at *Apple*™ CEO Steve Jobs. He made products that he and his friends wanted.

In 2000, portable music players started to become popular. Jobs hated the ones on the market. He loved music and wanted a device that was simple to use and allowed thousands of songs to fit in his pocket. There's an iconic story about the invention of the first iPod™. The story was shared on Quora™ by an ex-Apple™ employee. Apparently, Jobs wasn't satisfied with the size of the first iPod™ prototypes.

The story goes, as employees presented their work to Jobs, he spent time scrutinizing the device. He felt its weight in his hand and promptly said it was too big. The engineers told Jobs they would have to reinvent inventing to make it any smaller and that it was impossible to do.

According to the story, Jobs walked over to an aquarium and dropped the iPod™ in the tank. They watched it sink to the bottom, and as bubbles floated to the top, he said, "Those are air bubbles. That means there's space in there. Make it smaller."(5)

Stories like the *Apple*™ example give a clear picture to anyone who hears them of what it will be like to work on one of these teams. They also get a real understanding of who their CEO is and what his expectations are. He said, "we made the iPod™ for ourselves, and when you're doing something for yourself, or your best friend or family, you're not going to cheese out."(6)

Jobs is famous for being impatient and tough on the people around him, which comes from his passion for perfection, but that is countered by his ability to inspire. That's where the magic lies in stories. Being able to see a future and convince others to help you achieve the vision.

I trust the last three interviews have been helpful to shine the light on how incorporating the power of stories helps solidify your core values in the minds of your employees and lays a foundation for these values to begin to show up in their daily work activities. Learning from other leaders who have been in your shoes is a powerful way to reaffirm your decisions and make a massive movement forward.

Of course, that learning doesn't stop here, the next chapters are filled with more riveting accounts of successful leaders, leading in innovative and exceptional ways, designed to inspire you. And, this is where it gets really good, because the next few chapters break down and describe in detail the power behind the V.A.L.U.E. Culture system. From vision, to accountability, leadership to uniqueness of your people and engagement you are about to unlock the potential of your team and create a workplace culture that is truly unparalleled—one that celebrates every individual's unique contributions, encourages innovative thinking and collaboration, and sets everyone up for success! I've peppered in more interviews throughout the chapters so you can see how leaders from all types and sizes of organizations are building strong, successful people-centered cultures. All the work you've done until now is about to pay off as you apply the V.A.L.U.E. Culture fundamentals to create a workplace culture that is uniquely yours and which truly honors the value of every person in your organization.

The next five chapters are going to be a deep dive into all the elements of the V.A.L.U.E. Culture system and how they can be used to create a workplace culture that truly reflects your company's uniqueness and honors every individual in your organization. You'll explore questions designed to help you develop a better understanding of the core elements, as well as real-world examples from businesses both large and small who have implemented this system with immense success. With each chapter, you'll gain increasingly valuable insight into what it takes to create a people-centered culture that encourages innovative thinking, collaboration, and sets everyone up for success.

CHAPTER 8:

V—VISION

"Vision without action is merely a dream. Action without vision is merely passing time. But vision with action can change the world."

- NELSON MANDELA

Great leaders see things as they are, not worse than they are. Then they see it better than it is. Next, they find a way to make it the way they see it.

Be a Visionary.

If you are going to be a strong leader, it is critical that your actions are based on a strong vision. A visionary doesn't do things for the sake of doing them; rather, *the visionary makes very calculated decisions that will succeed in fulfilling their vision.*

When complications arise, they see them as anything but complications. Instead, they see possibilities. *Most visionaries will simply view an obstacle as a learning experience they can use for self-development.* They feel that challenges enlighten their mind to new understanding. For them, challenges show the future success of the organization. Culture must be future-focused to be successful. You must paint the future others can see themselves in. To do that, you must use their input to form a grand vision.

Understanding that *having a vision* differs from being *a visionary* is important. The person who possesses vision sees potential developments and events that may occur in the future.

On the other hand, the visionary produces a particular outcome based on thoughts and goals that once only resided in their minds. *The visionary is the one who takes action to make the vision become a reality.* As you become more confident in your role as a visionary, here are some helpful tips you can use. A visionary is not a victim of circumstance but rather a creator of circumstance and productivity.

STEPS TO BECOMING A VISIONARY LEADER

Now that you understand who a visionary leader is, it's time to transform the person you are today into a visionary leader for tomorrow! Becoming a visionary leader requires a transformational shift in mind and behavior. To achieve success as a leader one must develop a clear and compelling vision for the future, inspire others to follow that vision, and take bold and calculated risks to turn your vision into reality. While it may seem like an intimidating task, with the right approach, anyone can become a visionary leader. By following the steps listed below, you can transform yourself into the visionary leader you aspire to be.

1. Appreciate People

I mean ALL people—not just certain people you care about. *Every person on Earth has a special mission or a unique purpose in life.* A visionary leader needs to appreciate people because they understand people are the foundation of any successful organization. Learn to appreciate the special and not-so-special talents, skills, and personalities of others because you never know what lesson you'll learn from them. By showing appreciation, a visionary leader can cultivate a positive and productive work environment, foster employee engagement and loyalty, and inspire individuals to perform at their best. Furthermore, an appreciative leader can help build a strong and cohesive team where individuals feel valued and supported and where they are more likely to work toward shared goals.

There are many ways a visionary leader can show appreciation for their team. One of the most important ways is simply by being present and attentive to the needs and concerns of their individual team members. This may involve taking the time to listen to their ideas, recognizing achievements, and providing constructive feedback to help them grow and develop. Additionally, a visionary leader may demonstrate their appreciation by offering opportunities for growth and creating a positive, supportive work environment. By showing genuine appreciation and care for their team, a visionary leader can help create a thriving, successful organization.

2. Accept Responsibility

A visionary leader needs to accept responsibility for the success or failure of their organization or team, as they understand their leadership decisions and actions have a direct impact on the outcomes. By taking responsibility, visionary leaders can demonstrate accountability, integrity, and trustworthiness, which can build credibility and earn the respect of their team. A leader who accepts responsibility can help to create a culture of ownership, where everyone takes responsibility for their actions and works together to achieve a common goal.

Leaders seldom accept the position that they are a victim of circumstance. *You alone are responsible for the things you experience, your choices, and the outcomes of those choices and experiences.* Placing blame on others for your choices or mistakes will prevent you from learning from those mistakes and improving your life.

When a visionary leader accepts responsibility, they are willing to be held accountable for the team outcomes. This means you're willing to take ownership of both successes and failures and are willing to learn from your mistakes to make improvements moving forward. By modeling this behavior, you can inspire your team to take responsibility for their work, hold themselves accountable, and work towards continuous improvement.

Accepting responsibility also means being transparent and honest with employees. When something goes wrong, a visionary leader should communicate openly and honestly with their team, taking responsibility for any mistakes and outlining a plan for moving forward. This will help build trust and respect within the organization and can foster more integrated teamwork and collaboration.

Ultimately, a visionary leader who accepts responsibility can create a culture of trust, ownership, and continuous improvement, which drives the success of the team.

3. Strive to Learn and Improve

A visionary leader knows and understands the job of self-improvement is never-ending. As you advance through life, this will be a constant. *Working to improve yourself, the lives of those around you, and the world will make you one of the top visionaries that the world has ever seen!* A visionary leader needs to strive to learn and improve because they understand the world is constantly changing. To remain successful, they must be adaptable and continuously grow and develop. By modeling a growth mindset and willingness to learn, you can create a culture of improvement within your team, where employees are encouraged to seek out new knowledge and skills and embrace change and innovation.

To model the behavior of learning and improvement for your employees, you must first be committed to your own personal and professional growth. This may involve seeking out new opportunities for learning, such as attending conferences and workshops, taking online courses, or reading relevant publications. By sharing your own learning experiences with your team, you demonstrate the value of growth and inspire your employees to follow suit.

In addition to personal learning, you can foster a culture of learning and improvement by providing opportunities for your team to learn and develop new skills. This may involve offering training and development programs, mentorship opportunities, or job shadowing experiences. By investing in your employee's growth and development a visionary leader demonstrates their commitment to the success of their entire team.

Lastly, a visionary leader can model the behavior of learning and improvement by being open to feedback and actively seeking out opportunities for constructive criticism. By welcoming feedback and acting on it, you show your team you are willing to learn, grow and value input from them. This can help create a culture of open communication in all departments. By taking steps to improve yourself and looking for ways to improve the world, you'll begin to think about solutions more creatively.

4. Discover the Positive Effect of Challenges

Be willing to understand and approach all situations as if they're valuable lessons and you can learn something from them. Transform your thinking from believing something is bad to believing that *no matter how negative it appears at first glance, there is ultimately something positive to be gained from it.*

A visionary leader needs to embrace challenges because they understand that challenges are opportunities for growth and development for both themselves and their team. By embracing challenges, you demonstrate resilience, creativity, and innovation and can inspire your team to approach difficult situations with a positive and proactive mindset.

To show your team that challenges can have positive effects, you can model this behavior by approaching the challenge with a positive mindset. This may involve reframing the challenge as an opportunity for growth, seeking out innovative solutions, and being willing to take risks and try new approaches.

You can also encourage your team to approach challenges with a positive mindset by creating a culture of support and collaboration. This may involve fostering teamwork, encouraging cooperatives, and providing resources and support to help your employees overcome the challenge while recognizing and celebrating successes along the way.

A visionary leader who embraces challenges can help create a culture of innovation and advancement, where employees feel empowered to take on new and difficult tasks and are motivated to improve and develop their skills. By embracing challenges you can have a positive effect and inspire your team to achieve new heights of success.

5. Take Action to Make Your Dreams Come True

If *you're seeking to become a visionary, you must be both a dreamer and a doer.* Setting goals and having dreams is wonderful, but thoughts and dreams are futile if you never put anything into action. A visionary leader needs to take action to make their dreams come true because they understand that without action, their vision will remain just a dream. By taking action and making progress toward your goals, you demonstrate the courage, determination, and commitment needed to turn vision into reality

Sharing your journey towards achieving your vision with your employees is important because it can help to create a sense of shared purpose and inspires your team to work toward common goals. By being transparent about the vision and the steps you are taking to achieve it, you can build trust and create a sense of unity within your team.

When you share a journey towards achieving your vision with your employees, first be clear about your goals and the steps you will or are currently taking to achieve them. Communicate the vision and objectives, and provide regular updates on your progress. Choose milestones to celebrate, so your team feels part of the journey with you. Look for opportunities where you can invite your team to collaborate or share ideas about your goals and incorporate them into your plan for achieving your larger vision. This creates a sense of investment and will give your employees a chance to see you appreciate their unique perspectives

The last step is being open and transparent about the challenges or setbacks you encounter along the way. By sharing the ups and downs, you demonstrate your resilience as a leader, and it will inspire your team to persevere through difficult times.

A visionary leader who takes action to make their dreams come true and shares that journey with their employees can inspire a sense of shared purpose, build trust and unity and create a culture of collaboration that leads to a strong team.

Once you decide to become a visionary leader, you'll need to lead with vision. While a mission statement focuses on what your company is doing now, your vision is what you want to create for the future. I'll refer back to Bob Brown from *Yamaha*™, whose view on leadership and vision is worth hearing. "I think from a leadership perspective, a big part of it is understanding the vision and being able to articulate it and demonstrate it," he said. "Personally, to me, that's a big part of leadership. You can't just say the words; you must also demonstrate them. I think people respond much more strongly to that. It's not just words on paper. It's action, and it's something they can see. That makes it more tangible and real than just speaking about how being a part of that culture benefits you and why they should appreciate it. Explaining why I love working at *Yamaha*™ and doing that sincerely and honestly goes a long way as well."

6. Using the power of story

Stories allow you to connect the vision in an engaging way to your employees so they understand and align with your goal. Your vision becomes a reality when reflected in the beliefs, actions, and goals on a personal level which all stories do.

To develop a compelling and inspiring vision, ask yourself the following:

- What is the relationship between my vision and my corporate vision? Our belief system often overlaps with our business systems. It's important to live by a shared set of principles in our personal and professional lives.
- What are my values?
- Why are imagination and creativity important? Regardless of where my company is today, can I see potential and move towards developing this atmosphere?
- How can I encourage my employees to participate in your corporate vision?
- If I could set one record in my industry, what would it be?
- What are some of the resources I will need to achieve my vision?

- What culture would give my clients and customers confidence in my ability to deliver the products and services they need?
- What are the major obstacles I'll likely encounter as I pursue my vision in daily life?
- What visionary leader has impacted me? What can I learn from them?
- How would I describe my average employee? What environment would allow them to do their best work and enjoy coming to the office?
- What type of culture would be a big mistake?
- What will my company look like in 10 years? Can I create a culture that will work long-term?

Visionary leaders are those who take the time to appreciate the people around them, accept responsibility for their own actions and decisions, strive to continue learning, and discover how challenges can lead to positive effects. By taking action to make your dreams, and those of your employees, a reality and using stories to connect with and inspire others to follow your vision, you'll build a solid foundation for culture success.

Answering those questions will empower you to take the necessary steps as you become more confident in your own abilities and gain an appreciation of those within your network. With such an approach, visionary leadership can be achieved.

VISION LEADS TO PURPOSE AND PEOPLE NEED PURPOSE

Your vision can help bring clarity to an employee's purpose. A leader's core job is to help people find purpose in their work. But in reality, most leaders fail to make the connection. When asked about their work experience, most employees only tolerate their jobs. They feel their job is basically good but not extraordinary. They don't love what they do, but it pays the bills. Sounds anti-culture, doesn't it? You as a leader have the power to change that perception.

As a leader in a culture change, you have the power to change thought patterns and improve employee engagement by communicating your vision clearly. By doing this, you can help employees find purpose in their work and create a culture of enthusiasm and collaboration rather than mere tolerance. When people are given an opportunity to understand why their job matters and how it contributes to the bigger picture, they become motivated to do more than just pay the bills and fulfill obligations. Through visionary leadership, you can bring clarity and energy into your organization, helping all employees achieve their full potential in reaching collective goals. By connecting employees through your purpose, you fuel a change in perspective in them. You show them they are doing something that matters. With the right leader, any job can become purpose-filled.

Before we shut the book on this chapter regarding vision, I want you to digest one more powerful concept of connecting employees with a purpose from Garry Ridge, Chairman Emeritus of *WD-40™ Company*.

Q. Garry, I understand you believe that with the right leaders, any job can become purpose-filled and that that idea is a central theme to the culture at WD-40™ Company. Please expand on that.

Ours is a culture based on a couple of beliefs. One of the beliefs is that one of the biggest desires we have as human beings is to belong.

Most organizations don't create cultures where people feel like they belong and contribute to something bigger than themselves. It's based on:

1. Belonging
2. Purpose
3. Values
4. Learning

We believe these are four of the most important elements of building a connection and culture. Imagine a place where you go to work every day, and you make a contribution to something bigger than yourself. You learn something new. You're protected and set free by a compelling set of values. And then you go home happy at the end of the day.

If I unpack that a little bit, leaders simply need to look at what elements of those 4 things are not embedded or lived within the organization. Does your organization have a clearly understood purpose?

When I say clearly understood purpose, at *WD-40™ Company*, our purpose is to create memories. If you look at our purpose statement, we exist to create positive lasting memories. We do that by solving problems in factories, homes, and workshops around the world.

We're in the memories business. Now, you might want to say that we're in the squeaks business, but that's not the purpose. You have got to take what you do and Simon Sinek it—find you why.(7)

It's not about what you do. It's about *why* you do it and how you do it. Why we exist is to do what we did. And, how we do it by creating a culture of learning and teaching that delivers a highly engaged workforce who live our company's values every day.

I had a model I put together: people, purpose, and values. Then you have strategy and execution, which is where most organizations spend most of their time. That's when you learn. Learning is important because learning is the fuel for passion. And to create that passion, you have to create a safe and inspiring learning environment.

Having a vision means you have the opportunity to create a culture that excites you and your employees. Your desire to make change is something to celebrate. As your culture shifts, be enthusiastic and set a positive tone. Maintain open dialogue so you can find ways to tweak roles and better utilize skills or interests. Work at connecting people throughout the organization to align them with the grand vision. You have the ability to connect your team members with their work in a way that shows them the impact it has on the company as a whole, your customers, and on their co-workers. You can do this by sharing stories highlighting how your vision helps your employees accomplish their dreams too.

Now is the time for you to create your vision. Use the space below to map out and formulate the vision you have.

My vision is:

Now that you have crafted your vision, use it to rally your team around a shared purpose. When everyone is on board and understands their individual part in the bigger picture, your workplace culture will become energized with an atmosphere of collective success. This enthusiasm and collaboration is the foundation for a team that strives for excellence and accountability – laying the groundwork for the next chapter in achieving success.

CHAPTER 9:

A—Accountability

If you're like me, you likely want to work with people who do what they say they are going to do. I don't appreciate those who look for ways to blame others or make excuses when things aren't going their way. I prefer to work with people who show up, carry their weight on projects, and contribute in valuable ways. That's accountability, and it starts with you. Being accountable is not someone else's responsibility. It's yours. It's about taking ownership of the ideas and actions needed to move an idea forward. After all, you are in the driver-seat–no one else.

When everyone is working together for a common cause and understands their individual part in the bigger picture, the workplace culture becomes charged with enthusiasm and collaboration. This kind of collective spirit creates a culture of accountability and excellence, allowing your team to reach its collective goals more effectively. By creating a vision that everyone can buy into, you have laid the groundwork for holding each other accountable for successful results.

Accountability is about buying in, not weighing in, meaning that everyone must be invested and committed to the shared vision in order to achieve their collective goals. You will know accountability is in place when *It's not my job* transitions into *It's all of our jobs.*

I'm going back to my conversation with Daniel Lawrence from *Bots for That™* so that he can tell you himself about accountability and his experience with it in the workplace.

Q. Daniel, do you believe that people need to be accountable?

The answer is yes! Everyone needs to be equally accountable if they are going to succeed.

We have our annual strategy, and we have a quarterly plan. That quarterly plan gets very, very tangible, very real, and very practical. The outcome is that everybody has some part of it in delivering it.

If any one of us misses, we all miss. It is jointly accountable. So much as if two of us fail, well, guess what, we all failed. If I don't get the deals in and get them signed, I fail, and there's no money to go around for extra bonuses.

If we don't finish projects on time, we don't get the money, and there are no bonuses. All those things are very collaborative, and all joined up very closely. We all know that we've all got to succeed for us all to succeed. There's no I did okay. We either *all fail*, or *we all succeed*.

CLEAR DEFINITIONS BUILD ACCOUNTABILITY

Garry Ridge from *WD-40™ Company*, supports what Daniel said. He feels the first necessary step is ensuring everyone understands what they are being held accountable for, just like a great football coach does for their team.

Q. Garry, what does a great coach do for their team?

The first thing is to define what they're accountable for. Most people let people down because they haven't defined what we will hold each other accountable for. The book I wrote with Ken Blanchard, called *Helping People Win At Work* (¹) is a business philosophy around not marking people's papers but helping them get an A.

The first definition is what does an A look like? One of the things that's very important in our organization is that we define A's. If I'm your coach, we'll sit down at the beginning of the year and say, "Let's look at your role. What are the key components of your role? What are the three to five most important factors? What does an A look like if they walked in the room today?"

My job as your coach is to help you get that A. Great coaches don't run on the field. Great coaches spend time on the sideline, observing the play. They never go in and grab the ball. They never kick the ball. They never go to the podium.

They spend a lot of time in the locker room building trust and culture around the team. If you're a coach at our company, number one, A, is very clearly defined by those you coach. The responsibility of getting that A is on the player; your job is to show them areas where they could improve their play to help them get that A.

Gary's coach analogy is a strong one to consider. In our human-centered workplace, coaching is a strong form of leadership, which takes me to my next point, "Top-Down Accountability." What do I mean by that? Accountability starts at the top, visibly and expected. You must be willing to emulate what you want to see in others. Set a good example. Be the type of employee you'd like to have working for you. You can't ask others to behave in a way you are unwilling to; that means accountability has to start at the top if it is going to permeate through the company all the way down to the customers.

Harry Hynekamp put it more succinctly. He said, "anyone in the *AMB Sports and Entertainment*™ family understands what it's like to walk in each other's shoes."

Q. Harry, what does it mean to walk in each other's shoes as it pertains to the workplace?

On the accountability and alignment side, one of the ways an organization can go sideways very quickly is when they're separated from their associates or their customers.

We try to make sure that never happens. All of our associates can participate in something literally called the *Walk In My Shoes program*. They'll work a concession stand on event day, or they'll work security, or as a part of our guest services team, so everyone knows exactly what it's like to be on the front-line with our associates serving fans, guests, and customers.

Additionally, I think from the standpoint of accountability and alignment, leadership is also very visible to all of our associates, fans, guests, and customers. From a leadership perspective, we are side by side, arm in arm, with all of them. When we are working events and working our business, we all are responsible to lead by example.

Q. Is there another core value that you can share with us?

Sure. Innovate continuously.

After every event, we review fan, guest, and customer feedback and we talk about what we could do better so that the next event can be even better than the last one. It also helps to identify trends and themes regarding potential areas for future innovations we need to consider to improve the experience for our associates, fans, guests, customers or the business itself.

Everyone within your business is always watching you; as they say, *Actions speak louder than words.* Since great *businesses relentlessly pursue the best and innovate*, it is up to you to take risks, be proactive, and do things others don't like to do. *So, do* things others don't like to do. Creating a V.A.L.U.E. Culture isn't about being brilliant or having the most amazing skill set. It's much more about getting in there and getting things done, even when that means pushing yourself outside of your comfort zone. Everything you do should be done well and with a willingness to go above and beyond expectations to make sure you don't develop a reputation for doing things poorly or just enough to get by. Always do a little more than expected; that is true accountability.

As a business leader, Jana Adams, executive director at *Touchstone Energy Cooperatives™*, which is a national network of electric cooperatives across 45 U.S. states, has seen how great leaders connect with their employees through accountability and can build strong relationships and cultures that thrive for generations. Her perspective on leaders and how they build a human-centered culture through instilling accountability throughout an organization is worth considering.

Q. Jana, real leaders recognize their employees as what?

Leaders recognize employees are real human beings with lives outside of the office, and they bring those experiences to work with them, but that doesn't excuse them from meeting expectations.

Everyone carries something, if not multiple things, with them. We're going to be helpful to folks, and we're going to help them out in times of need. But we'll also expect effort and accountability, not just allow people to coast.

I've seen far too many businesses hold on to employees and allow them to stay on, even though it was widely known within the organization they were not performing up to standards. People think that's the kind and empathetic thing to do. I reject the notion of allowing them to stay on when they are not contributing; we are obligated to help them achieve. We can coach them or maybe find another position in the organization, but if they're not accountable and not doing their job, it's much more of a *culture-subtract* than a *culture-add*.

Q. Jana, tell me a little bit about models of accountability that have worked for you.

Accountability equals dependability. It creates a harmonious work culture. It strengthens your leadership. A team without accountability struggles to thrive. Leaders should set an example for the rest of the employees. But that doesn't mean they are the only ones who need to be held accountable. It's up to the entire organization.

When you convey and instill the idea that culture is how you work, it becomes clear that it's everybody's job. You should always be aligned with the core values and what your organization believes is important, good, and worth caring about. In terms of making sure it's part of everybody's job, it's practicing what you preach. There are lots of different ideas about how to incorporate that into practice.

At one organization I've been a part of, we had our core values and specific behaviors that exemplified those values. It starts to help people think about the process and how they can incorporate these into their day-to-day work.

Another tool I use that I love is the RACI model for

decision-making.([2]) RACI simply stands for responsible, accountable, consulted, and informed and usually shows up in a chart or matrix showing what level of responsibility each person has for a task, activity, or deliverable. This is more project management, but it's related to how to instill core values.

It shows who's responsible, who's accountable, who needs to be consulted on a project, and who supports and influences the project. If you look at those different areas in implementing a strong culture, everyone supports it. You start to realize that everybody is involved. If you have those different models about advancing any project, and you put the culture piece through that, people start to see I'm involved in that, and so is everyone else.

Accountability makes the difference. It ensures that you are always doing your best work, taking responsibility for your actions, and contributing to the greater success of the organization. For you to be the leader your company needs, assigning accountability to yourself is the first place to start, and setting a good example can have a positive ripple effect on your team.

THE OZ PRINCIPLE—A DIFFERENT ACCOUNTABILITY MODEL

I love to give you options so the culture you build reflects your leadership style. Let's look at another great accountability model—*The OZ Principle of Accountability*. The model of accountability is based on the book *The OZ Principle: Getting Results Through Individual and Organizational Accountability* by Tom Smith and Roger Connors.([3])

The core idea of the book is when people take personal ownership of their organization's goals and accept responsibility for their own performance, they become more engaged and work at a much higher level. It's not a new concept; the book has been around since 1994 and uses the *Wizard of Oz*™ storyline to illustrate how personal accountability impacts results.

If you remember the story, the characters, Dorothy, the Tin Man, the Scarecrow, and the Cowardly Lion, are all off to find the Wizard who can solve their problems. They each are portrayed as victims. In business, leaders may find it easier to look outward for the cause of a problem—bad economy, supply chain issues, regulations—than to look internally to see what is going on. Focusing on accountability can mean making hard decisions. Employees and leaders looking for an easy, quick fix can fall into victim thinking. A victim mindset erodes productivity, morale, and trust.

Using the OZ principle, you're either *above* or *below* the *line of accountability*. If you are above, you take ownership, accountability, responsibility, and opportunities. If you fall below the line, you offer blame, excuses, denial, and drama. We all know which side of the line helps drive a culture change faster. Yet, it's much easier to fall below the line than to take on responsibility and accountability.

How can you identify if you are functioning below the line? Here are some simple questions to ask:
- Do you feel like you lack control over present circumstances?
- Do you sometimes blame others or point fingers?
- Do discussions center around what you can't do instead of what you can do?
- Do you confront tough issues or ignore them?
- Do people feel they are treated unfairly?
- Are you defensive when team members give feedback?
- Do you say, "It's not my job?"

THE BLAME GAME ISN'T PART OF ACCOUNTABILITY

You must shift the view of accountability from a way to place blame to a personal choice of ownership. Taking ownership must become a discussion even when nothing is going wrong. Too often, accountability is only discussed after there is a problem because we are looking at where we should be placing blame.

Your job as a leader is to turn the view of accountability into a positive one. This perspective is a way to overcome challenges and results. Moving everyone to a point where they see accountability as a personal value will take time at first, but over time, it will be a tool for growth and development that will lead to improved business performance.

Here are some simple suggestions you can use to show your team, as their leader, that accountability starts at the top and you are committed to embracing the idea of a 360-degree accountability model:

- Inviting feedback from others on your performance.
- Being truthful.
- Acknowledge problems.
- Own the situation and circumstances as well as the results.
- Ask what else I can do to drive results.

Just like the Cowardly Lion in the *Wizard of Oz*™, accepting accountability takes courage and involves seeing things from multiple perspectives. It may mean admitting an action you did that didn't get the results you wanted. Finding ways to turn that around, or learning from it and using it as a tool for future success, will be the hallmark of good leadership and foster a culture of accountability in your organization.

With accountability comes transparency. Transparency is another driver for today's leaders. Whether it's in the daily decisions or the reasons behind your cultural initiative, share the why and be fully transparent. Keeping a secret means people won't trust you.

Once anyone believes you're not above board about a process, they will assume it about all processes. If you're pondering on what to share, err on the side of more. People want to trust who they work for and their leaders. Building trust means your team will be more willing and able to engage in the risk associated with change. Be clear. Be open. Be transparent. They will appreciate you for doing so.

ACCOUNTABILITY BUILDS RELATIONSHIPS

Accountability encourages employees to communicate with each other, get to know each other at work, and develop lasting relationships. You want to build relationships through your own accountability as a leader to form a winning team.

Conversely, when you make a mistake, you have to own it and communicate it. Changing a culture won't be a smooth linear process. Being responsible is a way of being and thinking and *not making excuses*. Being accountable is about policing your own actions because you have a responsibility to yourself. *You must be able to depend on yourself before expecting others to do so. Your ability to accept responsibility has a positive impact on others.*

The Scarecrow in the *Wizard of Oz*™ sought out wisdom. To shift culture, you must use your wisdom to guide you through the process. Ask questions. Think differently. Create relationships. Stay engaged. Your team needs to see you fully engaged with the process and hear how you remain accountable. As we mentioned earlier, leaders must emulate what they want to see from others.

Still using the *Wizard of Oz*™ analogy, Dorothy was all about getting it done. She used her skills and talents, which she had throughout the journey, and took ownership of her circumstances to get the results she wanted and reach her goal: getting home. She didn't let anything dissuade her, and she demonstrated a true spirit of resilience and care for her team. Personal accountability gives everyone buy-in to your culture change.

Accountability isn't about overloading people with projects and checkpoints. Organizations are responsible for promoting individual accountability to drive a successful culture shift. You can create an accountability process in four easy steps:

1. Clearly define the results wanted.
2. Determine a timeline for a progress update.
3. Coach them for success.
4. Repeat the process.

Showing multiple touch points of accountability will help your leadership team to get along and work together. An accountability system breaks down barriers between employees, gives them a common goal, and provides them time to work together in unique ways. Building an accountability system will also serve to reinforce your vision.

Accountability keeps everyone on the *same page*. From entry-level positions up to upper management, you and your work team should have the same mission. Each member should be given a clear understanding of how they can be a part of that mission. They should clearly understand that follow-through is vital and expected.

Accountability is essential in creating a successful workplace culture. When everyone has clear expectations and understands the importance of their contributions to the team's success, they are more likely to be motivated and engaged with their work.

An effective accountability system can help reduce conflict between employees while promoting collaboration and creative problem-solving. With an accountable team that shares common goals, it will be easier for your organization to reach its objectives and foster an atmosphere of trust and respect among all members of the leadership team.

CHAPTER 10:

L—Leadership

We are headed into the L of our V.A.L.U.E. Culture. L is for leadership. Your leadership can be an incredible coaching tool that leads individuals to work as a team and gain wins for their organization. Lasting cultures are built around a people-first model with strong leaders like you. Leadership is both the glue that holds the initiative together and the driver that spreads it throughout the organization.

You may be surprised we're just now reaching the leadership portion of the V.A.L.U.E. Culture formula. You've already seen the word "leader" numerous times in prior chapters. That's because each area requires something from you, the leader. However, one word you haven't seen is "boss." That's because there's a big difference between the two. You can be a leader who doesn't need to be a boss, or you can just be a boss that doesn't know how to lead.

In the 35 years I've been in the workforce, it's easy to pick out the bosses I've had who are also great leaders. The leaders are the ones who work to create a supportive and empowering work environment, communicate effectively and frequently, and actively listen to their team members so that they begin to know them on a human level and understand their needs and perspectives. The bosses are the ones who direct without motivation or inspiration. They fail to build relationships or take the time to understand the needs and perspectives of their team. Bosses often create an atmosphere of fear and stress. The difference between a leader and a boss lies in how they interact with their team members; while a leader will strive to build relationships and create an atmosphere of collaboration and trust, a boss is solely focused on managing their team.

As I've led training events and listened to the participants talk about the bosses who inspired them and made them want to do more each day, certain traits emerged consistently. A people-centered leader prioritizes their team members' well-being, development, and engagement above all else. They recognize that their success as a leader is directly linked to the success and satisfaction of their team. I believe great leaders also focus on helping their team members grow and develop both personally and professionally while ensuring their contributions are valued. In short, people-centered leaders put their team at the center of their leadership approach.

In this chapter, you'll hear from experts on what makes a great leader, and you can grade yourself on where you stand in your skills and approach. Leadership is personal and will require you to do some soul-searching to discover your own strengths and weaknesses, so you can use your natural abilities to the fullest. Reflect on the value you place in understanding different perspectives on your team, the effectiveness of your communications, and the importance you place on building trust. I am happy to share the skills and tactics you can learn to become a more effective boss in a leadership position so that you can build a V.A.L.U.E. Culture inside your organization and be both an effective boss and a supportive leader

I had a conversation with Adam Schwartz, the founder of *The Cooperative Way*™, a consulting firm helping co-ops define their mission, so employees and members remember it. He said true leaders have a calling to help others be successful, and it's easy to tell the difference between bosses and leaders.

> ***Q. Adam, how can you tell the difference between a leader and a boss?***

I'm a huge fan of the servant leadership model. A leader's true calling is to help others be successful. I've been fortunate. I've had some wonderful bosses and supervisors in my career, and I've had some awful bosses and supervisors.

What I say is I've learned from every one of them. I think that being genuinely caring and empathetic is key. Good leaders learn the appropriate amount of personal information about their employees, recognizing that some are willing to share more than others and respecting that. I think good leaders will showcase those skills of empathy and accountability. They also display curiosity and do not feel like they know all the answers.

I think good leaders understand that the frontline folks doing the job are often in the best position to suggest improvements.

The world is full of bosses. There are far too few leaders. One thing that's been popular for years is this notion that you don't quit a company; you quit your boss. That hasn't gone away. I think we'll continue to see it in the top five reasons why people tend not to be happy.

If you've got a leader who is very good at the task but doesn't know how to bring the best out of people and doesn't know how to coach and mentor, that's becoming more problematic, particularly in today's environment.

As Adam said, the world is full of bosses. As I began moving along my career path, it didn't take long to understand there is truly a difference between a boss and a leader. While the words get used interchangeably, there is a definite difference. A boss has authority because of their position and ability to impact your paycheck. They typically focus on getting things done or being in control rather than developing the people in their team. Leaders inspire and use their influence to help guide others toward a common goal. They motivate, support and help move people toward their full potential. For your culture change to be successful, leaders, not bosses, need to drive the change, not command it.

Just as the Covid-19 pandemic forced many organizations and employees to adapt rapidly to new ways of working, it also created an unprecedented opportunity for employees to reflect on the qualities of their leaders and how they navigated during challenging times. Adam's mention of the *Great Resignation* reminded me of something recruiter Mark Allred said: "The Covid-19 Pandemic gave people time to think about what mattered."

During any challenging time, employees can see their leaders in action and how they respond to stress and uncertainty. They watch them handle communications challenges, decision-making, and problem-solving. They witnessed them succeed and fail at motivating their teams in various environments. The pandemic, or any other challenge, allows employees to gain new insights into their leaders' strengths and weaknesses and how they contribute to the organization's success.

Challenging times also highlight the importance of empathy, compassion, and transparency in leadership. I've heard from multiple employees how they came to appreciate the leaders who are responsive to their concerns and provide clear and consistent communications about their plans and decisions. On the other hand, leaders who are seen as distant, unresponsive, or untrustworthy created lower morale and higher disengagement among their employees.

As a business leader, have you seen something similar in your organization when you've dealt with the challenging world, market, or economic times? I know Mark, Director of Talent Development and Growth at *Reveal Global Intelligence*™, had a few other nuggets of wisdom he shared on the impact the challenges, like the pandemic, have had on how employees view leadership.

Q. Mark, thanks for being willing to discuss the event, the elephant in the room of what happened when the world shut down, and how we coped with life following that pandemic event. Care to share your thoughts?

I wrote a blog about Covid-19 being the unsung hero or the unlikely hero of the American worker. When Covid-19 happened, and we all went home, we got quiet while being quarantined in our homes. We stopped to think, and many folks said I don't like my job. It changed that mentality, and everything like culture, leadership, and development came to the forefront of their mind. They started considering other things. So, leadership is absolutely a piece of it.

Q. Mark, what do you think about leadership during crises?

It impacted everyone, so we all had to start to figure things out. Many people like the idea of working at home or at least an employer showing some flexibility. Work-life balance continues to show up. When I'm recruiting, the common question is, what is that environment like?

Money is still on the table. If you, as an employer, aren't

doing your homework regarding fair compensation for the work you are asking folks to do, you'll have a problem. That information is getting so public. It's easier for job seekers to go out and find a competitive salary for the role they are looking at in their geographical region. So if you've fallen behind the times and you're not paying fairly for your work, that could also be a problem.

That's where leadership matters. Being adaptable. Recognizing there is a new set of employment drivers. Being responsive and talking about the changes.

Mark shared a starter list of traits great, effective leaders demonstrate. As I've worked with my personal coaching clients who were considering career changes and from those who attend my corporate training events, it's become apparent businesses aren't teaching leadership. Many people are promoted into leadership roles based on years of service or a skill set, yet they are unprepared for the people part of the equation. This lack of training makes effective leadership scarce.

Since all businesses need good leaders, you can stand out by becoming a people-first leader, not just a boss. Becoming a more *effective leader is the first key* to building a V.A.L.U.E. Culture-based culture in your organization.

Here's what good leaders do:
1. Lead by Example.
A boss likes to sit on the sidelines of their business and allow others to do the hard work. A leader is out in front of his people, showing the way. A leader is involved. A boss just makes a request and walks away. I've experienced this difference in the workplace and seen how it shows up in a number of ways. Leaders make sure that their actions lead the way, not merely

enforce how it should be done. For example, a good leader consistently arrives early and greets each team member to set a positive tone for the rest of the day. Leading by example is a powerful way for a leader to influence their team and create a culture of trust, respect, and mutual support.

2. Leaders are Driven by Purpose.

A leader who is driven by purpose is clear about the goals and directions of the organization and is committed to using their leadership to achieve them. These leaders establish a clear vision. There is an overall goal or mission. *The people following the leader must be inspired and empowered.* The people must understand the mission. Purpose-driven leadership is very different from providing a to-do list without any context.

Leaders delegate. Bosses micromanage. A leader trusts their people, a boss struggles to relinquish control. A leader surrounds themself with people that complement their weaknesses. A boss hires people who don't make them feel threatened.

The leaders I've seen excel in leading with purpose are those who prioritize values and encourage accountability. Their actions align with the core values, and they hold themselves as well as their team accountable for results.

A boss always has a weaker team. The team can't accomplish as much because they're not empowered. The team is also weaker because the boss doesn't want strong employees that might shine brighter than they do. When leaders foster teamwork, they understand success requires collaboration and mutual support.

3. Leaders Value Respect.

A boss wants to be feared. On the surface, they might appear to be similar, but the differences are striking. A leader will use their enthusiasm, skill, and expertise to encourage others to respect and follow them. A boss uses fear and threats to gain compliance.

Leaders have the best wishes of their followers. Those who follow a boss secretly want them to fail. Successful leaders I've worked with understand respect starts with their own actions and behaviors. Successful culture change happens when employees feel they are treated with dignity and respect, regardless of their position or seniority. Leaders who value respect also address disrespectful behavior when it occurs. They take a firm stance against bullying or harassment and take steps to address it when it occurs. These leaders' actions and words emphasize their commitment to creating a workplace where employees feel valued and respected.

4. A Leader Develops New Leaders.

A true leader constantly creates employees with the knowledge and experience to take their place. A boss is afraid of competition. A boss is afraid they'll be replaced and is too self-centered to be concerned about the career aspirations of their employees.

When I'm working with companies, I encourage them to take a look at who they have in their career pipelines. Developing new leaders is important for succession planning and the lack of opportunities is one of the main reasons I get coaching clients who are ready to find their next opportunity. Professional development is a critical piece for the long-term success and sustainability of an organization.

One way leaders can develop others is by being a mentor. I've had the ability to tap into the knowledge of numerous leaders as I've moved from a career in journalism to corporate public relations. I've had mentors who helped me as I was preparing to build my own company. Mentors play a significant role in the development of new leaders by providing guidance and support, sharing knowledge and experiences, encouraging avenues of growth, serving as a soundboard and offering networking opportunities. I know my mentors helped me develop a list of skills to grow and they gave me the confidence needed to become an effective leader myself. Imagine what you could instill in your team members.

5. Leaders Know How to Motivate

Leaders know that no two employees are the same. They know their employees well enough to know how to inspire them. A boss simply says, "It is what it is. This is what needs to be done. You can always look for another job if you don't like it." Leaders use positive techniques for motivation, while bosses tend to criticize. A leader will say:
- "I appreciate all the hard work you've done"
- "Let's celebrate our successes together"
- "It's ok to make mistakes - we learn from them"
- "We are in this together"
- "I am here to support you"
- "What can I do to make your job easier?"
- "Thank you for taking the initiative"
- "You are making a difference here"
- "Let's think of creative ways to solve this problem together"
- "Your feedback is valuable and appreciated"

Motivating a team is an important part of a leader's role, and I've seen several successful strategies you can use to help keep your team motivated and engaged. Along with making sure you are setting clear goals and expectations, recognition, and rewards can help boost morale and motivate your team. You'll find more on the value of recognition when you read chapter 12. E—Engagement. Motivating a team requires a leader to take an active and proactive approach using a combination of techniques to create a positive work environment.

6. Leaders Take Responsibility

When the team fails, *the leader* is still *out in front, taking the brunt of the criticism*. A boss is trying to absolve himself of as much responsibility as possible. A boss is quick to blame their employees. A leader is quick to blame him or herself. The ownership action is crucial for building trust and credibility with your team.

Early in my career, I had a wonderful leader, who wasn't just a boss. When I was hired, he told me he wasn't a micro-manager—that he wouldn't have hired me if he'd been afraid I couldn't do the job. He told me his door was always open and that if I needed something, tools, information, assistance—his job was to make sure I had the things I needed to do my job. He also created a culture of trust by always having my back. I remember a specific budget meeting, our CEO became irate over the numbers I was presenting. I had worked through the presentation with my boss and we both agreed on the invest-ment needed for the program. Throughout that meeting, my manager had my back. He intervened with the CEO saying he had verified my numbers and he agreed with the conclusions. He told the CEO he signed off on the budget and the presentation. His actions set the tone for years of positively working together.

Leaders also understand the importance of being held to the same standard as others on their team. Daniel Lawrence, co-founder of *Bots for That*™, pointed out how we, as leaders, need to *measure ourselves*. I wanted to share his nuggets of wisdom with you.

Q. Daniel, why do you review your successes and failures along with those of your team?

We measure ourselves quarterly, quite tightly. We have a particular progress meeting every fortnight (every two weeks) to review where we are, what's going well, what's not done, what's changed, who's had some successes, who has some failures, and I'm fairly open about everything that happens.

I like to think I take responsibility and accountability for all of it. Whenever I do a podcast, someone always asks, what do you do? I say, "I'm the guy who takes the credit for nothing and the blame for everything." That's how I like to think I lead.

I don't think it's always the case because people are people; we are all big complex beings. But that's how I like to think I would always take control of it. And then you hope that sets the theme for everyone else to do the same. I think it largely does.

I don't really see anyone in our company that doesn't take the same approach. They all take responsibility. They all take accountability for the outcomes. They take responsibility for getting their sleeves rolled up and getting stuck in because we're a smaller company. That's the only way that we can succeed.

There is no one else who's going to take care of that; you've got to do it. Sometimes that means getting your fingers in other people's pies and just getting on with it, getting it done. I think that does happen.

Look back over your work history. You've probably had plenty of bosses, and, I hope, at least a few leaders. Working for someone who fits into the boss category is not enjoyable. You feel like you're operating in the dark with little support and few development opportunities while working for a leader feels like you are part of a team that is focused on your growth and success. *It's much more enjoyable to work for a leader.*

LEADERS CAN MAKE THE DIFFERENCE—CLIENT NUMBER ONE:

As a professional coach and trainer, I wanted to share a few personal stories about being a boss or a leader and how it can dramatically change an organization's culture. A client named Kelly, a PR professional shared the aftermath employees endured after a long-tenured CEO retired from her company and a new person was handed the reins.

Kelly said all the employees knew who the board would put into place long before the announcement was made public. Everyone felt like the internal interview process was for show only. That made it even worse. But she couldn't say anyone was surprised when the announcement came.

What was surprising was how quickly one person could deteriorate a culture. In less than six months, people who had been there for years stayed in their office, trying to fly under the radar.

The CEO went from being accessible to hiding behind his executive assistant. Only a limited few had access to him. People began to feel taken advantage of and unvalued. People who had been high performers and achievers lost interest in the work and just did the status quo. Those with retirement options took them, and others began looking for new opportunities.

Kelly said she was very thankful she could find a way out, and now she is at a place where she is excited again. Her new opportunity makes her feel her voice is heard, and she's rewarded for the value she brings to the table daily.

Kelly said, "It's good to know there are great leaders in the world. You just have to do the legwork and look for them."

LEADERS CAN MAKE THE DIFFERENCE - CLIENT NUMBER TWO:

I want to share with you another client, Dave, who was in the financial industry and shared a leadership experience that left him feeling stressed, uncomfortable, and looking for a way out. I asked Dave about his career, and here's the story he shared.

I had started a business but was at a stage where I still wasn't sure it would work. My wife had lost her job, so it was really a case of doing what you had to do to get by. A guy from church said they needed someone at his company to do calls following up on unpaid bills.

I could do the work from home after I had gone in and learned their systems. Part of that was sitting in listening to how others made the calls. The guy I was learning from was a jerk.

He yelled at everyone. He made the clients miserable. I knew I wouldn't sit and yell at people on the phone daily. It wasn't just the clients either. The whole environment was miserable.

People didn't enjoy being in the office. They were being asked to work in an unpleasant environment. One day, I went to lunch, sat in my car, and almost had a panic attack. All I can remember is sitting there staring at the front door. I remember trying to convince myself to walk back through the front door.

Does any of this sound familiar? Could your employees be experiencing the same feelings? As I worked with Dave, he continued sharing more stories about his experience.

Once I could make the calls from home, it was better. I let people talk. Sometimes it was bad paperwork or lost invoices. Screaming didn't help get to the bottom of the problem. Some were in legit trouble and stressed out.

Being yelled at by everyone wasn't going to bring the money in. I tried to find a way to work with people. When I was cordial, they would talk to me. I had to do it in a way that didn't make me miserable also. I hated being asked to do things in a way that was unnatural to me and really just wrong.

Dave ended up leaving that company and moving on to another opportunity. I know we can all understand why. How many of you would have done something similar? I walked away from a company after working there for 20-plus years. *What was the problem?* Bad leadership. Being a great leader is part skill and part personal development. If you combine them effectively, people will love working with you. Leadership is about cultivating employees who are genuinely happy to be there. The more you do for your employees, the more they are willing to do for you. With the right leadership, you can cultivate longevity in the workplace because you'll build a loyal workforce.

The next section lists the characteristics of impactful culture leaders. Use this list to do your own self-assessment and analyze the areas in which you excel.

CHARACTERISTICS OF CULTURE LEADERS

These skills will help you as you lead a culture change. They are the characteristics of a standout culture-building leader

- **Listen.** Remember, you don't know everything. Your employees will have excellent suggestions that can prove beneficial.
- **Share information.** True leaders understand knowledge

sharing is powerful. Your job will be to communicate clearly that a culture change is coming. How you frame it and your words will impact how receptive employees are to the initiative.

- **Be fair.** Nothing breeds resentment and discontent like being mistreated. Don't have favorites.
- **Extend support.** Confident employees accomplish more. Be their cheerleader. Encourage them when they are unsure of a new challenge.
- **Show empathy.** Meet your employees where they are and strive to understand their needs and fears. It allows you to accurately understand how your employees work each day.
- **Avoid micromanaging.** Remember, you hired the person because you felt they had the skills you needed. Now let them do the job you hired them for. Nothing ruins morale faster than when your boss doesn't trust you.
- **Show appreciation.** People love to be thanked, and words don't cost you anything. Make people feel appreciated for the work they do.
- **Give good feedback.** People like to know how they are doing. They also want to know when things aren't going so well. They'd rather know sooner than wait six months for review time. It's your job to develop your employees for the future.
- **Trust.** Trustworthiness is the most important trait a leader can display. Trust comes from engaging others. By learning who they are on the inside. What matters to them? What their priorities are. Trust is about really listening, so people feel heard. Listening is the beginning of clear, consistent communication.
- **Communicate.** Communication is the key to building teams and encouraging collaboration. Some people

are born with the natural ability to communicate well, while others may struggle. No matter what category you fall into, you will likely *benefit from paying attention to improving your communication skills.*

With better communication skills, you will be able to lead a culture change effectively. Mastering how to listen, share information, show empathy, extend support, and trust, while giving good feedback and showing appreciation will reflect in your employees. You will motivate people and build strong teams that can accomplish great things together.

WHY BETTER COMMUNICATION HELPS YOU LEAD

Communicating effectively is the most crucial skill a culture change leader can exhibit. You could have top-notch knowledge and job skills but fail to effectively lead change if you're lacking in the communication department.

Proper communication will prevent misunderstandings and save you time, so you won't have to go back and explain yourself repeatedly. You know you've gained good communication skills when you can communicate your thoughts effectively with as few words as necessary!

Communication is a two-way street. Being understood is essential, and as more people understand you, everything around you will run more efficiently, and you'll more often get what you want!

Try these strategies to improve your communication skills:

- **Avoid arguing.** If you run into a snag in a conversation and it morphs into an argument, step back and realize what's happening. It's easy to get swept up into the blame game, but ultimately it's not important who's at fault.

What's important is the *mutual understanding of the issue at hand and a desire for a solution that benefits everyone.*

- **Don't be afraid to compromise.** You may be tempted to try and win, but that's not the best way to reach a mutual agreement. You may be happier with getting your way, but it may come at the other person's expense, which can cause further issues. Find a good compromise that you both can willingly accept.
- **Work on listening.** Your listening skills are even more important than your speaking skills. After all, how will you know what you should say, and when, if you haven't effectively listened? *Listen more than you speak; you'll also gain profound wisdom from others!*
- **Keep your focus.** Communication will get overly complicated if you worry about too many issues simultaneously. Avoid bringing up the past or other issues and focus on one topic.
- **Stay calm and take responsibility.** Adopt a calm and relaxed manner of handling situations. When things remain low-key, it's easier to communicate and get your point across. Take responsibility for what you say. *Don't be afraid to admit mistakes when you're wrong.*

Becoming a better communicator doesn't happen overnight. I know, I've been honing my craft for almost 30 years. But if you keep practicing and tweaking your skills, you'll be surprised at what you can accomplish. If you're encouraging communication, trust must be in place, so employees feel they can have meaningful conversations. Bob Brown, the Vice President of Finance and Operations Support for *Yamaha*™, has a great example of how weaving communication into your people processes leads to success.

Q. Bob, how do you communicate with your employees?

One thing we do every quarter is hold an all-associates communication meeting. It's eleven meetings throughout the day. Every one of our six buildings on all three shifts. The executive team speaks in front of every employee across the campus on the same day.

We share information about what happened the past quarter, where we performed well, where we need to improve, what's coming up In the next quarter, what new challenges might be coming in, or what's different or changing. Then at the end, it's an open question and answer.

They're not scripted. We don't pre-screen questions. You're welcome to ask whatever you like. We try to be very open and honest in our answers.

Q. Bob, what do you attribute communication success to?

I think that a big part of communication is personal trust. If you're just speaking to people in a pre-recorded message, it's not two-way communication. Even just knowing that you're sitting there in front of the person and you could ask the question, even if you don't, adds an element of trust as well.

I think that part of trust is having that open line of communication and being accessible. We have very much an open-door policy. In our last quarterly associate meeting, our President was talking about compliance and how it's important in whatever your role is in the organization to be compliant, whether that includes handling chemicals that could be hazardous appropriately or about free trade zone compliance.

He said if you're not sure you're compliant, you don't have to wait until something bad happens. If you're unsure that you're doing everything possible, feel free to talk to me about it, and we'll figure it out. So, when even your president has an open-door policy for everyone who works here, all 2,200 people, I think that demonstrates a lot of trust.

> ### Q. Bob, tell me why building trust is essential.

Building trust is essential. If people trust you, they are willing to be honest and vulnerable. They are willing to take risks. Without it, change won't happen. If you want to build trust, you need to understand trust is built by what you do, not necessarily by what you say. It's about authenticity.

LEADERS ARE THEIR EMPLOYEES HEAT SHIELD

Leaders who support and protect their employees, particularly during times of uncertainty and crisis, build loyal teams. They take responsibility for their employees. When employees know their leaders have their backs, they are better equipped to handle challenging situations and perform their work with greater ease. The *heat shield* analogy emphasizes the importance of leaders taking the brunt of any negative impact or consequences, shielding their employees from harm. Trust and strong leadership are essential to a strong culture because they allow for a sense of stability and support while promoting growth.

One way great leaders can demonstrate responsibility is by being the one to take the heat. Rich Sherian, the co-founder of *Menlo Innovations*™, has a great story about the importance of having his team's back.

> ### Q. Being a great leader also means having your team's back. If you want your team to get on board, they can't be afraid of

trying something new. Rich, please share your insight on this.

Part of my job as a leader was I had to elicit support. I was one executive out of many. There were shareholders. There was a board for accountability. There were quarterly reports. We had to deliver it to the public. There was a great business responsibility. We were a tech firm, and I was leading the technology part, the R&D part of the tech firm.

Most of the money in the company was spent on my team. The shareholders were counting on the results my team produced. There was a great responsibility on my part. I couldn't just wave a magic wand and say, "Okay, we're going to be joyful now." It still had to produce results. I felt like I wasn't really producing the result.

I think the first element of leadership is a kind of active discontent, just not being satisfied with what's status quo or what's normal, or simply accepting that's the way it's always been. I think active discontent says things can be better. I think a really big first moment for any leader is to say, "You know what? Can things be better? How are you going to do that? How are you going to make the change?"

Q. Rich, That is a great point. What was your next step?

I realized the next step was selling this idea to my executive team peers, my boss, the board of directors, and a couple of shareholders, which was a big learning moment, was to stop talking about what I wanted and start speaking in the language of the people I was selling to.

In other words, I wanted to do some technical things with my team. I wanted to create code differently. I want to do that. My boss really didn't care about that. He wanted to see results for the corporation.

So, I had this translate my vision into something that aligned with what he would support. That was my next big moment. When you go to create a cultural transformation, you must turn into a salesperson. You must communicate its value. You must communicate why this matters to others and what results you will produce for them due to whatever cultural transformation you go through. Then the delightful part happened.

Q. What was it, Rich, that changed?

Once I broke through the barrier with him and learned to speak his language, he became my most ardent supporter. I wouldn't have written two books on this idea. I wouldn't have created *Menlo Innovations*™ were it not for Bob Niro's role in my life.

As soon as I crafted the message in a way that Bob understood, Bob did two things. One, he became my biggest cheerleader whenever I slowed down or had self-doubt.

When you're making big changes, it isn't a smooth journey. It's not a snap of your fingers, and everything works. It's a long, tough, hard journey with a lot of unknowns. You don't know if you're succeeding or not every minute of the day. Bob Niro would put his gentle hand on my shoulder and whisper in my ear, "you're doing the right thing. Rich, I've got you covered. Keep going."

Q. Rich, What did Bob Nitro's support do for you?

I will tell you, I really, really needed that. From a leadership perspective, I learned in that moment that if you have someone who's working for you that's trying to lead some kind of big change, become their heat shield. Change agents are under attack, always. The attack is that's not the way we do things here. I was still the new kid on the block at that company. I'd been with the company for sixteen years at that point.

They said, "Rich, you don't know how things go here because you've only been here for sixteen years." And, it was absolutely true. I was still pretty much the new kid. I was the youngest executive on the team. Many of the people had been there for twenty-five or thirty years. I still had the stuff to learn about how the company worked. That was key.

Q. Rich, will you share about when you brought your eight-year-old daughter to work with you and how that changed your outlook?

Absolutely! It was a big moment when I brought my eight-year-old daughter to work with me one day. It was a "take your child to work day" moment. And she was going to watch her dad, the VP, work.

Can you imagine a more boring day than that? What on Earth would an eight-year-old see? Is she going to be inspired to a career by watching her dad, the VP work? She cleverly and wisely brought her coloring books, crayons, and stickers and sat on my test table all day while I did the work of a VP.

At the end of the day, I said, "So, Sarah, what did you learn today?" What she said surprised me. She said, "What I learned is you're really important here because nobody here can make a decision without asking you first."

And she was absolutely right. I created a hero-based organization. I was number one here. The way I got into my position was through hero-based leadership. I had to learn to step back from that.

Q. Wow Rich, children really observe and share it in a simple yet powerful way. What did you do?

I had to learn to *step back* from hero-based leadership. I think that's another key point for a leader of change. I needed to allow my teams to "run the experiment." Basically, I needed to become the heat shield for my team leaders. After all, I had a heat shield above me with Bob Niro; I needed to build a heat shield above them.

I had to give them the latitude to try things—run the experiment. Let's try stuff, and let's not get too upset if the stuff we try doesn't work. What I love about the word experiment is it almost gives you permission not to succeed. Because you can later say, yeah, it didn't work, but it was just an experiment.

Q. Rich, what are the three phases you use?

One is to make *mistakes faster*. The real emphasis is on the word *faster*. Nobody likes to make mistakes, but if you make them quickly and find them out when they're small, you can correct them before they kill you.

Number two is *let's run the experiment*. Let's try new stuff. And finally, number three is *it's okay to say I don't know*. Acknowledging that there's a ton to learn and we're not going to know everything and that we're going to run experiments and do things we don't know how to do is okay.

Mistakes will happen along the way, and by setting ourselves up, with repeated language from leaders, all the way down to the frontline, you create a spirit, attitude, and energy within a team.

Those three actions work because of the groundwork Rich and his team laid to build trust among the employee base. It took time and effort, but Rich reached a place where his team grasped the vision and bought into the implementation plan. And, so can you. Be willing to make mistakes, make them faster and run the experiment, get and give feedback often, and you'll begin to see the fruits of your labor spreading throughout the organization.

BUILDING TRUST IS A MUST FOR LEADERS

Trust is key to creating a V.A.L.U.E. Culture in today's workplace. Think about what Rich said. For his employees to do those three key things, there had to be a huge amount of trust. I know the leaders I trusted demonstrated they were trustworthy by being dependable and consistent. They were approachable and friendly. It's easier to trust someone you like. I've experienced trust in the workplace because leaders supported my team and me. They respected the ideas I brought to the table and listened to my perspective. They didn't always agree, but I knew I was heard. Trust comes when the eyes see what the ears hear.

Garry Ridge, Chairman Emeritus of *WD-40™ Company* and teacher of leadership says this about building trust, "You must behave in a manner that matches what you are communicating."

Q. Garry, tell me why you think trust in leadership is important.

Trust is extremely important. Number one, it comes from leadership. In leadership, it is important to ask, "Is the leader's ego eating the empathy instead of their empathy eating their ego?"

Your ego is the opposite of trust. Are we comfortable being vulnerable? Do we care about our people? Not only in word but in deed. Do we love our people enough to applaud them and reward them for doing great work, but are we brave enough as leaders to redirect them when their behavior is working against growing a great culture?

When I went to school in Australia many years ago, my science teacher gave me a Petri dish. The science teacher said we will grow a culture in this Petri dish. What's important is the ingredients that you are putting in the Petri dish. Are you putting in the right ingredients? Like the kind we are talking about in a successful culture. That's important. Then what's important is watching that Petri dish every day.

You feed it the ingredients that grow great culture and extract the ingredients that don't grow great culture. I have an algorithm that I adapted from some of Simon Sinek's work that says: *culture equals parenthesis, values plus behavior, close parenthesis times consistency.*

You've got to have the ingredients. You've got to have the behaviors. And you've got to pay attention to it every day.

Trust comes with humility. That doesn't mean downplaying your accomplishments or self-confidence, but it does mean sharing credit with your team. It comes with admitting your own mistakes along the way. Building trust isn't about perfection. Trust comes with integrity. It comes with being helpful. It's being a servant leader. It's genuinely seeking ways to help someone achieve their goals. It's about collaborating, not dictating.

If you are trying to build a V.A.L.U.E. Culture, you must have trust as a foundation piece. Building trust in a team requires time, effort, and intentionality. I encourage my managerial clients to set the tone by being transparent, fostering open communications, and being approachable. You can do numerous activities to bring your team members together and help build trust. One of the simplest ways to start is with an open-door policy. Encourage team members to share their thoughts and opinions and be available so anyone can come to you with questions or concerns. Hold regular team meetings and update your team on company news and progress. Encourage collaborative projects. By providing opportunities for team members to work together and rely on each other, you help build trust.

LEADERS TAKE THE FEAR OUT OF FAILURE

Now that you know trust is necessary for successful leadership, let's see if we can use that trust to eliminate the fear factor. There is fear in leadership. I've felt fear, and almost every other person I know who has been promoted to a leadership role or has stepped out on a leadership journey has had that moment where they wonder if they will be able to meet the expectations. Learning to push through, even when we're scared, is critical. Robert F. Kennedy said, "Only those who dare to fail greatly can ever achieve greatly." Without this attitude, fear of failure will hold you and your team back. Without trust, no one will step out and tackle new challenges or learn new skills. If they fear reprisal if something goes wrong while growing, you discourage a person from volunteering for new opportunities.

Q. Garry, what about fear and leadership? Is there something you can share that can fill the gap?

One tradition of the *WD-40™ Company is their Learning Moments.* This is a time of sharing both the positive and negative outcomes of any situation. It's shared openly, and everyone hears. No one is afraid of reprisal from their managers or supervisors.

If something doesn't go as planned, anyone can say, "I had a learning moment; here's what happened, and here's how it will be better tomorrow." On the flip side, "I had a learning moment; here's what happened, here's the great results I got, and here's what I want to share."

By taking the fear out of the equation, *WD-40™ Company* is creating a culture that isn't afraid to try new things and is more apt to grow and develop than one where fear rules.

> **Q. Garry, can you share why the WD-40™ product is called WD-40™?**

WD-40™, the product itself, was created due to a mistake. Can you believe it?

The forty in the name represents the inventor's fortieth attempt to get the formula right. That means there were thirty-nine chances for someone to get frustrated, get reprimanded, be made to feel not capable, or just give up, and success wouldn't have been achieved.

Mistakes are what allow us to grow and develop. When you give employees the safety to fail, you allow them to fail forward. When you do, that means you're building a growth mindset inside your organization. Trust comes with integrity. It comes with being helpful. It's being a servant leader. It's genuinely seeking ways to help someone achieve their goals. It's about collaborating, not dictating.

> **Q. Garry, I want to ask you a new question. What do you think about the phrase, "leadership isn't about you; it's about the people you lead."**

You are right! Leadership is not about you. When I was given the privilege to lead the company back in 1997, I was scared, but I wasn't afraid. I was reading some of the work of the Dalai Lama on a flight from Los Angeles to Sydney. He made a statement: our purpose in life is to make people happy. If we can't make them happy, at least don't hurt them.

What I saw around me, not necessarily in my company, but around in leadership, was leaders hurting people. I didn't understand why they were doing that. I didn't have the answer.

At the same time, I read Aristotle's statement that pleasure in the job puts perfection in work. I thought to myself, *If we could create a culture where we didn't hurt people, and we actually helped them, and they liked what they did, everything would change.*

Q. Garry, how do you spread that thought process through the organization?

Leadership doesn't start and end at the top. There are leaders on all levels of your organization. The ongoing leadership development of your people is going to give you a competitive advantage in today's world and in the upward trajectory of your organization. If your workforce becomes stagnant, it will die a slow death. This investment will build confidence in your employees. When people see that you value them and are willing to invest in them, they begin to recognize their worth. You'll begin to see key performers stand out.

Communication, being a heat shield, trust, respect, and serving as a visual reminder of what you want your employees to model should be at the top of your leadership trait list.

There's another piece to effective leadership you must master if you want to build a lasting V.A.L.U.E. Culture. It's identifying the next generation of leaders who will carry on the vision created. Unfortunately, there are times when these people are hidden gems in the workforce, and you have to work to bring them to the frontline.

LEADERSHIP HIDING IN PLAIN SIGHT

Every company has leaders hidden in plain sight. And, when you build a V.A.L.U.E. Culture, those leaders begin to emerge. Having a support system helps to develop their abilities even more. Your job as a leader is to support those hidden leaders to learn how to become visible and use their influence for good. These people are already hard workers and your leadership will help advance their skills in new directions.

They are good at their job. These hidden leaders usually lack the influence piece. Most people don't understand how to use influence to impact their sphere of people. The sad truth is most workplaces have numerous hidden talents already inside their walls that will remain invisible until supervisors and leaders are taught how to identify them.

Companies don't need to go out and hire more people. Their current employees are waiting for the manager to get to know them personally and issue an invitation to become engaged and empowered. This is where a people-centered culture becomes more impactful.

Building a culture in a way that grows leaders internally is a competitive advantage for you and the company.

HOW CAN YOU IDENTIFY THESE HIDDEN LEADERS?

How can you make sure you aren't overlooking employees, your hidden leaders, who have more to offer?

First, look at your departments. Are there individuals doing consistently good work but don't often speak out? Are there quiet people who seem overshadowed by other, more powerful personalities? Is there a rising star who, for whatever reason, has not yet moved upward inside your organization? It's time to give that employee a new look. As a leader, you must be on the lookout for these situations and determine how to engage these employees. It's your job to notice emerging *leaders* who may not notice the leadership skills they have within themselves.

Identifying hidden leaders can be challenging, but there are several strategies a supervisor can use to uncover these individuals:

- **Observe behavior:** Pay close attention to how individuals interact with others in the department. Has someone displayed leadership abilities in a committee or project setting, but those skills haven't been made aware of by their senior managers? Look for those who are frequently sought out for advice or who take extra responsibilities without being asked. Hidden leaders often exhibit qualities such as initiative, problem-solving skills, and a positive attitude.
- **Solicit feedback:** Ask colleagues, peers, and other supervisors for their opinions on individuals who may have leadership potential. These individuals may have a reputation for being helpful, resourceful, or knowledgeable. They may also have a track record of successfully completing projects or initiatives.
- **Look for individuals who exhibit key leadership traits and model your company core values:** Hidden leaders often exhibit key traits such as integrity, creativity, accountability, and adaptability. They may also be good communicators, active listeners, and able to inspire and motivate others.
- **Encourage professional development:** Provide opportunities for individuals to expand their skill sets, take on new challenges, and assume leadership roles. Hidden leaders may be more likely to step forward when given

the chance to demonstrate their abilities.

- **Foster a culture of recognition:** Hidden leaders become more visible and come to the forefront when they feel their contributions are valued and recognized. Acknowledge and reward individuals for their accomplishments, and create opportunities for team members to celebrate each other's successes.

By using these strategies, a supervisor can identify hidden leaders within their teams and organization and work to develop their skills, and provide them additional opportunities to grow and thrive within the company. By implementing better communication and trust, you will be able to more effectively identify potentially hidden leaders within your teams. These people may have valuable skills and knowledge which can help grow the entire organization if given the chance. Giving them additional opportunities to develop their skills and shine will not only help them reach their fullest potential but also create a sense of visibility that builds stronger teams and increases morale throughout the company.

VISIBILITY OF LEADERSHIP MATTERS

To be a leader, you must be willing to be seen. There is no leadership without visibility.

Visibility at work is an important factor for leaders to consider in order to create effective and successful working environments. A leader's visibility in the workplace implies that they are engaged with their team, understand their business needs and goals, and actively collaborate with their colleagues. This level of engagement helps to ensure that the organization is heading in the right direction. In addition, visibility also helps to boost employee morale, foster a sense of belonging and promote a culture of collaboration and innovation.

Research shows that when leaders are visible in the workplace, it encourages employees to speak up, express their ideas and actively participate in decision-making. This can show up as improved productivity and better job satisfaction. Visible leaders also set an example of trustworthiness and accountability, which can help to build strong team dynamics and create a healthy organizational culture.

Furthermore, visibility at work goes beyond managing people; it is essential for staying connected with the organization's goals, mission, and values. A visible leader will be able to spot opportunities for improvement and make informed decisions that are aligned with the company's objectives. They will be able to effectively communicate their ideas and vision to their team, creating an atmosphere of shared understanding and collaboration.

In order to get visibility in the workplace, leaders should strive to create open communication channels with their employees. They should aim to have regular meetings where they can discuss organizational needs and issues in detail, and provide feedback on tasks or successes achieved by their team members. By actively listening to the opinions of their staff, a leader can gain insight into how they feel about the work environment or particular projects, helping them better understand what motivates them or what may need improvement. Leaders should also make themselves available for one-on-one conversations or informal chats on a regular basis as this helps employees feel valued and appreciated for their contributions.

Developing visibility in the workplace is an essential part of successful leadership since it enables leaders to get in tune with their team members' needs while keeping up with business objectives. Therefore, leaders should make it a priority to stay connected with their staff while promoting effective communication within the organization.

As a leader, visibility starts with you. You can increase the visibility of your team members which in turn makes employees feel they are truly part of something bigger. It gives them an emotional attachment to the company. An emotional aspect increases the feeling of value, which leads to loyalty. They begin to feel more confident in their abilities, which means they are more productive. Visible leaders tend to make the teams they are part of shine brighter. Other people want to work with them, and the caliber of work improves across the board.

Visibility leads to great opportunity and responsibility, which becomes a cycle on repeat. As you accomplish new things, new projects and skills should be made available to you and your team to keep motivation high and encourage a growth mindset. This creates a positive loop for both the employee and the company.

Visibility is also something you want to consider as you are choosing who should be involved with your culture initiative from the very beginning. An employee with visibility means other employees are watching and they have influence that can help you push your culture program forward. Giving your most visible team members a role in your culture plan addresses their need to feel recognized and makes them valuable contributors.

Visibility in the workplace is essential for effective leadership as it helps build trust between leaders and their team members. When employees know that their leader is showing up, taking part in conversations, and leading by example, they feel more secure in their roles and are motivated to perform better. Leaders who are visible also demonstrate consistency and transparency, setting clear expectations while remaining flexible should unexpected circumstances arise. Furthermore, visible leaders can motivate people in inspiring ways, creating an environment where innovation is encouraged and failure is embraced as part of the learning process. By being visible in the workplace, leaders encourage collaboration between team members while reinforcing a sense of ownership over outcomes that ultimately leads to higher performance standards across the organization.

CHAPTER 11:

U — Uniqueness of Your People

I believe the best leaders take the time to get to know the people on their teams individually. One of the best bosses I had knew I was a huge Alabama Crimson Tide™ football fan. During football season, he always asked if I'd watched the game and how I thought it went. He collected stamps, and when a tribute collection to Coach Bear Bryant was printed, he gave me a sheet of those stamps. None of this had anything to do with my work, tasks, or skills, but it connected us personally. It showed me he valued knowing me as a person and he knew what I was interested in. In turn, I worked harder for him. I respected him. I went above and beyond when he needed someone to do extra because he recognized something about me that was different from everyone else. He celebrated the uniqueness of his people. He made me feel like I belonged.

A basic human need is met when you construct a V.A.L.U.E. Culture in the workplace. Everyone wants to feel like they are unique and that they belong. A sense of belonging is crucial to satisfaction, happiness, and mental well-being, whether on a personal or career front. Since the beginning of time, there have been groups for people to belong to - tribes, families, and neighborhoods. Belonging is necessary in the workplace to bring out the best in each employee. The less secure employees feel about where they fit in or belong, the more insecure they feel about their position and ability to share ideas. When they belong, they feel their uniqueness is accepted. They feel safe. They bring their best selves. After all, belonging is more than just being a part of an organization. A sense of belonging means connecting with people in a way that can benefit both parties. I asked Bob Brown about this very topic. He has over 2,200 people at the *Yamaha*™ facility in Georgia.

Q. Bob, with so many employees, how do you recognize their uniqueness?

It's true that we have over 500 people that have been here for more than 10 years. There's a lot of people that have been here for a long time. And we've increased our headcount by 600 people in the last three years, so there's also a big pool of newer people.

One thing we hadn't anticipated as we added all these new people was how important culture is in helping people feel like they are part of the same team. It can be a little bit intimidating when you come into a company. You realize there are all these people with this long tenure. You want to leverage that experience, knowledge, and history as a company.

Q. Bob, how do you make your culture solidify?

The culture solidified when we realized strengthening the feeling of belonging was tied to our employees living and working in the same community—it made a big impact.

We also needed to be very welcoming to new people and make them feel like they were a part of that culture. People didn't have to be here for twenty years before they felt like they were part of the family.

Q. What did you do to achieve that?

One of the ways we've done that is really recognizing that fifty-five percent of our workforce lives in Coweta County (Georgia). Many of them have students in the school system here. They have friends and relatives that have worked here or might work here.

By recognizing that, we've adopted a personality of being engaged in the community. That's something *Yamaha*™ has always done. But before, we kind of did it quietly behind the scenes.

Over the last few years, we've seen that our team here really likes to see us out in the community doing things, having an impact, and being good corporate citizens. It gives people a lot of pride to be a part of working here. We've made that part of our culture.

It's a strong corporate citizenship type of policy. Being engaged in the community matters to our employees. I get people that will stop by my office and say, "hey, I was at a band competition, and you guys sponsored it." It was so cool to see our brand right there at the competition. I think including community is a part of our culture's success, the uniqueness; it's not something I've experienced elsewhere.

It is important for organizations to create an environment that fosters a strong sense of belonging and pride. Focusing on values like helping the community, going above and beyond, and creative problem-solving can help build a culture of distinction that is attractive to potential new hires. Communicating these core concepts during the onboarding process is key in ensuring that new hires are fully aware of how they fit into the organization's mission and understand how they can contribute to its success. Doing this helps create an atmosphere in which employees feel confident and inspired to perform at their best, setting the organization up for long-term success.

NEW HIRES NEED SENSE OF CULTURE

A strong culture creates a sense of shared values and beliefs among employees. Strong cultures are also crucial to ensure new hires are properly introduced and integrated into the program. If this doesn't happen, new employees may feel disconnected from the rest of the team and struggle to understand and embody the organization's culture, which can lead to a host of issues down the line.

Walking into a new workplace can be a daunting experience for anyone, especially for new hires who may feel like outsiders in an unfamiliar environment. However, the experience is even more challenging for those who don't see anyone who looks like them or shares their background. It can be a very disheartening and isolating experience, leaving one feeling like they don't belong. It's important for new hires to be able to see others like themselves in the workplace as it is a source of comfort and reassurance, giving them the confidence to contribute their unique perspectives and talents to the team. Seeing others like themselves can provide a sense of belonging, a feeling that they are part of a community.

I reached back out to Rich Sheridn and asked him to share his experience with new recruits in a multi-generational environment. Here's what he had to say.

Q. Rich, how do you build cohesion in a multi-generational workforce?

This answer is very simple. I think one of the ways you build a multi-generational workforce that works is having a multi-generational workforce. We've had people retire from here, and of course, we have a lot of young people here as well. I think we have an unnatural advantage because we pair people. I think, in some ways, this gets down to almost basic human relationships stuff.

You can't build a relationship with another human being if you don't spend time together. Because when we're apart, and I think this has been the biggest challenge of the pandemic for all of us, our brain does this weird thing when we're not in the same room together. We start making up stories in our heads.

We start inventing a new truth, a new reality in our heads. If you repeat that conversation with yourself often enough, it goes from I think this is the way it is to this is the way it is. But because we pair people together, we're always knocking those stories down.

You can imagine someone might hang out with me and at first think that *I'm the old guy*. They have a fear or a stereotype of me or my generation; however, after spending time with me, they might think that I'm not quite like they thought I was going to be. This can happen within and across all generations as well.

I want you to take a few minutes to consider Rich's comments. Building inclusion can be accomplished by adding opportunities for people to build relationships. Inclusion is how we positively champion diversity—by allowing individuals to find their similarities and learn about the experiences that made them who they are. Building a V.A.L.U.E. Culture allows you to champion relationship building. Connection is a cornerstone of all great workplace cultures and it needs to start from the moment you hire someone new.

Garry Ridge, with the *WD-40™ Company*, shared why hiring for culture fit is a cornerstone practice successful companies implement to build culture, and to keep a successful culture leaders must hire for values.

Q. Garry, companies that are successfully implementing a culture change based around values, looks like what?

If you ever go to our careers page, you'll see it points you to our values. We hire for values alignment first. We do that by having meaningful conversations with the people to try and understand what they stand for and what they don't stand for.

I can teach anybody with a certain level of competency to do something better in a function. However, it's the values alignment that's so important to us. Now, people are coming to us because they want to be in an organization that has been seen as one where it respects its people and the culture is strong.

You get referrals and redirections. We didn't experience *the great escape* many experienced during the pandemic. We don't have a huge issue finding people to come and work in the organization because we have such a high reputation for having a strong culture.

Q. Garry, that really speaks volumes about how culture is working for you. What does your culture promise people?

Everyone knows our cultural promise is we'll be a group of people that come together to protect and feed each other. That's why we come together. Over the years, we've never laid anybody off in any downturn. We've been able to maintain our position. And in fact, through COVID, we had some of the best results we've ever had. And it's because people weren't going home every night worried about whether I was going to be able to feed my kids or pay for my doctor.

The security Garry's employees felt is evident. Clearly, employees believe in *WD-40™ Company's* promise to come together and protect each other. The feeling of security happens only when an organization clearly articulates a set of deeply rooted beliefs and expectations. By defining core values as part of a culture program, you plant the seed for this critical piece. Communication of values must start at the beginning with hiring and be repeated and demonstrated frequently to become ingrained in the company DNA. Celebrating the uniqueness of each employee you bring on as a team member starts during the interview. I think it's a disservice to them, and your current employees, if you fail to look at how their values align with those of the organization. In my own experience, if you have multiple qualified candidates based on skill level, looking at their culture fit is the best way to determine how successful they will be as an employee and how well they will interact with and blend with your current team. I remembered something Harry, with *AMB Sports™*, said; specifically, he mentioned something about the fact that *selection is key.*

Q. Harry, do you feel that selecting the right people is the key to your success?

We all live and breathe our Core Values. And it starts with who we bring into our business to join our team. We are definitely selective, whether it's an associate who's going to be a game day host, or someone who's going to lead our ticketing team.

Do they have the right attitude in terms of fitting into and adding to our culture? You hear a lot of businesses say they are hiring. We select. We intentionally use the word select. We call it *Draft Day* because we are making picks in terms of who's going to join our family. Our questions and our interview processes are centered around our Core Values. We select good humans with a service mindset and who want to be great in all they do!

Q. Harry, how do you know that the value talk doesn't end during the interview?

We know the value talk doesn't end in the interview because they continue in the training people receive, and they serve as a guide for everyone in terms of their roles and responsibilities.

For example, innovate continuously. *Mercedes-Benz™* Stadium just celebrated its fifth birthday in 2022, but the team is already crafting a vision for the next level of innovations for *Mercedes-Benz™* Stadium.

We've been open for five years. But, from a design perspective, the stadium is a bit older than that. The team is literally in the planning phase for the next level of *Mercedes-Benz™* Stadium innovations to come. And it isn't about just making a change for change's sake. It's about the level of investments to bring new technology and new experiences.

So that's the vision. So, what's the next evolution of an amazing venue like *Mercedes-Benz™* Stadium going to look like? How do we continue to make it the envy of the world? The vision starts there in terms of what are the goals we want to achieve.

We want to create new experiences. We want to drive additional revenues. We want to create new activations, and new premium spaces, both inside the stadium and out. For us, as

Arthur Blank would say, *there's no finish line.*

Q. Harry, what is the point of integrating passion, purpose, and profits?

The whole point of integrating passion, purpose, and profits allows everything to work—it's the key. We're constantly listening and responding to the voices of our fans, guests, and customers. They are driving not only the things that are innovations but also different ways in which we can be even better from one event to the next.

Q. It sounds like you put everyone first. Would you agree?

Yes. Putting people first is what we do. We are in the people business. We just happen to sell tickets to amazing sports and entertainment events as well. One of the values we have is to *include everyone.* When we're thinking about something, we look at it from the perspective of who will it impact and benefit. Is it a small group of our associates, or a small group of our fans, guests, or customer base? Then that's really not the scale we're looking for.

We're looking for something that's scalable and really does *include everyone.* I would say our Core Values fundamentally are that guiding post to all the decisions we make, and the great part about that is that they're so well known, clearly understood, we easily hold one another accountable.

They're so entrenched no matter what meeting you're in; as soon as we're not living up to those in some way, a team member will call it out. That's what the core values do. They just help us hold ourselves accountable to always doing the right things for the right reasons.

Building and maintaining a culture starts before employees complete their first task. The interview process is key, and successful culture-based organizations aren't afraid to hire based on the culture they are designing. Personality and attitude won't change, but skills can be improved and taught. Once the decision to hire has been made, encouraging employees to build their personal brands continues the celebration of their uniqueness. Also, it turns them into brand ambassadors for your business. Let's look at how personal branding for your employees is accomplished.

ENCOURAGE EMPLOYEES TO BUILD PERSONAL CAREER BRANDS

Celebrating your team's uniqueness starts by taking a look at what makes each member special, and what talents they bring to the table. The next few sections revolve around personal branding for employees and how this impacts the successful implementation of a V.A.L.U.E. Culture.

Branding used to only be in the marketing department; now, it's a *key strategy* throughout your organization and not limited to your business or products. Celebrating and encouraging team members to develop their personal career brands is a vital component of the V.A.L.U.E. Culture. When you do, you'll see employees overcome their fear of speaking up in meetings and begin to share ideas. You'll identify those truly engaged employees who act as your public relations team. They'll become influencers who empower their co-workers and learn the value of building relationships across company departments and be an example in your industry.

Just because you see an employee posting about or creating content that enhances their career brand doesn't mean they are out looking for a new job.

An employee's brand is their reputation—how they are viewed in their career field. Their reputation allows them to position themselves as an expert in their field. When an employee positions themselves as an expert, recognized by their peers, you look smart for hiring them and will help attract new talent interested in personal development and growth.

Influencers aren't just on social media. They are also people in your business who have a following and can gain engagement in your industry. When you celebrate your employees' uniqueness, you will identify influencers in your midst.

Your best bet as an employer is to identify who has the potential to be an influencer inside and outside your organization. You want to engage them as part of your V.A.L.U.E. Culture implementation team. These employees are more likely to listen to what you have to say, and if they feel they have input, they will be more apt to share your message.

You need to show them it's up to them to take control of how others see them in the workplace. They need to create the reflection they want others to see, especially those interested in moving up. You can help employees learn to communicate their value and impact so that it allows decision-makers to know the asset they are to the company.

This taking ownership of what you bring to the table enables employees to see how they can positively help the company achieve success and how that ties into their success and enjoyment. Visibility is a keystone to personal branding.

Many companies fear employees will leave when they begin to help them build out their career brands. Actually, the opposite is true. It takes much more to lure them away when they feel encouraged, celebrated, valued, and invested in.

When your employees make themselves more marketable

by sharing their growth on social media, it ultimately positively impacts your company and its bottom line. There's also the internal benefit of you beginning to understand what it is about each employee's job that they love.

Encouraging employees to build personal brands also gives you an accurate database of what skills and talents employees have and enjoy. Imagine if you could build teams where you already know the members have the talent and desire to be on it. Think how much greater the chance of success for these projects will be.

When you invest in your employees' personal brand development and encourage them to share with their network, you are also building trust for your products and services. When statements come from real people and not the company, it's more believable.

People believe their friends and acquaintances. And, since people, now more than ever, turn to social media for their information and recommendation, encouraging your employees to post content that reflects well on both parties becomes a highly trustworthy and effective way to higher your value as a business.

CELEBRATE YOUR TEAM'S UNIQUE TRAITS THROUGH PERSONAL BRANDING

Put simply, personal branding is what people think about you, your values, your skills, and your beliefs when you aren't around to tell them. In a business setting, personal branding with employees strengthens your culture. Also, when your employees build personal brands they become a great recruiting tool because people are learning about the awesomeness of the company from employees who are sharing their work experiences with the world. The key is teaching them how and what to share. It's a great way to showcase the diversity of your workforce.

Let's start with your employees since they are the company's heart. Here are a few quick questions to get you thinking about how your employees currently feel about their place inside the organization and how they might express those feelings to others outside your walls:

- Do your employees know their worth? How do you know?
- Do they see their value? Do they feel they are vital and essential to the team? Is it reflected at evaluation time?
- Do they see their involvement and recognize their importance within the ecosystem of the company?

Perhaps the most important piece of information that any human being can possess is a clear view of who they are and how they fit into the world around them. We characterize this idea in several ways: self-worth, self-value, and self-importance.

When employees feel respect, they also have confidence in their abilities. New situations are not seen as chances for failure. Instead, they are seen as opportunities to succeed. Finding personal confidence is an extraordinarily potent personal outlook.

With the confidence that comes from self-respect, employees can accomplish more. Confidence acts essentially as a solvent for fear and doubt. It dissolves away all the negative emotional shackles that hobble success, making getting the things they want out of their career seem more possible to achieve.

The formula is simple—help your employees build their self-respect and confidence, and they gain the work life and community they desire, and your business will benefit as well. This becomes the building block for their personal brand as you begin encouraging them to share their work experience with others.

EMPLOYEE PERSONAL BRANDING HIGHLIGHTS DIVERSITY IN WORKPLACE

When you identify weak spots inside your organization and think you need to attract new talent, understanding *how* to attract the right new talent is essential. However, knowing how to manage and motivate the talent you currently have is also crucial in today's competitive environment. One of the ways you can do that is by infusing into your existing workforce the same energy and excitement they felt on the day they accepted your initial offer to work there. You can reignite that initial excitement of the unknown while accentuating the desire to learn new things and the willingness to engage with co-workers and learn about them as people. What if each of your employees were sharing experiences that reflect these same feelings on their own personal social platforms? When your employees begin sharing their unique experiences, talents, and skills, others begin to see your organization as a place they would fit in and enjoy working. This sharing helps promote the diversity and inclusion found inside your walls.

Potential employees want to see different genders, races, and nationalities reflected in their employees. Employees who share about the company they work with on their personal feeds help portray diversity in the workforce. The even more important aspect of encouraging your employees to build their own personal brand is that they are sharing based on the core values and behaviors that are the foundation of your V.A.L.U.E. Culture. In turn, your business is seen as more innovative, productive, and creative than others. These characteristics attract more potential employees you can choose from when the need arises. (Not to mention potential customers too).

Today's business world now recognizes the need for diversity in the workplace. The business landscape has been evolving, and companies have learned diversity is a strength rather than a weakness.

A diverse work team has many benefits, including
- Increased productivity
- More creativity and out-of-the-box thinking
- Greater innovation
- Faster problem solving
- Reduced employee turnover
- Marketing your team's uniqueness is more inclusive and sensitive to various demographics
- Enhanced company reputation

Diversifying your business becomes easier when you look for ways to celebrate the uniqueness of your team.

YOUR EMPLOYEE'S UNIQUE BRAND WILL GROW YOUR COMPANY'S EXTERNAL BRAND AND HIGHLIGHT YOUR CULTURE

As employees share their personal brands by posting online, it also increases visibility for you, your company, and your products. Visibility expands because people who may not follow you will see their content and become interested in what is taking place inside your company. Another benefit is that other employees view these postings and see opportunities for growth and development. By sharing content, individuals inside the organization are cementing themselves as subject matter experts, and employees, in turn, see them as people they should learn from or emulate. It builds credibility in your management team as well.

Personal brand building improves customer satisfaction also. Your customers notice what is said about your business and your employees. When they repeatedly see employees participating in development opportunities, it makes customers feel like they have a highly trained, competent member of your team looking after their needs.

When you vertically integrate an employee's personal brand (internal and professional network growth) with your employer brand (culture designed to attract and retain talent), and your company brand (external to customers, investors, and partners), there are unmistakable benefits. Let's look at a few strategies you can use to build into your culture program.

IMPLEMENTING PERSONAL CAREER BRANDING— THE STRATEGY

To ensure your employees understand the benefits of creating and managing their personal brand, show them how building their brand can expand their network, open the door to potential new opportunities, help them keep up with industry trends, and develop new skills.

As you initiate a personal branding program, have your employees begin by assessing where they are right now. Next, have them identify their areas of expertise. Then help them determine the right audience they desire to attract. For some, it may just be family and friends. For others, it may be potential clients and leads. Once the audience and purpose is determined, the next step is choosing the right tool to use.

When personal branding is discussed, most people automatically think about social media. While there are many other aspects to your personal brand—reputation, network, co-worker relationships, resume, interview skills, and professional development—social media is one of the most powerful tools a person can utilize. Why? Think about it. Word of mouth is one of the most potent ways believable messages are spread, and social media is our voice today.

SOCIAL MEDIA TRAINING DESIGNED TO HIGH-LIGHT YOUR UNIQUE EMPLOYEES

Providing social media training is a necessity if you want to empower your employees to become brand ambassadors for your organization. According to a survey from *Social Media Today*, three out of 10 companies aren't actively considering their employee engagement on social media. When employees were asked, nearly 75% said they had never received training on how to engage on social platforms professionally.

Training can look different from company to company. If you nurture a group of sales professionals, providing training on generating leads can be highly beneficial. For others, learning how to use specific platforms that speak to different audiences may be more helpful.

No matter the training, it should be designed to motivate employees to become brand advocates for the company on whichever platform they utilize. It should always come with a warning about how to protect their personal information online and to beware of identity theft scams. Once you've helped them create a safe platform, help them show off what makes them a great addition to your company.

IDENTIFYING THE UNIQUE STRENGTHS OF YOUR TEAM

As you look at developing training programs inside your organization, identifying the strengths and weaknesses of each employee can be a great starting point. There are particular activities or actions potentially preventing an employee or department from excelling. Here's a list of common issues your training program could address:

- *Social skills.* Not everyone is skilled at communicating and getting along with others. Consider a program that includes communication skills training, conflict resolution training, and team-building exercises. Encourage your employees to attend industry events, conferences, and seminars to improve their networking skills. Networking events can provide an opportunity for employees to meet new people, build relationships, and develop their social skills.

- *Social intelligence.* Think about the people you know who thrive, both at work and socially, they have social intelligence. *The ability to manage one's emotions, recognize emotions in others, and make appropriate decisions to override other weaknesses.* Support them by recognizing they have valuable social skills and abilities that benefit not only themselves but also the people around them. By acknowledging their social intelligence, you can help build their confidence and encourage them to continue using their skills to create positive outcomes in both their personal and professional lives.

- *Public speaking skills.* Public speaking skills develop quickly but require practice. Give each member of your team regular opportunities to present their work to the group. Giving employees a chance to gain confidence in presenting can pay off in the future for both you and the employee.

- *Writing effectively.* Being an effective writer is crucial for success in many fields, as it is often a primary means of communication in the business world. Therefore, it is important to encourage individuals to develop their writing skills and provide them with the necessary resources and support to do so. However, it is important to acknowledge that not everyone can write at the same level, especially for those whose first language is not English. In such cases, it is essential to provide additional language support, such as grammar and vocabulary training, or even a proofreading service, to help individuals overcome language barriers and communicate their ideas effectively. Ultimately, by supporting individuals in their writing efforts, we can help them achieve their goals and contribute to a more successful and inclusive society.

- **Knowledge.** Having a well-informed and knowledgeable workforce can help a company stay competitive and adapt to changes in the industry. Employees who understand the latest trends, best practices, and technologies can help their company remain relevant and innovative. Additionally, having knowledgeable employees can improve customer satisfaction, as they are better equipped to answer questions and provide solutions. By investing in the professional development of their employees, business leaders can also increase employee engagement and retention, as employees are more likely to feel valued and motivated when they are given opportunities to learn and grow. Business leaders can improve the industry knowledge of their employees by providing training and development opportunities, encouraging participation in industry events and conferences, and facilitating ongoing learning through mentorship and coaching.

- **Education.** Is a lack of education negatively affecting someone on your team? Take a look at your employees' educational backgrounds and offer advice, support, or an opportunity for them to pursue further education or training. Offering tuition assistance can be an effective way to help employees improve their skills and knowledge, which can lead to better job performance and career growth. By investing in their education, employees are more likely to stay motivated and engaged, as they can see a clear path for advancement within the company. Moreover, providing support and guidance to employees can help them identify areas for improvement and choose the right educational programs that align with their career goals. Whether it's covering the cost of tuition or providing flexible scheduling options, offering educational support is a valuable investment that can benefit both employees and the company as a whole.

- *Visibility.* Many great employees are stuck in a cubical all day, and no one realizes how amazing they are. Or they are afraid to speak up and showcase their talents and ideas. This is where visibility comes in. Being visible in the workplace means actively participating in meetings, sharing ideas, and networking with colleagues. It means taking on new challenges, volunteering for projects, and collaborating with others. *Find ways to make your employees more well-known to others in the company so that they feel included and confident in their abilities, value and recognized for their contributions.* Additionally, being visible can help employees build relationships with colleagues and create a positive work environment. Business leaders can encourage visibility by providing opportunities for employees to showcase their work, such as through presentations or internal newsletters. They can also foster a culture that values visibility and encourages employees to speak up and share their ideas.

- ***Capitalize on an employee's strength.*** To capitalize on the strengths of employees in a group, a supervisor can take several steps. First, identify the individual strengths of each employee through performance evaluations, self-assessments, or feedback from colleagues. Once identified, you can assign tasks and projects that align with those strengths, allowing employees to showcase their talents and contribute to the team's success. Additionally, you can provide training and development opportunities that build upon employees' strengths and help them develop new skills. This can lead to increased job satisfaction and engagement, as employees feel valued and recognized for their contributions. Moreover, the supervisor can encourage collaboration among employees, allowing them to leverage each other's strengths and work together to achieve common goals. By creating a culture that values and capitalizes on employee strengths, the supervisor can foster a more productive and successful team.

Once you identify areas needing work, use that to provide a great starting point for building an employee advocacy program focused on personal branding. Look for ways you can help employees create the backbone of their brand. Perhaps you can offer a day where a professional photographer takes headshots, or maybe you can have a workshop on creating a personal website. Consider providing conversation starters related to your industry or images you have created that highlight employees' work or your products. By giving them pieces designed to enhance their professional outlook, you will be viewed as a partner in your employees' success.

Knowing and owning their professional brand is a big step toward developing an engaged workforce. When everyone becomes aware that they have a brand, the next step is to ensure they understand the importance of cultivating it. Their brand really is your professional reputation.

Don't limit training to just social or digital media. Think about ways you can involve coaching, mentoring, and even on-the-job learning or shadowing efforts. Each of these can help employees define their professional goals and act as a way to transfer knowledge.

EMPLOYEE BRANDING + V.A.L.U.E. CULTURE = DIFFERENTIATORS

Just like culture is a differentiator and a selling point for someone looking for a new career opportunity, an employee's personal brand becomes a differentiator, both inside and outside of an organization. Let's say your company has not implemented training to help employees develop their brands. How can you begin moving the needle in your favor?

Remember, an employee's brand isn't just a business card or a social media profile. It's much bigger than that. Their brand is how they present themselves, both on and offline, to your clients or potential clients, co-workers, supervisors, and others in your industry. It's what they stand for—their values. I like to say it's the secret sauce that sets you apart from everyone else.

The question becomes: is what your employees are showing online a reflection of the company culture and purpose you want the world to see? Are their posts showcasing your company values, highlighting skills, emphasizing experiences, telling your company stories, reflecting the personality of our organization, and building the vision of the company. Every post, comment, or online interaction made by your employees can be a recruiting ad if you help train them to show off the right traits, values, and experiences.

Decide to actively coach your employees on how they are a reflection of your company brand. When you work with your employees to build your brand intentionally, you control what shows up and how your industry thinks of you. Your employee's brand should be designed to attract people you want to employ or clients you want to secure. The whole intent of developing strong employee brands is to draw people to you. It's a way to communicate your company's worth as an organization and the worth of the people who work for you.

The other thing you are building is credibility.

HIGHLIGHTING YOUR UNIQUE EMPLOYEES CREATES CREDIBILITY

By highlighting the uniqueness of your employees you are making deposits into a credibility bank. How does employee branding do this? You are building trust between yourself and your employees, as well as between the company and your clients. Credibility is currency, especially in today's world when trust is at an all-time low. Trust not only boosts the personal reputation of your employees, but it also boosts that of the company. If you're a leader of a team, it can help motivate and improve team performance.

For employees who rely on commission or have sales-based positions, growing their personal brand means their "calls" get answered—whether that's a real call, a DM, or an email—because they've built a reputation of credibility. The more your employees and leaders share their authentic selves—what makes them different and the best at what they do, the more people can relate to them and are willing to give them their time. Building credibility means more sales, repeat business, and ultimately higher compensation.

Credibility also makes it easier to get referrals. There's no more powerful proof that your employees' personal brands are working than when current clients or others in your industry pass along referrals. Referrals say clients trust you to solve a problem they care about.

However, building a personal brand doesn't stop with your employees. As a leader or CEO, you must also manage your personal brand. You need to craft a brand that shows your leadership style and helps people connect you to the core values you are building your culture around. Building your own brand solidifies what people can expect from you and allows them to see your vision in action. Your personal leadership brand also highlights the principles you stand for—coaching, philanthropy, customer service excellence, or integrity in business. Your employees, and clients will look at your social profiles to provide credibility by checking to see if your work persona matches the personal one you show the world. It's not enough just to have a company page. When you build your brand with a mix of industry knowledge and personality, it makes you more likable. People begin to feel like they know you on a personal level.

Establishing a credible reputation matters. How you show up defines how people interpret your leadership style. The values your reputation showcases are what you want your team members to emulate. These highlights make you more relatable and respected by your clients and team members. Your dedication to learning tells your employees you value continual growth. Your clients will see you're always striving to stay updated. When you highlight your own accomplishments it shows you value personal development. Exemplify the behavior and content you want your employees to mirror. As you achieve milestones and sharpen your skills, share these steps and wisdom as they relate to your career.

Think about the company you work for; what are the values, ethics, and culture you want to promote? How can you connect those within your personal brand? Your customers, and potential new hires, will connect with you not because of what you do but because of who you are. Connecting with you on a personal level will also strengthen their buy-in with the culture you are creating.

When you connect value, vision, and purpose with your personal brand—big things can happen. Creating your personal brand, and helping your employees build theirs, begins with understanding why you chose the path you are on. Your skills and passion are there for a reason.

As you work on building your personal brand, focus on sharing your knowledge and helping others who are a few steps behind you on the journey to build their brand. This combined effort will be beneficial for you, your team members, the company, and the clients that buy from you.

You can even make building personal brands a teambuilding activity in your V.A.L.U.E. Culture implementation.

EMPLOYEES BUILD UNIQUE BRANDING STATEMENT

One great exercise you can work on with your staff or employees is crafting a powerful branding statement. A branding statement is simply your personal brand, summed up into a single powerful statement describing exactly what you do for your audience, clients, employer, or team.

If you made notes on your strengths, values, and accomplishments from the earlier part of this section, you can take those answers and put them together to form a statement that sums up either who you are personally, or how you want your brand to be professionally perceived. If you didn't take notes, take a moment and think about those traits now. Then use the following template to craft your first personal branding statement.

I help (target person/company/division) to (achieve X) so that they can (outcome).

Or, if you're a business owner, think of it as **We at (your business) help you (what need do you meet for your client) by/with only/without (unique benefit).**

Your personal brand doesn't mean anything or do any good if you keep it to yourself. Test it out. Take a few moments and share with others what you came up with. Using my branding statement exercise can be a great way to kick off an internal discussion with your staff on your vision for the culture your organization should display.

When you are all comfortable with your branding message, share it with all of your employees. You must become articulate and confident in sharing who you are and what you do. When you combine those things you leave the person you're sharing with the feeling you're truly aligned with your values and your actions, which differentiates you from others.

How does it feel when you say your branding statement? Does it sound authentic? Would your best friend say the words you use sound like you? Is it strong enough to convince someone to give you a chance or to leave a competitor?

Like goal setting, branding statements become real when you write something down and look at it, read it, and say it over and over. Creating your branding statement moves you closer to living out your personal and company's purpose.

Developing a personal brand takes employees on a journey of examination. There is choice and decision-making involved. Building confidence and connecting on a personal level creates real awareness, and then employees bring their best unique selves to the table, and the organization and themselves as individuals truly benefit.

CHAPTER 12:

E—Engagement

If you're like the average professional, you spend about one-third of your life at the office. That's almost 90,000 hours. *Feeling committed and connected is important for your health and happiness.* Lack of engagement is more than just not enjoying something you've been assigned to, it is when employees struggle to find meaning, intrinsic motivation, and a sense of purpose in their work.

I had a time in my career when I literally had to give myself a pep talk each morning on the way to work to convince myself I needed to show up. I had a position that required wearing multiple hats, so I couldn't focus on areas where my skills excelled. Doing multiple things meant doing some things well enough to get by but not in a manner I felt utilized my full potential. Not living up to my own internal expectations created an inner conflict and a feeling of disengagement on my part. Over time I became less engaged with the job, feeling like my efforts were unappreciated and my skills were underutilized. This led to a lack of motivation and an overall sense of dissatisfaction.

Feeling disengaged isn't uncommon for today's workers. Many employees seem to be missing out on the engagement piece. Global polls by *Gallup*™ show that only *twenty percent* of employees are engaged at work, and *low engagement is associated with high stress and poor morale issues.*[1]

While a lack of enthusiasm and lackluster participation can indicate you have an issue with engagement, I wanted to share with you the importance of using real data to gauge where your employees currently fall on the engagement scale. Adam Schwartz, consultant and founder of *The Cooperative Way*™, believes using real data is critical and that data provides concrete evidence to help you determine how to increase engagement.

Q. Adam, the last word in a V.A.L.U.E. Culture is engagement. I know how passionate you are about this concept because it can be measured with data. What are some other ways to monitor engagement?

Great question. It's monitoring participation. It's a good check to see how engaged your employees are. For example, are they showing up at your *Employee Appreciation Day*? Are you doing some fun, exciting work at work to keep people engaged and interested?

Engagement can look different to different people, and it can be challenging to measure. When I work with my corporate clients, one of the first things we determine is which engagement indicators are critical for their culture's success. It could be productivity, communication, attendance, initiative, collaboration, attitude, or loyalty. These signs give you a great sense of whether your team is engaged or not. As we dive into why engagement is an important component of building a V.A.L.U.E. Culture and how you can use your unique culture to create an engaged workforce, I feel it's vital we start with the definition of engagement.

WHAT IS ENGAGEMENT?

Let's look at the standard definition. Engaged means:
- To attract or involve.
- To get someone's interest or attention.
- To cause someone to become involved.

Engagement is the ultimate goal of building a V.A.L.U.E. rich Culture. A workplace where employees, supervisors, management, teams, committees, and more are actively taking part in moving toward a successful future.

Employee engagement is how employees feel about their job and the culture inside the organization. Engagement is the emotional piece of the equation. Emotions are a fundamental part of our human experience.

Engaged employees are connected to the organization's larger mission because they can see the benefit and find value in the company's product or service. They also connect when the principles and activities align with their own personal value system.

In one corporate training session I ran, I asked participants, "if you could do anything and a paycheck wasn't a concern, what would you do?" Over two-thirds of the room indicated a form of service. Whether that was helping elderly members of the community, working in shelters, feeding the hungry, or even working with abused or neglected animals.

The company I was holding the training for believed service to the community was important and worked to provide opportunities for employees to give back. However, a big movement in the culture occurred when these same training group members began associating their need to serve or help others with actions in their daily job.

From a customer service representative who can solve a problem over the phone to a service manager who can show empathy and concern over faulty equipment, engagement increases exponentially when personal values can be tied to corporate outcomes. It's also where the personal connection to your desired culture begins to take root.

ENGAGEMENT BEGINS WITH CONNECTION

Connecting employees to a company's purpose is one of the most powerful ways to grow engagement and foster a sense of purpose and motivation. When employees understand and align with the mission, they are more likely to feel invested in the organization's success and passionate about their work. A strong mission can also help employees see how their individual contributions fit into the bigger picture, which can help make them motivated to exceed their goals. Engagement shows in the excitement that comes when new learning opportunities are presented and when positivity becomes the norm throughout the organization. By emphasizing the company's purpose and the positive impact it has on the customers and the outside world, employees can feel that their work is meaningful and that they are making a difference.

Another key ingredient in building a successful company culture is fostering strong relationships and engagement between employees. When people feel connected with their colleagues, they are more likely to collaborate, communicate and support one another, leading to higher levels of satisfaction and productivity. Building these connections requires intentional effort, such as creating opportunities for employees to socialize and bond outside of work, promoting a culture of transparency and open communication, and encouraging teamwork and collaboration. When employees feel comfortable sharing their ideas, asking for help, and working together to solve problems, the result is a more cohesive and effective team.

Rich Sheridan, with *Menlo Innovation*™, shared his observation concerning building relationships and how vital they are to cultural success in the workplace. Engaged relationships are defined by how each person inside the company treats the other. I asked him a few questions to learn how engagement and relationship building are connected.

> *Q. Rich, you said that engagement is about being connected with each other. Please share more about this.*

My co-founder says *culture is a summation of all the relationships inside your organization.* Put them all together, and that's your culture. I love this definition.

How I describe our culture is how we choose to treat one another. Are we going to be mean-spirited? Are we going to be demanding and fear-based and let that become our culture? Or are we going to be encouraging and supportive with a growth mindset? Are we going to focus on our team members' personal and professional growth while we're getting work done?

I think *mission* and *vision* are important, and you accomplish those things with the culture you've created. Quite frankly, if somehow, tomorrow, software development became illegal, or everybody figured out how to do it on their own, and they didn't need us anymore, we'd still have our culture.

We would look and say so what else can we do? We could build play structures for children. We'd figured out how to do it because we have our culture. There's likely a lot of companies that can't achieve their mission statement or goals because they don't have the culture. But when you have the culture you want, particularly a positive one, you can do anything you want. Companies that have high engagement continue to grow and reinvent themselves because their employees become problem solvers.

One way to grow engagement is through actively listening. That means not being distracted when conversing with co-workers or teams.

Relationships and engagement are built and nurtured through communication and listening. Let's investigate the concept of active listening further. Nothing makes a person (in this case, your employees) feel more valued than someone giving them their complete attention when they are having a conversation or sharing ideas. Nothing makes employees feel more unworthy than attempting to share an idea or concern with their supervisor only to feel distracted by texts, emails, or the pinging of DM's on a screen. Listening is a key skill to develop if you wish to grow engagement inside the workplace.

LISTENING GROWS ENGAGEMENT

Listening is an important part of the communication process, it fosters a positive work environment and encourages employee engagement. When employees feel heard and their input is taken into account, they are more likely to be motivated and invested in their job. Listening is fifty percent of the communication effort, which means it is just as important as speaking in order to effectively convey ideas and feelings. Without actively listening to the other person, a conversation can quickly become one-sided and unproductive. Furthermore, good listening skills not only help people understand each other better but can also help build trust among coworkers and create a more collaborative work environment therefore it's worth your time, as a leader, to develop the art of listening.

You can amp up your leadership skills exponentially if you

implement these strategies to strengthen your listening skills:

WHEN SOMEONE IS TALKING TO YOU, BE *FULLY* IMMERSED IN THE CONVERSATION.

Most of us can't do two tasks at once (or at least do them well); stop what you're doing when another person speaks to you and give them your full attention.

- Look them in the eyes and focus on them directly.
- Pause what you are doing and give them your full attention.
- Step closer to them and create a feeling of a personal conversation, but be careful not to invade their personal space.
- If you're unable to pause what you're doing, let the person know. Ask the communicator to stop speaking and briefly explain why you're unable to give them your full attention.
  - Say something like, "Can you please just wait a moment? As soon as I'm finished with this task, I can listen to you more fully and give my complete attention."
- *Avoid attempting to communicate with others while watching videos or scrolling through emails on your computer screen because these distractions will hamper your efforts to listen carefully.*

LOOK INTERESTED

Your nonverbal communication skills are important while you're listening. If you're looking disinterested and uncaring, the person trying to communicate with you will likely pick up on these subtle hints. They may be flustered or less likely to share their thoughts effectively if the look on your face is annoyed or disinterested. Make a conscious effort to have a look on your face that encourages them to share.

Body language is also integral to listening. As soon as you're ready to listen, turn your body toward the communicator.

- **Leaning toward the person speaking** also demonstrates that you're paying attention to the speaker's every word.
- **Refrain from multitasking** that requires you to turn your body away from the speaker.
- **Smile.** Positivity is key when it comes to mastering body language. Most of us don't notice how often we have a sour expression on our faces. However, grimacing and frowning significantly reduce your chances of connecting with someone else on an emotional level.
  - Frowning also sends signals to your brain that you're doing something difficult, which increases your stress levels and prompts even more nervousness and discomfort.
  - When you smile, you push yourself to relax a little more, and you encourage the people you connect with to relax too.
- **Mirror others.** Although you shouldn't go into a conversation with a plan to copy everything that someone else does, mirroring can be a great technique for improving your chances of a good first impression.
  - When someone nods or scratches their nose, doing the same (though not too frequently) can help you to develop a deeper sense of connection with that person.
  - Try to be subtle when you're mirroring someone else, as doing too much can look a bit off.

- If you're not comfortable with replicating what someone else does all the time, fill in the gaps between mirroring moments with an open and easy posture. Have your arms by your sides, not crossed, and your palms open.

MAKE AND MAINTAIN EYE CONTACT WITH THE SPEAKER.

In most western cultures, eye contact sends the message, "I hear you. I'm listening." Furthermore, holding eye contact with the speaker says, "You have all of my attention at this moment." *Be aware that the meaning and impact of eye contact vary from culture to culture.* If you're involved with cultures other than your native culture, it's recommended to learn about that culture's view of eye contact.

FOCUS YOUR THOUGHTS ON THE PERSON'S WORDS.

Refrain from thinking about how you want to respond while the person is speaking. *Fight the urge to speak overtop of them or before they are finished.* Sometimes when you're engaged in a conversation, you start to concentrate on what you're going to say next and not fully absorb the context of the speaker's words.

You may even be tempted to respond before the other person is finished. Make the extra effort to hold your comment to yourself until they're through talking.

- Use "I" phrases, not You" statements. For example, "I felt unappreciated when..." instead of "You never appreciate anything I do."
- Your goal in listening is to grasp what the speaker is

trying to convey to you so that you hear *them*.

- *While they're speaking, don't worry about what you're going to say or how you are going to say it. Instead, focus on the words and body language of the other person.*

SHARE WITH THE PERSON WHAT YOU UNDERSTOOD THEM TO SAY.

When the speaker ceases talking, take the opportunity to check out what you heard. *Repeat the highlights.* One way to tell your conversation partner that they're effectively communicating is to simply restate their points. You can repeat key phrases in an affirming tone. You can even give them a quick summary of what they just said in your own words to show you were fully listening.

1. **State back to the communicator what you believe you heard to make sure you are clear.**
2. **Ask questions that clarify what you heard to let them know you understand.**

As the listener, stating what you heard allows the speaker to correct or clarify their remarks. The speaker can then reply, "Yes, that's right. or "No, allow me to be more clear."

Asking clarifying questions empowers both listener and speaker to gain a better understanding of the conversation, while also demonstrating respect for the other person's point of view. Research has shown that people who take time to ask follow-up questions are considered more thoughtful and engaged than those who do not. By actively engaging with the speaker through open-ended questioning, listeners can uncover more information about the topic at hand and gain valuable insights into the opinions of their colleagues.

BE PATIENT.

It's important to maintain patience, especially when working with people who may be shy or unable to communicate very well. If you're not patient, you may end the conversation prematurely or scare off your conversation partner. Patience means taking a few extra moments, pausing when needed, and showing through body language that you are actively listening to the speaker. It also involves being aware of what is not being said, as well as reflecting on the conversation before responding. Furthermore, patience allows for more thoughtful responses and prevents misunderstandings from occurring due to rushed conversations. Ultimately, having patience in conversations helps build trust between individuals by demonstrating respect for their views and opinions.

Through active listening strategies, such as being fully immersed in the conversation, making eye contact, carefully considering each word spoken, confirming the message is accurate and asking for clarification when needed, leaders can create meaningful connections with those they are speaking with.

AN EXAMPLE OF ACTIVE LISTENING

While this is an exercise in listening, it's also a great way to practice a coaching style of leadership as well.

Let's say you just finished a big project, and you want to have a debrief with everyone involved. To prepare for the meetings, schedule a time when all parties will be free of distractions, alert, and fully attentive. Make a note with bullet points you want to address. Enter the conversation with the attitude that you are looking for a win-win solution.

Ask all participants to agree to use 'I' messages and active listening. At the meeting, decide who will speak first and who will be listening first. Agree that the listener will not interrupt or respond to comments—only paraphrase what she or he hears (for now). The listener may ask for clarification if needed. (Did you say...?).

The speaker will say 2-3 sentences, then stop and allow the listener to paraphrase. If the listener misunderstands or further clarification is necessary, the speaker will provide the needed information. After the speaker talks for five minutes (or until she or he has finished his or her part of the discussion), switch roles. Repeat the same steps and continue to switch roles every five minutes until everyone feels they have been heard and understood.

When all parties feel understood, you are ready to address the issue at hand. Active listening is the first step in the problem-solving process.

Effective listening takes place when you understand what you're being told or asked.

I wanted to give you a real-world look at how active listening in the workplace can work, so I went back to Harry Hynekamp and asked him about how the team at *Mercedes-Benz™* Stadium incorporates listening as a piece of their culture-building initiative.

Q. Harry, it seems that the team at Mercedes-Benz™ Stadium takes listening to the next level. Please share.

I'll give you the Green Team as an example. It is a collection of associates that are interested in and passionate about the environment and sustainability. It's a passion of theirs and ours. Any associate can join those meetings, share, and contribute. It's why we have three beehives at the stadium today. It's a reason why we have a recycling center for all those difficult to recycle at home items. We listen and respond to the Green Team and how we can continue to add to all our zero waste efforts across *Mercedes-Benz*™ Stadium and our businesses.

Whether it's feedback from our customer surveys, associate surveys or skip level meetings held by the leadership, we're always listening and responding. And you have to do both to build trust and a thriving caring culture. Right now, we're doing something fun called a "Lunch Lottery" that further helps us listen to one another.

Q. That sounds so fun! I know as an employee I would be engaged in the activity. Tell me how it works.

Associates receive a scratch-off Lunch Lottery card. You scratch off two spots, revealing two other associate names and then schedule and have lunch with the people named on the card. By having lunch with the people on the card, everyone gets connected with two team members from entirely different parts of our business.

For example, I got a Lunch Lottery card and it's my responsibility to contact two associates and have lunch. I get to meet and learn about two team members from entirely different parts of our business. We go to the press box. I show the press box my Lunch Lottery card, our lunches are paid for by the organization, and we get to listen and learn more about and from each other.

We also do Hours of Power get-togethers where everyone is invited, there is a specific theme, it might be about what the security team is doing or the HR team is doing. The team gives a twenty-minute update, and then the rest is all about networking, connecting and having some fun together.

We do Associate Huddles; our GM for the Falcons™ has come in and kicked off a huddle talking about the team. We talk about Core Values. There are so many opportunities to create connectivity with folks, listening and responding. If you're interested in something, raising your hand and getting involved is pretty easy.

Strive to strengthen your listening skills. As my mom always reminded me, I have two ears for a reason, use them both. You'll be a better communicator, and your relationships with others will thrive!

Once you have worked on your listening skills and decided where to include listening opportunities in your culture building, it's important to take what you hear and use it to help develop your team members or address issues or concerns. To be effective, leaders need to become internal coaches within the organization and use good listening skills as a framework for more.

COACHING IS KEY TO BUILDING ENGAGEMENT

Let's look at engagement between supervisory levels and employees. It shouldn't just happen at evaluation time. Just like you cultivate a garden, relationships need to be nurtured throughout the year.

A way to improve your culture and your team's performance is to turn your supervisors into coaches. A coaching approach allows you to combine the best aspects of business, psychology, and emotional connections to help individuals achieve their goals and improve their performance.

There are three main reasons why a coaching leadership style works:

1. **Collaboration:** Through teamwork in the form of a partnership, the employee and supervisor can accomplish more than any one person can alone.
2. **Foundation:** With the right foundation, employees can take on greater projects more often, using suggestions and a direct plan of action from the coach/supervisor.
3. **Knowledge:** Through the expert knowledge of their supervisor, employees can learn to set goals, make better decisions, restructure their career life, and move towards becoming proficient.

An internal coaching environment will help employees with the following:
- Goal setting
- Handling problems efficiently
- Designing strategies
- Making good decisions
- Prioritizing actions
- Increasing sales
- Planning
- Budgeting
- Finding a balance
- Increasing work performance.

The coaching model builds stronger and more effective relationships because the employee genuinely feels someone is invested in them. Not just for the company's benefit but for their personal benefit as well.

Here are some ways you can set your supervisors up with the skills to be excellent coaches. Start with these nine simple suggestions they can use when meeting with their team.
- **Acknowledge:** Acknowledge what the team member

is saying and respond positively, demonstrating your empathy towards their experiences.

- **Paraphrase:** Reiterate what you hear the team member say. This takes putting the active listening and communication skills shared earlier in this chapter to work.
- **Ask the "duh" questions:** Engage your employees in having a simple discussion about the obvious elements of their situation. You may have an idea about what's wrong, but it's always more effective if you can help lead an employee to figure out the issue and solution on their own. A clearer understanding of some of the unstated issues will benefit all parties.
- **Look at the big picture:** It is necessary to step back from the situation in order to see the larger picture. Everything happens within a particular context.
- **Identify the ideal:** By discussing the ultimate goals, we outline what success looks like—what the situation entails, the emotions that stem from the success, and the ultimate outcomes.
- **Clarify:** It is important to keep the conversation going and always spell out what you hear the team member saying. Everyone needs to be on the same page throughout the conversation to reach the desired result..
- **Define the process and your role:** Keep in mind that this process is for the team member; make sure you clarify your role as a coach is to help them grow and improve. It's not about having all the answers or micromanaging. Sometimes as a coach, a supervisor may know the best solution, but it's better to ask more questions and let the team member work through and arrive at their own conclusion and solution when possible.
- **Explore strategies:** Suggest multiple ways of handling a

situation. Make sure to engage the team members in the discussion and encourage them to be open to thinking outside of the box. Unconventional is often innovative and can solve problems and invigorate new outcomes

- **Listen and Reflect:** Be consistent in reiterating what you hear your employees say. Engaged listening is all about being attuned to what your team not only says but what they feel. Things are not always black and white, emotions play a big part. Reflecting on the emotions of the team member and actively listening to their point of view helps create a sense of trust and understanding between all parties. This can lead to higher levels of employee engagement, as employees feel supported and valued in their work environment. Additionally, this allows for more meaningful conversations and deeper understanding, leading to better decision-making and problem-solving abilities within the organization.

Building a successful culture means not only management, but all individuals in a leadership role need to actively participate in good listening skills. When your supervisors and managers utilize these skills with their team members it creates an environment of mutual respect and understanding. This can lead to a more efficient and productive workplace, as employees feel heard, appreciated, and valued. Moreover, research has shown that employees who are trusted are more likely to take initiative and be creative problem-solvers. Additionally, good listening skills foster an atmosphere of collaboration which helps to foster innovation and creativity within the organization. Therefore, when leaders take the time to actively listen to their teams and engage in meaningful dialogue, it allows for better communication and a higher level of trust amongst everyone involved. When listening and coaching are working effectively, the next driver of engagement comes naturally. It's all about developing talent.

TALENT DEVELOPMENT BUILDS ENGAGEMENT

Investing in talent development is another way to build engagement and grow your V.A.L.U.E. Culture from within the organization. Advancing current employees makes smart business sense because filling positions with internal candidates is less costly than hiring externally. It also builds morale and gives existing employees advancement opportunities to work towards; creating more engagement.

You reduce turnover by keeping top talent. You reduce risk from hiring an unknown. And, talent development enables you to build the teams you need for current and future business priorities who have already invested in the company's vision.

Implementing a talent development program can be this simple:

- **Align and communicate.** Ensure employees understand the business strategy. Then, you can align individual goals with your corporate priorities, so they know where to focus their efforts.
- **Offer e-learning.** Provide opportunities to acquire new skills and knowledge. Technology makes education and training more affordable and accessible. Many experts recommend a blended approach of classroom lessons and workplace experiences.
- **Coach and mentor.** Create a formal mentorship program and reward employees who guide and support others. Set clear objectives and measure results.
- **Embrace diversity.** An inclusive workplace can make

your business more competitive and innovative. Learn more about your employees' backgrounds and encourage relationships based on appreciation and respect.

- **Recognize potential. In addition to high performers who regularly exceed expectations, identify those employees who may have the ability to shine**, especially if they move into a different role that leverages their strengths. Remember that performance and potential often overlap.
- **Encourage collaboration.** Major accomplishments in most workplaces result from group efforts, so it makes sense to reward teams and individuals. Set team goals, use online collaboration tools, and build a sense of shared purpose.
- **Pay for performance.** At the same time, basing compensation on merit motivates employees to enhance their performance and helps to create a transparent and fair pay structure. Experiment with annual bonuses and other forms of incentive pay.
- **Broaden your perspective.** Overall, identifying and nurturing internal talent requires expanding your vision. Evaluate employees based on how they can serve the company in the future and how well they're performing in their current positions. Focus on organization-wide goals.

Engagement increases when employees are allowed to develop their skills and progress in their careers. Don't overlook your high performers when it comes to engagement—they are often the most motivated, passionate employees and can be invaluable resources when it comes to creating a culture of collaboration and innovation. Investing in the development of your high-performing team members helps encourage them to share their insights and ideas, which in turn helps keep them engaged and encourages further growth. Additionally, giving these top performers more responsibility within the organization can help foster a sense of ownership for their work as well as create an atmosphere of trust. With increased engagement from this subset of employees, businesses can benefit from higher morale, better communication, and improved performance overall.

Some research suggests nearly half of your high-potential employees are currently looking for their next job.(2) While you don't want to create a prima donna, you do want to let them know they are special and you recognize what their skills and abilities add to the company. Surprisingly, some high performers want more attention, not less. If you are practicing your listening skills and adding in coaching, you'll be able to determine how to handle each employee individually.

Overall, it's a good idea to let it be known that high performers are recognized. The more people are aware that you acknowledge their performance and dedication, the less likely they are to leave. Recognition isn't necessarily all about a current achievement. Employees also want to be recognized for their potential. Look for ways to challenge them so they can acquire new skills or responsibilities. If you aren't stretching them, they'll easily get bored.

Building high-performers and retaining them should be a driver of your cultural shift. They love to be seen and known to others inside the organization. Use this to your advantage as you implement your V.A.L.U.E. Culture leadership group.

ADD IN RECOGNITION FOR MORE ENGAGEMENT

Recognition is one way to build engagement. However,

recognition doesn't always have to come in the form of a pay raise. As a leader in your company, it's up to you to find ways to add recognition to your employee development programs.

Praise and rewards can do wonders to bolster an employee's self-confidence and morale. No one can deny the effect praise and recognition can have on your team. *Yamaha*™ uses their Kaizen™ program to make recognition happen company-wide. To get more understanding on the topic, I went back to Bob Brown of *Yamaha*™.

Q. Bob, tell me more about the Kaizen™ program. How did you make this happen company-wide?

Well, in a Japanese manufacturing company, the idea of continuous improvement is very strong. It's something we call Kaizen™. One of the ways that we've implemented that here is by having a Kaizen™ program every single person can participate in.

It doesn't have to be something that makes *Yamaha*™ $10 million. It's any small improvement that they made. We document it. The supervisor signs off. Then we record it. We compile all of these. I forget how many we did last year as a total organization, but the person who submitted the most had like two hundred.

It was a lot of little things, but those all add up. We really celebrate this. We recognize some of the best ones each month. We have annual recognition for people who submitted the best or the most. We also reward the employee. People get credit in the company store and Kaizen™ bucks they can redeem for branded stuff.

Q. How does it encourage teamwork?

The program encourages teamwork and allows employees a chance to work together and build relationships. A part of our Kaizen™, it's what we call our small group competitions. We do this twice a year. Typically, between six or twelve people, sometimes multi-departmental, and sometimes just within a department, following the eight-step process for improvement.

They identify something they want to improve and go through the eight-step process to realize that improvement. Then twice a year, the small group presents to the executive team, our leadership team. Maybe they're not used to presenting at that level, but there are no free passes. Everyone must be there to be a part of it. The projects are always amazing. The teams work together to come up with some incredible improvements. We try to celebrate to encourage people to engage in that way. Sometimes somebody might have an idea that is too big for them to even think about how I would implement that. But that's usually where the best small-team ideas come from.

Somebody sees something that's a problem or something that could be better and then creates this whole group around that opportunity to improve. They are given all the tools and resources, the budget, and whatever is needed to achieve that improvement opportunity. We tried to ensure we resource them with everything they would require to do it, no matter how big it is.

The individual Kaizen™ program does many small day-to-day incremental type improvements. But the small group program really empowers people who see something on the shop floor and gives them all the tools and resources they need to achieve it. It's not our VP of Operations going out there and saying, hey, go fix this. It's bubbled up from the bottom, which makes it cool.

As I listened to the concept of what Kaizen™ is and how it can impact a whole organization, I thought about other types of engagement and I asked Harry Hynekamp how recognition is displayed with the *Mercedes-Benz*™ Stadium team.

Q. Harry, it seems like you can't say enough about engagement in your organization. Share a bit more about that.

I use the recognition examples because they demonstrate what great and excellence looks like to us. These are simple things that anyone can demonstrate and do to deliver excellence for associates, fans, guests and customers.

Simple things anyone can do to drive value and to create value for themselves in terms of feeling like they're fully alive in the role they play inside our business as well as the meaningful and memorable positive impact they can have on everyone from associates to loyal fans.

Q. Harry, I know this to be true. When employees can see how they can contribute and that a company will recognize the effort, that's when you know your V.A.L.U.E. Culture is taking root.

Very true. Now, the problem is that when folks only think recognition comes from climbing Mount Everest, in other words it takes some kind of major achievement to be recognized. Then we're sending the wrong message. Because then you're sending a message that only a select few folks have got the ability to be able to go and do that.

When you praise someone, you let them know you're aware of their hard work, that you see them. You acknowledge they've put forth a great effort to accomplish something, you're celebrating their accomplishment and encouraging them, supporting them.

Recognition goes a long way and it shows employees that their efforts are valued and appreciated, which is essential to a positive working environment. The best news is there are many ways to reward employees without spending a lot of money. Here are some additional ways you can reward people for a job well done:

REDUCE THEIR SUPERVISION.

Some people are happier and do much better work when they're allowed to work on their own. Giving an employee more freedom can be an excellent reward. *By giving your employees less supervision, you're letting them know they're trusted and you have confidence in their abilities.*

If you truly trust your employees to do their work without supervision, allow them the flexibility to work on their own schedule or even from home occasionally. Of course, whether you can allow your employees to work at home will depend on the work they do. By allowing employees to work more freely with less supervision, businesses can reap the rewards of increased productivity, improved morale, and better engagement. Not only does this create an atmosphere of trust and respect between management and employees, but it can also help foster creativity and innovation within the organization. Providing flexible working arrangements, such as the ability to work from home occasionally or rearranging shifts according to individual needs, allows for higher levels of job satisfaction, which in turn leads to higher performance. Additionally, companies can benefit from greater cost savings due to reduced overhead costs associated with remote working arrangements. Ultimately, when employers demonstrate trust in their team members through providing autonomy and flexibility that aligns with their professional goals, they are more likely to stay engaged and motivated in their work.

GIVE YOUR TEAM MEMBERS WHO GO ABOVE AND BEYOND THE CALL OF DUTY A NEW TITLE.

Job titles don't always have to mean more money—they can be an effective way of recognizing and rewarding employees for their hard work and dedication. By providing increased responsibility alongside a new title, businesses can show their appreciation and give employees a sense of achievement. Furthermore, promoting an employee to a higher position within the organization gives them greater visibility which can help to further motivate them and boost morale. Additionally, such recognition encourages employees to stay with the company by increasing their sense of loyalty and sense of purpose in their work. All in all, job titles are an excellent way to recognize hard-working employees while also boosting engagement within the organization.

PUBLICLY RECOGNIZE PEOPLE THAT DO THEIR JOB WELL.

At your next staff meeting, present that person with a certificate. Create a bulletin board in the staff lounge with photographs of honored employees to continue recognizing them for their good work. Use your internal office communication platforms to send office-wide kudos for a job well done.

ENCOURAGE YOUR TEAM BY GIVING DISCOUNT COUPONS.

Provide usable vouchers to local businesses in your area. You could give a coupon for a free movie and popcorn at the movie theater, reduced entrance at a family park, or a coupon for a free turkey around the holidays. Not only does the employee feel recognized, but it also allows them to involve family or friends in their recognition by bringing them along.

When employees feel they matter, they're much more willing to give their all to a company. Use some of these ways to reward people for a job well done. Not only will your team enjoy their job and the workplace much more, but you'll also find they're more productive.

SIMPLE WAYS TO START

One of the simplest ways to start recognizing team members is by promoting them publicly. You can begin in your weekly team meetings. Make a point to highlight even small accomplishments.

Share the wins in your staff meetings or create an interoffice newsletter. If it isn't a norm now, consider adding this form of recognition. Building a V.A.L.U.E. Culture really is a series of small actions that lead to a big impact.

As a leader, I encourage you to think through where you have opportunities to add in recognition. The most successful recognition efforts don't have to be costly. In fact, I still have every note of thanks or commendation I've received from a client or boss. Some of them are tucked away in a folder, but a few of them still hang on my cork board in my home office. Each time I read them, I feel valued. Most of them are just a few sentences long. But what mattered to me was the fact they were heartfelt and delivered in a handwritten manner. That personal gesture was deeply appreciated and remembered.

Before we leave this topic, I also believe recognizing employees who work from home or seasonally is essential in order to build a positive and healthy culture. When employers take the time to recognize their employees' contributions, whether they are working on-site or remotely, or during peak seasons or other times of the year, they demonstrate appreciation for their employees, create an environment of shared respect, and foster a sense of community. Doing so encourages employees to stay with the company longer, and helps build strong relationships within the workplace while maintaining a productive and dynamic corporate atmosphere. Let's head back to the *Mercedes-Benz™* Stadium with Harry and see more great engagement ideas since his teams include both part-time, seasonal and full-time employees.

Q. Harry, how do you keep both part-time, seasonal, and full-time employees engaged and bought into the culture?

There are two main points. It involves collaboration and communication. Of course, everyone takes part in the onboarding process. We have new hire orientation, and they're shadowing, training, huddles, team meetings, leadership meetings, coaching, development, events, our day-to-day work, participation in giveback opportunities and more.

For example, Falcon's Feast was an event where our associates could be out there together handing out turkeys for Thanksgiving. Those turkeys were funded by team members just like me, giving $15 or $30 and by our offensive and defensive lineman.

We gave them away to families in need from the Westside, as well as our event staff who might have known a family, friend, or neighbor in need. That was once an idea that went from a few associates giving away thirty turkeys to giving away 1,500 turkeys.

Q. WOW! That is quite the engagement. Share with us other ways to bring people together.

Sure. Newsletters and briefings with the leadership team members also bring everyone together and on the same page for event day. We actually have our executive team go into huddles and briefings as early as 6:00 am. They join in with different teams throughout the year. We ensure we thoroughly brief associates on everything that's planned for on gameday.

In terms of communication and sharing, here's one example. We have a newsletter that goes out monthly. We also have a weekly one we call the *Guest Service Insider.* There is a little bit of everything, obviously information relevant to the upcoming event. But in the newsletter, we also share wellness programs covering social, mental, physical, lifestyle, and nutrition.

There are messages from frontline executives. We talk about the latest training initiatives we have. What we try to do is make sure we're communicating. We're collaborating. We're providing opportunities for training with everyone alongside each other.

We do a great job communicating, collaborating, and including everyone in different opportunities.

When we do give back opportunities, everyone is invited to join us and volunteer. That's just some of the ways in how we make sure we're all staying connected.

The best leaders actively search for and see the positive impact their people are making and tell them. Acknowledgment from a leader can be a truly powerful thing, so be sure to call it out and celebrate it whenever you can .

Throughout the book, you've read how important creating connections and building relationships is to the V.A.L.U.E. Culture process. It's also a key element in building high engagement in your workforce. As a leader, you need to be conscientious and make sure recognition opportunities are spread throughout the organization and everyone has access to participate in them.

NETWORKING GROWS RELATIONSHIPS AND ENGAGEMENT

Offering networking opportunities is another way to grow engagement. Our peer groups, both personal and professional, are extremely valuable and need to connect with one another. When opportunities arise, ensure your employees receive equal opportunities to build those connections and engage on a personal level.

That means if only men are invited to play golf at a company outing, you need to look at how equitable opportunities are inside your organization that includes women, minorities, single or married individuals, Gen Z, X or Boomers and Millennials. Networking can help build stronger interdepartmental relationships. Employees need to feel comfortable crossing gender and generational lines. Building cross-cultural, racial, psychographic, and sociographic relationships keeps silos from forming and groups from isolating themselves and disconnecting.

VOLUNTEERING GROWS RELATIONSHIPS AND ENGAGEMENT

Volunteering together is another form of networking. Offering volunteer opportunities is a fantastic way to get employees involved and work together collaboratively. Volunteer programs are effective ways for companies to build culture and meet Environmental, Social, and Governance (ESG) requirements. The first step for a company to consider is identifying the social issues employees are interested in. Once the issues are identified, local organizations can be found that address the problem and seek out ways to partner in volunteer opportunities. Again, you are aligning company values and employee values which builds culture. Therefore, encourage employees to participate.

A key aspect of successful volunteer programs is participation. You can offer incentives or even allow the activity to be done as part of the workday or as a team-building exercise.

ESG numbers are becoming more important since they are now considered by financial institutions before they will make some loans. A calculation is done as part of the analysis to determine the risk and growth opportunities an organization has available. Your culture program plays a major role in driving profitability and raising morale which boosts your ESG numbers. An increase in ESG also shows up in improved safety which is a benefit of a strong culture also. All of these areas fall under the social category of ESG. Community concerns also fall under the S—in ESG.

Employee engagement is crucial for any organization to achieve its goals and remain competitive in today's fast-paced business environment. Volunteering is a powerful way to connect employees to their communities and foster a sense of purpose. When organizations provide opportunities for employees to volunteer and give back, it can create a sense of pride and ownership of the company's mission and values. This can be particularly effective when coupled with a strong culture that emphasizes the value of employees and their contributions. When employees feel valued, they are likely to participate in company-sponsored volunteering initiatives leading to increased levels of engagement. This can create a virtuous cycle of employee engagement, where employees feel more invested in the company, leading to increased loyalty, productivity, and ultimately organizational success.

Let's go back to Garry Ridge and see how *WD-40™ Company* helps encourage employee engagement through volunteerism.

> **Q. Garry, what do you do to help your people become more engaged?**

We offer volunteer opportunities. It is a way for our company to connect with and impact areas of social concern employees may have. They are the heartbeat of the community, so we want them to share the local needs.

The ultimate form of employee engagement is when they become brand ambassadors for you. When employees enjoy where they are and what they do and want to share it with others, you've hit it out of the park. It's a natural occurrence when the culture is right.

We don't encourage them; they do it because they're proud. We don't run contests and incentives to have people get out there and voice positively about working for a *WD-40™ Company*. But our people, our tribe members, genuinely love talking about the memories we create for other people. Because we do it with a sincere heart.

I've seen great leaders build engagement simply by taking the time to get to know the people they manage. The leaders I've respected the most are the ones I felt cared about me and my future. They helped me identify areas of growth and celebrated achievements with me along the way. If the engagement comes from the people's hearts, then they are already motivated, and the culture is truly shaped.

Are you now engaged in what your team members can do and ways to recognize them? Do you see the potential for them and the company? Do you feel the power of how engagement can propel your team and organization forward, leading to greater success and innovation? Use that energy and propel yourself into forming recognition opportunities in your organization and watch your employees sore.

CHAPTER 13:

Roadblocks and Obstacles

A few years ago, I succumbed to peer pressure and agreed to sign up to participate in a half marathon. Let me set an accurate stage for you. *I'm not what you call athletic.* I had never completed anything longer than a 5K (and by completed, I mean walked and talked more than I ran). There were so many times while I was training for the 13.1 miles that I came close to quitting. I was listening to that voice of self-doubt get louder and louder in my head. It wasn't until I completed a 7-mile training run one day that something flipped in my brain, and I started to believe I was strong enough and fast enough to finish the half marathon.

There will always be obstacles and roadblocks to overcome when you begin to initiate change in the workplace. We live in a world conditioned to look at the negative. If those obstacles (including our people) remain unaddressed, it will prevent us from seeing beyond them and reach our desired finish line. To help increase the success of your culture build, you must keep a close eye on those prone to block or delay its adherence. These are your *Negative Nicks*, your *Suzy Skeptics*, and your *Doubting Donalds.* You must clear a path for *Advocate Amy* and *Supporter Steve.* You need the right people to share the right message.

It's important you realize your work isn't done just because you've launched the initiative. As a leader in the change movement, you must continue to be visible and check in to ensure V.A.L.U.E. Culture is being communicated throughout the organization, continuously. You might be surprised who is resistant to new ideas and plans, and those individuals will need to be addressed.

MANAGING CHANGE DURING YOUR CULTURE BUILD

For your culture initiative to succeed, you'll need to manage how people react to change. Change may look and feel uniquely different to each employee. We all know change is a constant in life. Humans are hardwired to crave stability. When something is changing outside our control, the initial reaction is to resist.

Think of change from an employee viewpoint. Your boss or supervisor is presenting a new idea. The idea changes the familiar processes. How do you imagine you would feel? Anxious? As you roll out the initiative, ask yourself how this change will impact each department. Will it impact the team? How can I help each individual better understand the details?

Including employees in early discussions is vital. The rollout isn't the first time your employees should hear of a culture change. Have them a part of the process from the beginning and see how much more they buy in.

Change is often hard, especially for your long-term employees or supervisors. They can feel threatened or left behind—or maybe they did not feel you took their ideas or criticisms to heart in your new plan. Change can be difficult for many reasons. People fear the unknown and often resist change because they are unsure about what the future holds and are afraid of the unknown. Change often requires people to adjust to new ways of doing things, and fear can make them feel like they have lost control of their work. Your employees could be afraid that these changes in the workplace might result in the loss of their job or position. Society loves to highlight failure. Fear of failure makes it hard to encourage people to do something unfamiliar. If there's a chance they will fail, they tend to avoid trying something new all together.

What's strange is that amazing companies are started by someone willing to risk failure. Still, then they stall because the idea of failure shuts down innovation, creativity, and the implementation of new behaviors. For your V.A.L.U.E. Culture to succeed, you need to embrace change agents. These are the people inside your organization who say "What if..." and actually try it.

Many resist the idea of change because they are skeptical of new ideas and are comfortable with the status quo. Jana Adams, with *Touchstone Energy*™, added more about the damage skeptics can do to derail your culture program.

Q. Jana, why are changes so difficult?

You're going to have the skeptics. There are going to be people who say, "I don't want any part of this because I do my job fine. I don't need to change anything." Those are the obvious ones. Then there will be the people who are skeptical, who think this is just some new trend. This new management fad is coming in.

They're the kind of quiet killers of a culture. You have to be very, very wary of the skeptic. Honestly, you'll probably have the early adopters who are all gung-ho but then tire themselves out. It's about a measured pace. You're not saying, hey, here's a piece of paper; this is our culture; let's go run out and do it.

It's built from within.

People naturally start to join in the process because they see the benefits. They see happier employees. They see the better service to their community that comes from having that strong and defined culture.

At times, resistance to the new culture may be coming from all of the different perceptions and world views your employees bring to the office with them each day. Since your workforce is likely to reflect a multitude of generations, it's important to look at how that lens filters their interpretation of your new cultural implementation.

As the leader, it is important that you manage the process across the different generations. The largest emerging workforce is the Millennials (born between 1980 and 2000) who have developed their work characteristics from parents who were doting and living very structured lives. You will be required to create a unique dialogue with them. They have ideas and opinions and don't like to be ignored. They have been trained and genuinely believe they have a right to have input. You will need to make them feel the cultural shift is a partnership. They also like experiences and want to enjoy their work, workplace, and the people surrounding them. So, work fun into the equation. They crave positive, fulfilling professional experiences. If you have Millennials who aren't socializing with others, you have a problem. Involve them in planning the rollout and employee engagement activities. They expect to have a life outside of work and believe their career should allow them to fulfill both personal and professional desires. To get them on board, you must create an atmosphere where they feel they have a say and contribute. Millennials in the workplace want work that both enables them to contribute to society in positive ways *and* that rewards them appropriately. You must help them understand how your business is having a positive impact and how their work directly contributes. Getting your multi-generational workforce on the same page can be challenging yet extremely rewarding. It's one of the biggest talent management necessities leaders will face over the next few years.

Regardless of the generation, you need to encourage open dialogue. Different generations may see the company values displayed yet not understand why they matter. A difference in understanding could lead to employees closing up and shutting down. Your goal as a leader is to get people talking so you can create a collaborative mindset. Help them embrace the diversity of work styles, attire, habits, and language. More dialogue is always better than no dialogue. Don't get labeled as a leader who tolerates negative behavior. It will derail your best intentions if employees see the opposition isn't being encouraged to change.

Know ahead of time you will need to be flexible in your approach. One size doesn't fit all when you are communicating change. Think in terms of defining great outcomes and less about defining how they *need* to be achieved.

OPEN UP TO FLEXIBILITY

As the modern workforce continues to evolve, leaders need to consider the desire of both current and future employees for more flexibility in their work schedules. While offering options such as remote work, flexible hours, and job sharing can attract and retain top talent who value work-life balance and the ability to manage their time effectively, it's important to also consider how the lack of employee interactions can impact workplace culture. Leaders need to find ways to maintain a sense of connection and community among team members, even if they are working remotely or on flexible schedules.

Daniel Lawrence, co-founder of *Bots for That™* and whose company is located in London, has felt the impact of a remote workforce on the culture inside his company.

Q. Daniel, how has a remote workforce impacted your work culture?

I think we're missing out by not physically interacting. I think that's creating a bigger challenge than we've ever had. I think it's the same for anyone. So professionally, it's a challenge.

Without social interaction, it's those little things, the little water cooler moments where you overhear a comment and you interject. That's where the correction of culture happens more naturally. It's very difficult if you only talk to someone for 35 minutes in a 40-hour week. You're missing out on so much.

I think that's the biggest challenge that we've got to overcome. I think culture is going to suffer; values are going to suffer.

It's going to make the challenge harder because employees could end up speaking more with a client than they do with their colleagues. The risk is then they start seeing client culture as predominantly ours, and that could well be a mistake. It could not be in the best interest of us.

As a leader in the workplace, you can take several steps to help overcome the impact that having a remote workforce can have on company culture. First, you can prioritize clear and consistent communication to ensure remote employees feel connected to the company and its mission. This can involve regular video or phone calls, team meetings, and one-on-one check-ins. You can promote opportunities for virtual team building, such as online games or virtual coffee breaks. You can also create policies and guidelines that support work-life balance, such as flexible schedules and mental health resources.

It's important to encourage remote employees to share their feedback and ideas, and make sure that their contributions are recognized and valued. Finally, embrace technology and innovation to facilitate seamless collaboration, and provide training and resources to help your remote employees use these tools effectively. Doing these steps will help you build a strong and supportive workplace culture, even in a remote or hybrid work environment.

MASTER EMPLOYEE BUY-IN

An employee who doesn't buy-in to your culture can have a significant impact on its adoption by the rest of the workforce. Workplace culture is shaped by the attitudes, behaviors, and values of everyone within the organization, and if even a single employee resists or undermines those cultural norms, it can create friction and disrupt the cohesion of the team. If you address such behavior early on and take steps to reinforce the importance of the company's culture, it can help to prevent further disengagement and ensure that the rest of the work-force is aligned with the organization's values and mission. One surefire way to kill the culture's momentum is to let employees continue using the old ways. Rich Sheridan talked about this very point.

Q. Rich, what is the difference between the people who say, "we can't do this" versus the people who say, "I can't do this yet?"

Suppose you're going to move an organization forward and you're going to create an intentionally positive, joyful culture in our world. In that case, you need people trying stuff and celebrating those small victories every step of the way.

What if when we tried something new, and it worked, we celebrated the fact *we did it*! We had to figure out how to do something that we had never figured out before. And when we switched to *I did it*, the learning moments became a joy, not a burden. It increases your confidence in trying to learn new things, which is ultimately what I think all leaders need within their organizations.

Q. Rich, share an example with us.

Just recently, I've learned an important huge lesson about can from my now two, almost three-year-old granddaughter Coco. You know, two-year-olds try to do stuff all the time, right? She is a wild child. She climbs stuff. She does crazy things. But she keeps trying stuff.

Coco, got a scooter. At first, she kept falling, tipping it over, but she kept working at it until she figured out how to get it to work. She didn't have it yet, but she didn't give up. Add the word *yet* at the end of every sentence, opens up a world of possibilities

In the end, she got it! She yelled I did it. I watched her do this, and that is an amazingly important phrase for all human beings. There's always stuff that we do as humans that we learn how to do. And, we need to celebrate our wins.

Q. Rich, how can you help your employees embrace change?

The number one mistake is believing you can just click your fingers, put up a poster, and do a rah-rah speech once a year and that someone else is going to change your culture.

We do have posters at *Menlo Innovations*™. One says,

"Technology changes quickly; People change slowly." Then another poster says, "People don't resist change; they resist *being* changed."

One of the reasons people resist any kind of change is because *it threatens an existing rewards system.* I'm not talking about compensation. That is the least effective kind of reward system. I'm talking about what's my job. What's my title? What's my span of authority? Can I tell people I'm working hard today? Can I tell them I'm working crazy overtime hours and the company can't live without me?

When you start messing with how things work, you must understand you are pulling rewards away from people. We must change the way we change. If you don't replace the existing reward, you just take away a reward of equal or greater value. People will revert to the old way of doing things, even if it is pain-filled.

Ultimately, it's important for leaders to communicate clearly and consistently about the importance of workplace culture and take action when necessary to uphold those standards. It's important to have a conversation about what you will do with the people who choose not to join your cultural movement.

Just like when I was preparing for that half marathon, mindset is critical to the success of your culture rollout. For me, it was repeating the mantra "Strong enough, fast enough." That simple phrase kept me putting one foot in front of the other on my journey to cross the finish line. As Rich shared, maybe it's adopting the fearless mindset of a child and saying "I Did It!" when we are faced with new ways of thinking and doing things.

The mindset of a leader plays a critical role in the success of implementing a culture change, as they set the tone for the entire organization. Leaders who believe in the change and are committed to its success are more likely to inspire and motivate others to follow their lead. A positive and optimistic attitude from leaders can help create a sense of excitement and energy around it, making it easier for others to embrace the change.

As I continued researching roadblocks to workplace culture, time and consistency are crucial factors in successfully implementing a culture change. Here's why. Culture change takes time to take root and become fully integrated into the organization. Leaders need to be patient and recognize that culture change is a long-term process and not a one-time event. In fact, Garry Ridge from *WD-40™ Company* cautioned about the need to have patience during the growing phase of your culture.

Q. Garry, what is your caution when it comes to culture change?

Leaders, you must remember that time is your friend. Consistency is important. You do not build a strong, enduring culture in six months. It takes time. You've got to set the foundation. You've got to work on it every day.

Q. Garry, how do you help employees to understand that change is coming?

Employees may be slow to believe a change is coming, You have to show the people you lead that you do have a larger goal but you also do have a backbone of steel. You've got to show care and can do at the same time.

Empathy and persistence play an important role in culture change. Empathy is crucial because your employees need to feel understood and believe you will address their concerns.

You need to be able to see the change from the employees' perspective and understand why some may be hesitant. I've already mentioned culture isn't a short-term project. Leaders need to be persistent in their efforts to communicate the vision, values, and goals of the change, as well as in their efforts to model the desired behaviors which reinforce the new culture. Honesty and transparency are also critical in creating a successful environment for culture change. Couple these with persistence and empathy, and you'll build the trust needed and gain the buy-in from your team.

Daniel Lawrence said it best, "I think the major roadblock is always openness. Some people are afraid to be honest with themselves. Some people are afraid to be honest with others. You need to be honest with yourself and put your hands up because nothing moves forward unless there's honesty. Honesty's the number one thing."

With his honesty ringing in our ears, let's see how we can go from our roadblocks and obstacles to now finding success. It's like preparing for running a marathon—your success measures are in place to help make sure you are making continual progress.

CHAPTER 14:

Success Measures

Building a strong and cohesive company culture is essential to creating a thriving and successful company. However, without a way to measure the success of these efforts, it can be difficult to determine if they are having the desired impact. Measuring the success of a culture program is more than tracking data and numbers, it is about ensuring that the work being done is truly making a difference. It is also about creating a culture that fosters employee engagement, motivation, and satisfaction. Measuring the success of a culture program helps an organization identify what is working and what needs improvement, which can lead to targeted efforts to further enhance an even greater culture. Measuring the success of a culture program is a critical step in moving from the planning phase into the implementation phase. Adding ways to measure the success of the program, makes it possible to know whether your program is making the impact you desire. Measuring success is a sign that the company is moving from theory to practice and from idea to action.

Once you've made the decision to launch your V.A.L.U.E. Culture, a forward-looking attitude will keep you focused. There will be mistakes along the way; however, you will continue to grow, and your culture will evolve as you move through the process and reinforce the desired behaviors and beliefs of your employee base.

Throughout this book, you have been introduced to the components your culture program needs to include and the tactics you can use to move forward. Intelligent planning, focused effort, and positive reinforcers with measurable indicators will keep you and your team on the path to success.

Garry Ridge, CEO of *WD-40™ Company*, shares how his company uses measurable tactics to keep his people engaged.

Q. Garry, what are the two ways to ensure culture change doesn't fade away?

One is it's embedded in the talent development program or what a lot of people would call a review system. We have our values as part of our regular conversations with our team members on an ongoing basis. We ask our people to share with us how they have lived our values in the last 90 days.

We only have two measurements of values. You either *live with them* or you *visit them,* and we say we don't want a lot of visitors. We're embedding this norm into the things we do. Our values are not framed up on a wall so that people point at them. Values should be on a very coffee-stained piece of paper that is referred to and used all the time to help make decisions.

Q. Garry, I love that point. What else can you share?

You've got to adopt and adapt. A lot of people adopt something, a training program. They adapt to it. I call that fairy dust. They sprinkle it over the business. They forget that the fairy dust will evaporate if they don't embed it in behavior. Then it'll be on to the next shiny coin: What leadership program do we do next?

We think if we do this leadership program, it'll change everything. Well, it doesn't. It doesn't because we live in a very fluid world—even more so than ever today.

Picture this: if you're flying an airplane, you have headwinds and tailwinds. You can maneuver through there because it pushes you back or forward.

What we have today is a lot of turbulence. Turbulence is unexpected. You can't take your eyes off the controls anymore around culture. You've got to watch it constantly because turbulence will move it around.

Q. What can we do to be effective?

In our leadership team, you either adopt, adapt, and embed our culture, or we'll share you with a competitor. People are escaping to or from cultures these days. This has been going on forever. I think that's why our measurement system, employee engagement surveys, and work have been so important.

We have to measure continually, particularly in the senior leadership group, if you don't want to be on this path with us, it's okay. You're a great person. If you're not happy here, go be happy somewhere else.

You've also got to be brave enough; you've got to love your people enough to redirect behavior. If you cannot redirect the behavior or correct it, then you have to take it out. If not, you must be prepared to look and see a big sour mess because that's how quickly it can change.

Consider your culture champions as you make decisions concerning promotions. Reward those who embrace and help move the initiative forward. Advancement must be tied to the new expected norms, not falling back on an old system of rewarding longevity.

You also need an analytical data-based method of gauging how well your new culture is embedded in the workforce. As I researched for this book, the preferred method emerged: surveying your employees.

SURVEY FOR SUCCESS

No program can be defined as successful without measuring your outcomes. Remember, positive results can look different for companies and departments. That's why it's important to set milestones from the beginning, and your leadership team and their team members agree on what success will look like. I have witnessed this myself when working with organizations concerned with internal culture. I work with clients to establish the areas we will measure prior to a culture rollout and then at regular intervals after the initial launch. For example, I think it's important that the core values and vision or purpose are easily understood throughout the organization and that people have bought into exhibiting the desired traits. The other necessity, which comes from open communications is, employees must be able to trust they can fill out these surveys honestly and without the fear of retribution, if their answers show some room for continued improvement.

I asked Adam Schwartz, founder of *The Cooperative Way*™, who has years of experience interpreting employee satisfaction survey results, about using satisfaction surveys effectively.

Q. Adam, what do you think about employee satisfaction surveys?

I'm a huge fan of employee satisfaction surveys and of

leaders responding to those surveys promptly. I want to ensure the employee knows that I am aware, "This is what you said. This is what we heard." I want to affirm their responses were documented and that there's no miscommunication between what you're asking for and what leadership heard.

There are ways to structure the survey to get maximum input from employees and know that the data you receive will be interpreted in a way you can get real direction. There's the format I'm a big fan of. It is the one to five, or one to seven strongly disagree to strongly agree to scale. It should be a double-blind survey. Meaning we are not going to know what a specific employee has said in the survey, but we will know if they completed it.

It is important employees can be guaranteed their anonymity. That is an absolute sacred vow that cannot be broken. Then you have an outside facilitator review the comments.

Following the data is crucial when determining which areas you need to work on. It's also crucial you share the results with the employees. You can't ask and not respond.

I think it's essential that we do this type of survey as a benchmark when we do it the first time, and we make a commitment that we're going to do it at least one more time in a year or two. We're going to measure progress or regression as it may be, and all of the results and all of the top-level data will be shared.

Q. Adam, how do you share your results with your employees?

Having an all-employee meeting is the best way to share the results. If you can't get everyone in one meeting, do it in two or three on the same day so the rumor mill does not take over the narrative that you want to ensure. The key point is making sure everyone hears the same message and understands management is taking the results seriously.

We're going to share the same information in each meeting. We're going to tell you what we've heard, and then we're going to say we're going to consider some of these ideas, and we're going to get back to you and give a date and honor it.

Everything we're going to do with respect to employees will be based on this information because that will get buy-in for future surveys. People are really paying attention. At the end of the day, people want to be heard.

I caution clients about the negative consequences they can face if they don't share the results of these surveys with their workforce. If employees take the time to provide feedback through a survey, they expect the results to be shared with them. Failing to do so can erode any trust you were working to establish. Employees will feel their opinions are not valued. You'll also miss out on opportunities for improvement. You want to create an atmosphere where continuous improvement is the norm. Finally, failure to share results means decreased participation in future surveys. Adam's comments triggered me to share what Garry Ridge, who leads the *WD-40™ Company*, said about the importance of collecting data.

Q. Garry, I understand that you have been collecting data at your company. What is it telling you?

The data allows us to measure and track the effectiveness of our culture over twenty years. The high marks are not just in the survey. They can also be seen in how the company's profitability has grown.

We've got an employee engagement of ninety-three percent and ninety-eight percent of our people say they love to tell people they work at the company. Ninety-seven percent say they feel their values align with the company's values. Another ninety-seven percent of our people say they respect their coach, who is actually their boss because we don't have managers.

Q. What type of support do you have?

We have coaches because the job of a leader is to help those they lead play a better game. We've got all those great measures, and by the way, over a 20-year period, we've taken the value of our company from about $300 million to nearly $3 billion, and we've increased our revenue more than six times.

We've been able to do that by taking our brand to 176 countries worldwide. So, if you think about it, we sell oil in a can. Why would anybody be passionate about selling oil in a can? Because we don't *sell oil in a can, we sell memories.*

We sell a place where people learn, grow, and feel like they belong. That's one of the biggest challenges in organizations—the people. If people don't feel like they belong, they'll leave.

You, me, and anybody else we know has at some time in their life, left a company, a relationship, or a party. Why? Because they didn't feel like they belonged. Our job is to help people feel that.

Other than employee engagement surveys, there are other things you can monitor to see if you are impacting your culture in a positive way. Some areas you can track are job satisfaction scores, productivity, turnover, retention rates, absenteeism, safety, customer satisfaction, employee referrals for job openings, and profits.

You can also look at your wellness program. Engaged employees tend to be happier at home and have lower health costs, so they won't be adding to your insurance costs.

At evaluation time or during your yearly goal setting, make a point to include culture initiatives as goals for your team to accomplish. Review it with them mid-year and create course corrections where necessary.

Evaluations reinforce that accountability and collaboration are essential in the workplace.

Measuring how effectively your employees have shifted to becoming brand advocates is another way to gauge your program's effectiveness. As a leader, it's up to you to determine the metrics you need to build support for your program at a board level.

I went back to Jana Adams, executive director of *Touchstone Energy*™, and asked her about electric cooperatives specifically and how they measure their return on the culture investment, and why it is important.

Q. Jana, with people you work with coming from different roles, how do you talk with them about culture ROI?

In our industry, we have a lot of engineers and accountants that move into the role of CEO. Everything needs to have a number associated with it and show a return on their investment.

As a CEO, you cannot put a number on some of this. You can't just say I'm going to get a fifteen percent increase if I start focusing on culture. What things can a CEO look at inside the organization to see if they are effectively changing culture in a way that positively impacts not only the employees but the bottom line of that organization?

By determining the areas of concern, you can determine what numbers to focus on to effectively measure how much impact your initiatives have. It's absolutely tied to the bottom line. I'm not an accountant, but I like spreadsheets and retention. If you have a good strong positive culture in your organization people are going to stay.

Change can be challenging, and some employees may not be comfortable with a new direction or new ways of doing things. Keep in mind some level of turnover in the workplace is normal, even without a culture change. That's why it's important to understand what your turnover numbers are normally. Pay attention to the feedback from your remaining employees. Do they seem concerned about the people leaving? Or do these employees seem relieved because there could have been potential issues you were unaware of?

When you have the right people in the right *seats* they stay. They have bought into the culture, and they understand the value. They believe in the company's mission, vision, and values and are committed to working toward these goals. These engaged employees will produce a high level of work and help drive your culture efforts inside the organization.

Measuring your initiatives and gauging the pace at which your goals will be accomplished will help you determine if you are on track to achieving the desired results. Identifying any potential weak spots in the workplace culture can be addressed before any potential problems arise, allowing you to keep the positive momentum going forward. Regularly assessing employee sentiment to get a true sense of how they feel about the culture is also essential. Surveys, open forums, and other formative feedback tools can help you to continuously refine and adjust your processes. Finally, make sure to measure both quantitative (e.g., increased productivity) as well as qualitative (e.g., improved morale) metrics in order to get a comprehensive overview of the success of your workplace culture initiatives.

As we wrap up this section, here's a checklist you can to measure the success of your workforce culture program:

1. **Track employee engagement** survey results and analyze changes over time to identify areas for improvement.

2. **Monitor job satisfaction** scores as an indicator of how engaged employees are in their roles.

3. **Measure productivity** and compare it against previous benchmarks to see if productivity is increasing or decreasing.

4. **Track turnover, retention, and absenteeism** rates to get a better sense of how employees feel about their jobs and company culture.

5. **Examine customer satisfaction ratings** to determine how successful the company is at delivering positive customer experiences.

6. **Analyze employee referrals** for job openings, as this can give an indication of the reputation of the organization among its staff members.

7. **Use profits as an indication** of the effectiveness of any cultural initiatives that have been implemented by the business leader; higher profits likely indicate a more successful culture program has been put in place by the business leader, while lower profits suggest there may be room for improvement when it comes to cultivating healthy workplace culture within the organization.

8. **Evaluate wellness programs** in terms of how they are helping employees stay healthy and happy; engaged employees often tend to have lower health costs and be more productive in their roles, so this should be monitored closely by business leaders interested in gauging their success with respect to workforce culture initiatives.

If you've been wondering how others have created inspiring workplace culture that include the V.A.L.U.E. Culture elements, look no further! In the next section, you'll find real-world examples that have worked, and these case studies will provide you with an even greater understanding of how you can create a culture of success. Companies such as *Panasonic™ Global Automotive*, the *Electric Cooperatives of America™*, and *King of Pops™* are paving the way with innovative approaches to keep their employees motivated and engaged. Learn from their strategies and apply them alongside other best practices you've read so far to ensure the highest level of success in building a truly unique corporate culture. Read on to get inspired!

SECTION 3:

You are Now Poised for Success

I trust you have learned that a V.A.L.U.E. Culture works for any business type. And, I hope that you have seen how each principle works harmoniously with the other to create a culture that celebrates your unique business vision and empowers your employees. The key to each of these is your strong leadership and willingness to openly communicate and invite your employees into the discussion. The great news is, now you are poised for your own success.

Up until now, I have shared examples from the workplace where each aspect of my culture formula was woven into their internal cultures. I also shared how adaptable my V.A.L.U.E. Culture formula can be and how successful companies of all sizes can include these elements in their culture programs. I think it's important to see real culture in action, so this section gives your examples of companies that are getting it right and their background and experience will be helpful and valuable to you. Reading how they overcame objections at all levels in the organization, how they developed their own sets of unique core values that reflect the personality of their businesses and worked to engage their employees in the culture transformation will give you an insider's perspective that will set you up for success inside your own organization.

First, *Panasonic*™ Automotive, Stephen Childs, chief human resource officer (CHRO) and passionate workplace culture builder, helped lead a culture *rebel-ution*. His mission is to create a culture where highly talented people want to come and stay.

Stephen Childs shares candidly what it took to define their culture, the roadblocks they encountered, and how they created a culture that is winning the war on talent recruitment and retention. Childs has been with *Panasonic*™ Automotive for 24 years and has watched the company grow from a $400 million organization to over $3 billion with 1,213 locations globally. Their workforce grew from approximately 400 people to close to 7,000.

Second, let's look at the *cooperative business model*, specifically *electric cooperatives*. Their purpose positions them perfectly to compete with the next generation of workers who want to feel their job is important and impacts others.

Scott Peterson, retired, Senior Vice President of Communications, and Holly Wetzel, Senior Director of Marketing and Member Communications, are with the *National Rural Electric Cooperative Association (NRECA)*™. *NRECA*™ is a trade association representing over 900 local electric cooperatives that power 42 million Americans' homes and businesses.

Jana Adams is the Executive Director at *Touchstone Energy*™ *(R) Cooperatives*. *Touchstone Energy*™ is a national network of electric cooperatives across 45 states that provides research and training programs and leverages partnerships that help cooperatives better engage and serve their members.

As a result, *Touchstone Energy*™ cooperatives are positioned to achieve superior member satisfaction and engagement that strengthens the cooperative, the communities it serves, and the electric cooperative community at large. Before coming to

Touchstone Energy™, Jana was with the *American Wind Energy Association™*, the *Personal Care Products Council™*, and the *American Public Power Association™*.

Steven and Nick Carse are brothers and co-founders of *King of Pops™*, a family-owned popsicle company whose purpose is to create Unexpected Moments of Happiness. They started with a couple of thousand bucks, a used ice cream pushcart, and, in their own words, a whole lot of luck.

Steven, who was laid off during the Great Recession, and his brother Nick left their job as a lawyer and became the second employee of a company, are dedicated to supporting communities in the south. The business has grown to include *King of Crops™*, *Tree Elves™*, and *Perfect 10™*.

This section also dives deep into how my industry, electric cooperatives, have adapted their messaging while holding true to their purpose, so they can retain and hire talented employees to meet the needs of a changing industry. It also delves into the challenges and roadblocks the industry faces as well.

Full disclosure, I've worked in the electric cooperative industry for over 25 years. I moved up through the ranks from a front-line member services representative who performed energy audits and helped members understand their home energy use, to a vice president of communications and public relations who managed both the internal and external communications programs designed to educate both our employees and our members. Today, my role has evolved into serving on community boards and developing our next generation of leaders in the workplace.

My goal in sharing with you from my industry is to give you a glimpse inside a value-based business system and how the cooperative model is aligned perfectly to meet the needs of an incoming workforce.

I hope all of these examples will inspire and encourage you to evaluate and begin to create a workforce culture that benefits both your employees and customers. From them, you can avoid some missteps along the way and set yourself up for success faster. I wanted to make sure that you received a well-rounded viewpoint so I chose three very different organizations, representing different types of industries, business models, and products. I know you will enjoy them.

If you are more inclined to keep the momentum going and want to stay working on your own culture build, you can jump to chapter 18 where I address the importance of a people-first culture and summarize with some reminders and words of encouragement designed to assist you as you move forward with your own internal plans. You can always come back and read these case studies at any time, and I encourage you to do so. We gain some of our greatest insights from those who have walked the path before us. This is a perfect opportunity for you to decide, are you ready to implement, or learn a little bit more?

CHAPTER 15:

Happy Hour and Ping Pong Tables Don't Build Culture

"A STRONG CULTURE CAN OVERCOME ALMOST ANY SETUP OR
POOR TECHNICAL DECISIONS. A WEAK CULTURE CAN'T BE
SAVED BY USING THE BEST TECHNOLOGY. CULTURE IS ALSO
WHAT BRINGS PEOPLE TO YOUR COMPANY. IT BEATS EVERY-
THING ELSE."
—STEPHEN CHILDS

Leaders know that creating and sustaining a unique, peo-
ple-centric culture is essential for any organization to be
successful. However, it can be difficult to foster this type of
environment in the workplace as it requires constant vigilance,
creativity, and an ongoing commitment from both leaders and
team members. It demands an understanding that diversity
of thought and opinion should be embraced, communication should flow freely and employees should feel heard and
empowered.

Leaders who take the time to gain the support of upper
management, learn from their peers, and listen to their team's
ideas ultimately create cultures that make their people the

centerpiece of their companies' success.

Panasonic™ founder Konosuke Matsushita had a saying, *People Before Products*—this was paramount to his overall business philosophy. With this idea as the background, you might think culture has been a driver for *Panasonic™* Automotive since its founding over 100 years ago. However, I learned that wasn't the case. That's why I felt the *Panasonic™* story is one you needed to hear. As you read their story, look for each of the V.A.L.U.E. Culture attributes and compare how they incorporated them into their culture, and see what might work inside your own organization.

Much of the *Panasonic™* Automotive culture inspiration was based on the founder's desire to create an organization purposely built to put people at the front of the business strategy. With this in mind, I talked to Stephen Childs, the current Chief Human Resource Officer (CHRO) and passionate workplace culture builder, about his take on it.

Q. Stephen. how have things changed at <u>*Panasonic™*</u>*?*

We've changed so much in my timeframe. When we originally started the conversation about culture, it wasn't *really* about culture. It was about change management or transformation. We were going through an internal transformation, and someone asked, "Hey Stephen, you want to be a part of this?" and I was like, "I'm all in."

Q. It is exciting to be a part of such a huge transformation. But I'm sure with that came a lot of growing pains.

It sure did. In 2015, we were growing at double-digit numbers, and the business metrics looked very good. We looked at sales volume, market share, revenue, profitability, quality, etc.

The key business success factors we focused on were not much different than most companies. However, we learned later that the core of our business was rotting from the inside out, and we didn't know it.

Q. That's a powerful image rotting from the inside out. Share more with my readers.

The company had faced several major transformations, including mergers and acquisitions, resulting in numerous systems and processes getting dumped together. Our product portfolio also changed significantly.

We transitioned from car audio head units and speakers to product offerings, including navigation, heads-up displays, smart entry systems, onboard charging systems, cameras, sensors, and other Advanced Driver Assistance Systems (ADAS).

Our company needed different technical skills, so upskilling our team was required. We noticed a drop in our Employee Opinion Surveys, and employees felt too much focus was on the products and not enough on the people. To top it off, our Glassdoor.com rating was 2.7, which meant hiring top talent was incredibly difficult.

Q. What did you do to get things back on track?

I was tasked with reaching out to some best practice companies to uncover ideas, processes, or tools we could use to improve our ability to change and adapt faster with more success. I started having these conversations about transformation and change, and one question kept surfacing, "What is your company culture?" I didn't have a good answer. I wasn't even sure what constituted a company culture."

Q. Stephen, what did you do next?

This led to a whole new journey of visiting companies that were on the *Best Places to Work* list. I wanted to learn what these companies had figured out about long-term culture sounded great to me.

Q. Well, that sounds easy; more comfortable seating, ping pong tables, food, is that all it takes to change the culture?

Great question. Each time I visited different places, I thought that that was really all it took. It wasn't until later that I realized something was missing from these visits.

I started having conversations with companies and was asked how you went through your transformation. And, they said, "Before we get to that, talk a little bit about your culture." It was stumping me. I'd answer, "We're people before products." They would ask, "What makes you people before products?"

They got me again. I said, "We're heavy into innovation." I explained some of the things we did to create an innovative organization. Then they'd ask, "So you built that into a culture model?" I'd answer, "Well, we really don't have a culture."

Whenever I had a conversation, somebody asked me about our culture. I came back and talked with the executive team and said, "Here's the problem. Nobody will share their change.

I made a list of fifteen companies and started making calls. The call would go something like this. "Hi, I'm Stephen Childs. I'm the CHRO of *Panasonic*™ Automotive. We're on a journey to define and implement a best place-to-work culture. I would love to take about 30 minutes to pick your brain and learn about all the wonderful things your company is doing." The biggest surprise I had while making the calls was that everyone I spoke to agreed to meet with me.

Q. What happened during the visits?

I would show up to meet with the Chief Human Resource Officer, and nine times out of ten, they would be involved in the meet and greet and then pass me off to people from their team to give me a tour and explain why they are *the best place to work*.

They gave me an overview of the cool things they implemented, including the use of bean bag chairs throughout the office, the placement of ping pong tables in key areas for employees to connect, the subsidizing of the café to keep food costs low, or how their happy hour was the most attended company event each week. As a highly social person, all of these sounded great to me.

Q. Stephen, it's like you were looking for a solution without really knowing what your problem was in the first place.

Yes. I returned with his newfound information and proceeded to make a lot of mistakes. I went back and talked with the executive leadership team, and we decided to move forward with just about everything we heard.

We launched our Monthly *Wind Down Wednesday* event, put in a nice gym area, installed some massage chairs versus the bean bag chairs, had cornhole tournaments, sectioned off a room with multiple ping pong tables, and subsidized our café to keep the food prices low.

Q. With your culture changes, what were the results after 12 months?

That is both fascinating and disappointing. Near the one-year mark, I couldn't wait to see how much things had changed. We collected data from their Employee Opinion Survey (EOS) and checked their *Glassdoor™* ratings; nothing changed. *Not one* of their key cultural measures made a significant difference.

Sure, we had more people playing ping pong, winning cornhole tournaments, and getting a nice rest in the massage chairs, but all of the key Culture KPIs remained the same. It didn't change our EOS or our *Glassdoor™* score. It basically just made work a little more fun.

To say it was disappointing to the leadership team would be an understatement. It was clear we didn't do something right, but we were not sure what it was.

Q. I'm sure you hit the road again to really figure it out. Share with us what happened.

To understand where things got off track, I had to revisit seven of the eleven companies I met with for benchmarking, but this time, something was different.

This time I met with their Presidents, CEOs, and Division Leaders and explained what and how we implemented the different activities, and the conversations went sideways from there. The key question I received was, *"What is your Culture?"*

My response was something around engagement, collaboration, fun, and people-focused. They all gave me some strange looks and asked to see the *Culture Model*. They lost me. What was a *Culture Model*?

The executive summary from that CEO tour was this,

"Happy Hour and Ping Pong tables don't make a Culture." Gulp! The lesson learned? Get the guts right—*not things*.

Think about it like a birthday cake. If the cake isn't right, the icing won't fix it. Culture is a set of behaviors and values that outline what your organization does and doesn't tolerate.

The other stuff is nice and is good to have when your *Culture Model* is in place, but it alone will not define your organizational goals or set the direction for how you lead the company. It seems we heard what we wanted to hear and missed some very big steps in the culture-building process.

> *Q. That's a huge awakening that the icing won't fix the cake. How did you change your organization's set of behaviors and values?*

It was important not to treat culture as just an *HR initiative*. It had to be a business process, and his team spent a disproportionate amount of time building an award-winning human resources infrastructure to ensure their ability to hire, engage, retain, and reward their top talent. Working on those key initiatives without a focus on culture was a big oversight.

We all know the best-recruiting strategy is retaining your people. When our primary foundation wasn't culture, we continued to see improvement. However, you notice that department silos still exist, leadership trust doesn't grow at the level you wanted, and while employee engagement improved, we had to work hard to maintain it.

The bottom-line business results fell short of what the leadership team expected, and the turnover rate was high. There was positive momentum, but the organization fell short of its overall goal of being the *Best Place to Work* company.

Q. Thanks for sharing your vulnerabilities. What secret did you need in your culture to make the breakthrough?

One critical ingredient to the *Best Place to Work* secret sauce was a plan to influence an intentional, distinctive culture that defines your organization's priorities, values, and behaviors and a high level of executive commitment to see it through. We had to go *back to the drawing board*.

We took the new research and the feedback from their survey to begin a two-year project designed to define the culture we aspired to have and align the executive team. The first focus area is a clearly defined culture. The next time someone asked me what our culture was, I wanted to be able to answer the question confidently. The executive team wanted to ensure our people came to work because they *wanted to*, not because they *had to*.

Q. Stephen, what did you spend the most time doing?

The executive team identified the company's mission, vision, values, and behaviors. This was the easy part of this process.

Panasonic™ has a set of seven principles that have been part of the company for many years. However, they were posted on a wall somewhere, but no one could articulate what they were or how they were important to our culture. These seven principles were very much aligned with the values we needed to have, but we had a lot of work to do to make them a part of who we were as a company.

Q. How did you do that?

Well, the real work came when the executive team met and began assigning behaviors with the Panasonic™ Principles. We went off-site as an executive team. We talked about the set of principles that had been on a wall for many years that nobody could contextualize. Then we said, "We're going to come up with some behaviors that match them."

One key message I heard during the last round of benchmarking was the need to involve *all of your employees* in the process of developing your culture model. That involvement translates into a high level of ownership and engagement.

One of the things we were told was not to let the executive come up with these behaviors. You've got to do that as a company. But we came up with our list first. Then we had meetings with all of our leaders and asked them, *what do you think are the most important behaviors that we should focus on as an organization?*

Next, we conducted a company-wide survey and asked what key behaviors we should consider as part of our new culture model. Then we took the consolidated version of what we heard and devised our seven behaviors. That's how we came up with the seven principles that *Panasonic™* really is.

The *Panasonic™* Automotive Culture Model includes these 7 core behaviors: *accountability, customer experience, learning agility, communication, engaging talent, influence, and courageous authenticity*.

The 7 principles are a contribution to society, fairness and honesty, cooperation and team spirit, untiring effort for improvement, courtesy and humility, adaptability, and gratitude.

Panasonic™ has put values on walls for years, and now we have matched them with seven key behaviors. We were able to establish the *Panasonic™* Automotive Culture Model. This culture model consisted of our Vision, Mission, seven behaviors, and seven principles.

It now shapes what is encouraged, discouraged, tolerated, and rejected. The defining of a culture needs a lot of care and attention. Once defined, it needs to be part of the company's DNA.

Q. Incredible! Stephen, what did you do to roll it out?

What we did next was probably the most important step in making this culture model work and continue to last. The executive team agreed that HR would not roll this out to the organization. That advice came through loud and clear from the other organizations that were highly successful.

It had to be implemented by the entire executive team. This meant that all executives had to take a high level of accountability for this model and be the spokesperson for their team.

When employees hear the cultural message from their functional leader versus it being rolled out like a PTO (personal time off) policy, the engagement and attention paid to its success are much higher.

We brought in leaders from around the country into a huge room, and the President introduced this new cultural model. He explained that this model would set the tone for what would and would not be tolerated. He explained the whole leadership team would be the custodian of this new model.

Q. Stephen, what did the President have to say?

The new model was explained in detail, and best practices were discussed. Something really powerful took place as well. They discussed the opportunity to *give leaders an out*.

I asked the room full of leaders, "Who wants to have a real relationship with their team?" After a joke or two about how having a relationship with your employee is against company policy, we dug into that question. Very few seemed excited to change the way they managed their teams. Our new model reflected the changes we wanted to see in leaders. The new model built strong relationships within the team and ensured each member's success.

I told the room full of leaders regardless of what they were told when they were hired, their new role would consist of these new leadership activities and processes. It didn't matter if we hired you one week ago, five years ago, or fifteen years ago. Here's what we care about going forward. We had to create a new leadership model that reflected the new culture.

Q. That is so true that leadership must reflect the culture. What was one of the keys to making this work?

One of the keys to the new model is increasing communication. At *Panasonic*™ Automotive, we have a saying now: "It's all about the conversation." We explained it wasn't about doing all of these new leadership activities perfectly; it was about communicating with your team and starting to do better.

Then we explained we would give them a lot of training over the next year, and the only expectation we had was for them to keep working towards improvement. Then we gave them an out. We explained that since we were changing the nature of the job, we also gave each manager the option of getting out of the leadership position without any negative effect.

Q. Stephen, how do you make building relationships within the team a primary objective?

We told leadership moving forward we're going to ask you to have a relationship with your team. You have to be responsible for the people in your charge, not be in charge. We explained the accountability model and that we would hold them accountable to this new model, and we knew this change wouldn't be easy.

We said, "Look, a lot of you are really going to suck at this at first. That's okay." We did a bait and switched on them. We said, "All we're asking you is that if you want to stay in this leadership job, you go into it knowing this is what we want you to get better at, and we'll help you get better. We'll train you."

Q. How did you help them to "get better?"

We brought in training and support to help retrain leaders. They reframed how they were evaluating leaders. We basically said, "If you're going to be successful in this organization, you have got to care about your employees."

Think about high potential development, their succession plan, their role, clarity, organizational design and development, and talking to them and getting to know them at a personal level. We built that all into their performance management process.

We also said, "We'll give you some grace. We're all going to figure out how to do this better." About six months later, we said, "Now, we'll still keep training you on these new leadership competencies, but if anybody is not meeting these behavior requirements, you're not going to be here. You've had plenty of time to get accustomed to what we're saying from a behavior standpoint."

"We care fifty-one percent about how you do it and forty-nine percent about what you do. Your job and technical expertise are important, but we care more about how you do it." Then we said, "If you're not going to do it to these behaviors and values, you're not going to be here."

Q. Stephen, I bet that was a tough conversation. What happened?

Some of our leaders took us up on our offer early on and moved them into individual contributor roles. Then we made believers out of a few who didn't get on board.

We started taking action on the behaviors we said we wouldn't tolerate. Trust formed, and the employees started to take personal accountability in ensuring behavior issues were visible. With this new visibility, we had many conversations with our leaders to help them align with the new models.

For the ones that did not align, we parted ways. Firing employees who didn't adjust to the new culture was critical for the journey's success.

Q. Stephen, with all that change in leadership, can you share a specific story that helps cement the culture shift for your employees?

Sure. One leader who other people called the *smartest person in the room* was definitely that, but he wasn't the brightest. After many conversations about his harsh and critical leadership style, he never made any real attempt to change.

He assumed he was indispensable because of his high-level technical ability and connections in the industry. This was a bad assumption on his side. After the President and I got the legal okay to terminate him for bad culture, we also explained the reason for the termination—he was a butthole.

We literally branded the termination. However, our language was not as nice as that. We explained we had a new culture standard in our company and anyone who didn't want to align would not be working for us. We basically said, "We've created a *no asshole policy* and we wouldn't tolerate anyone not willing to get on board." Then we terminated his employment, wished him the best, and announced it to the employees.

Q. WOW! That is bold. You didn't mess around.

That's right. We warned it might get worse before it gets better. Over the next six months, they terminated twenty-six people at all levels in the organization for being a serious culture fit problem.

The terminations were very powerful as they built a lot of trust within the organization. People understood how committed they were to culture change. That we are fully committed to making this new culture work for all of us.

If they were not interested in joining us in this new culture of putting people first, we would be more than willing to help them find a new role somewhere else; that is exactly what we did. After that, people got on board. They knew we were not just rolling out some flavor-of-the-day culture model and that we really meant it.

Q. Stephen, I assume that the new leadership model was followed. What happened with management and the hiring process?

We needed *Panasonic*™ Automotive to update its performance management and hiring processes to reflect the same.

We learned a little bit about how the brain responds to feedback and how to change that to improve the overall experience and engagement. Performance conversations can be hard and scary because you don't always know what you will get as an employee. Or maybe you do know what you're going to hear, and you're scared to hear it.

We had to make their *People Process* as transparent as possible. In prior employee opinion surveys, it became apparent people thought our Enhanced Development program for our inspiring leaders was secretive. So, we created playbooks for each key process that explained what we did, how we did it, and why it was important.

Q. I'm sure it was imperative everyone was on the same page with the new expectations.

Yes, you are absolutely right. We decided to brand the behaviors and principles through a series of 90 Day Learning Sprints. At *Panasonic*™ Automotive, creating the *Best Place to Work* culture has been a top priority and is key to our success moving forward. These sprints were a company-wide initiative, and we focused on a single behavior or principle every 90 days. Our executive team delivered the workshops.

Q. What about the hiring process? How did you change the focus of their interviews?

We created a whole new interview process based on the culture model. We spent 50 percent of the time during interviews on culture. The other part we spent on their technical capabilities.

Q. Stephen, what was the key to getting it to work?

Simple, trust was the key. Now, because it was simple, it was not easy, but we did it. Holding all levels of the organization accountable and changing people processes made a difference. That dramatically changed everything for us. It changed our employee opinion survey. Leadership and trust went from almost last to first. We were very transparent about everything.

One way we accomplished this was by creating internal playbooks. We basically pulled out each process and matched it to the culture model.

We took all of our people processes and turned them into playbooks. Everybody knew exactly how we did what we did and why we did it. Then we went on tour. We went to every facility and let people just ask questions about our processes while going through the culture. From then on, we just kept supporting it more and more.

Q. What happened during COVID?

Interesting that you would ask that. The results and impact of the trust we have built and earned showed up in big ways during the Covid-19 pandemic.

When Covid-19 hit in March 2020, they shut down a big portion of our business. It was pretty dismal.

We said, "Look, we're going to have to do something. We literally couldn't build anything. We were going to have to look at some furloughs and pay cuts, just like many other companies. So, how are we going to do it?"

We pulled out our culture model and said, "Here's what we're going to do. We're going to over-communicate with all employees about what we're doing, why we're doing it, and why we need to do this."

We shared what our business looked like, what we were thinking, and how we would handle pay cuts. We took almost all the pay cuts at the top and then worked down a few levels. At some levels, we didn't do any big cuts—and we avoided the ones that would hurt the most.

We understood the cuts would hit everybody differently. For furloughs, we just highly communicated why we had to do this. We went through the whole process. We cut people's pay. We did the furloughs.

Then October came. We were going to put everything back the way it was. But at the same time, we had our EOS survey that was due to come up. We said, "Man, we're going to get hammered on this employee opinion survey because it has been such a bad year." Some companies decided just to skip the year and say it was an anomaly.

We decided we were going to do it. We wanted to hear how we did during this timeframe. We went through the EOS survey, and when we got it back, it was the best EOS survey we ever had in the worst possible year we've ever had as a company.

This told us very clearly—it's not about how *well you're doing*; it's how *well* you're *managing that culture model* with your employees that matters because that was our best EOS survey. That, to us, was telling us we did something right. The last four or five years we worked on this thing wasn't in vain. It made a huge difference.

Q. This is incredible. All of that firing, hiring, and leadership changing also prepared you for a global pandemic that no one could have predicted. Amazing. What about a growth mindset? What can it do for a leader/business?

I believe that having a growth mindset is a key element to success. Today companies are increasingly required to adapt to new technologies and processes—and emphasize innovation. Smart business leaders know they must focus on innovation to make their organization genuinely stand out.

When you attempt to promote innovation, there's a need to shift workers' more traditional mindsets to encourage creativity and new ideas. Fear of failure or lack of risk-taking prevents people from getting creative. Employees can be hesitant to *break the mold* and try something new because of the fear of judgment.

Once employees realized it wasn't just them being held accountable to the new standards—that management was accountable also—the change took hold.

If you spend any time on change, the hardest piece is just getting the executive team to agree that they will do this together. They don't all have to agree on every part of the culture model, but at the end of the day, they must agree that there will be a culture model. They have to own it as an executive team.

It can't be launched from HR. Your HR processes need to become business processes. Culture is a business process. If they say it's important to the president, and they say it's important to all the executives, and they talk about it in their meetings, everybody will be in. Number one is getting that executive leadership team, not a communication team, to do it. It's not about a branded launch for some initiative.

The executive team becomes the branding mechanism for which this culture model must be infused into your business. Then you get all your employees involved. That isn't how most people try to run their culture. I always get called by companies with a culture that isn't working.

It's because they asked HR or their communication team to go launch this thing. They asked HR to talk about training and performance management. Every bit of that should be talked about by those functional leaders in the business when you do that; the priorities just change for the employees. It's a huge buy-in when all those things become business processes.

Q. Stephen, can you launch a new culture model and then forget about it?

Are you kidding? No way. You can't just launch and forget it. You have to make sure everyone hears the same message continually, and you have the plan to deal with those who don't come on board.

Every year we launch it again. We start the year with the three most important things and how we will do it. They know these are the behaviors and values we will use to do these three things. We're all pulling on the same rope with the same cultural narrative for every group.

Everybody's tied to those behaviors and values in their performance. It's hard to steer away from that cultural model. And when somebody does, because maybe they're not fully bought in, it becomes really apparent. It gets escalated back up through the chain of command quickly, so we can either get them on board, or we help them find a place, hopefully with one of our competitors so that they can ruin their culture.

We'll be glad to help you transition out. That's part of the conversation we have. It's hard to get off track if everybody has the same compass.

I really like that, "It's hard to get off track if everybody has the same compass." It's a powerful insight. For me, the willingness of the company to transition someone out for culture says a lot. I think it's important for employees to understand the expectations and behaviors a company believes will move them toward success. Employees who are not in alignment with the company's culture can keep others from fully embracing the culture change leadership is building. It is essential for a business to have an environment where individuals representing diverse backgrounds and perspectives feel welcomed, respected, and appreciated. However, allowing people who do not adhere to the agreed-upon values of the organization, or those who actively work against it, compromises both company morale as well as its overall success. By removing people who do not fit within the organization's culture, leaders are able to create a safe space where employees can collaborate without fear of negative reinforcement or judgment from other team members. In the end, this leads to more meaningful relationships, open dialogue, an increase in creativity and productivity, and ultimately more success in achieving organizational goals.

CHAPTER 16:

A Purpose-Driven Culture— The Cooperative Way

As the author, I want to introduce you to my industry and bring you into my cooperative world. People who have worked with me know I drank the co-op *Kool-Aid* and never looked back.

I want you to know where my mindset and experience come from. I think this will help you to understand why I wrote this book, *Culture Secrets*. I have seen the positive power that culture plays in the lives of my colleagues and the members of the more than 900 electric cooperatives in the United States. It's a purpose-driven culture where the V.A.L.U.E. Culture was built as part of our founding principles. In other words, we have a member-first, service mindset.

Now, let's get the meeting—ahem—reading started, and what better way than to share the seven principles of cooperatives worldwide? All cooperatives are built and operate under a set of seven principles. These principles are a crucial part of the cooperative model and are essential to their success. They serve as the foundation for the values and practices of cooperatives around the world, no matter their product or service. By following these principles, cooperatives are able to provide their members with fair and equitable economic benefits while creating positive social and economic impacts in their communities.

1. **Voluntary and Open Membership**—open to all persons able to use their services and willing to accept the responsibilities of membership, without gender, social, racial, political, or religious discrimination.

2. **Democratic Member Control**—cooperatives are controlled by their members, who actively set their policies and make decisions. Cooperative members have equal voting rights (one member, one vote).

3. **Member Economic Participation**—members contribute equitably to and democratically control the capital of their cooperative. Some part of that capital is usually the common property of the cooperative. Members may allocate surpluses for developing their cooperative, setting up reserves, benefiting members in proportion to their transactions with the cooperative, or supporting activities approved by the membership.

4. **Autonomy and Independence**—cooperatives are autonomous, self-help organizations controlled by their members.

5. **Education, Training, and Information**—cooperatives provide education and training for their members, elected representatives, managers, and employees so they can contribute effectively to developing their cooperatives. They inform the public about the cooperative form of business.

6. **Cooperation among Cooperatives**—cooperatives work together through local, national, regional, and international structures to serve their members.

7. **Concern for Community**—cooperatives work for the betterment of their communities through policies approved by their members.

The cooperative principles benefit communities in a number of ways, including economic development, job creation, and building social capital by creating a network of people who are committed to working together for mutual benefit. These principles lead to stronger, more resilient communities and are a powerful attractor to this incoming workforce.

Let's return to what my friend from *The Cooperative Way*™, Adam Schwartz, says about the cooperative business model.

Q. Adam, let's get right to the point. Can you share with us how cooperatives are positioned perfectly to compete for high-caliber talent and be even more successful in the coming years?

If I could just wave the wand, we would learn about the cooperative business model in school, in every country in the world. This would be something that would be taught, and it would be taught multiple times at different grades.

Curriculums have been developed from kindergarten through twelfth grade. Then there are college-level and graduate-level courses about co-ops. So that work has already been done. It exists; it is just not widely used.

Q. That's true, so how can you get more people to see and understand the potential of this business model?

Great question. Education in school and of course the stories from the 40,000 plus co-ops that already exist in the USA alone. I have a story to share about this. There was a business roundtable group that met in August 2019.

I'm talking about *JP Morgan*™, *Apple*™, and the who's-who Fortune 100 companies all came out with this meeting with a huge pronouncement. Those investor-held companies needed to do more than just care about the stock price. They finally said, "They need to care about their employees, customers, the community, and the environment." I think I was just like, *Um, hello. Of course, you need to do that!* I just sat there with an open mouth like Duh! I remember thinking to myself? *Okay, it only took you 125 years to figure that out.*

TELLING THE RIGHT STORY

Remember earlier, in section 2, chapter 8, when you learned visionary leaders use the power of story to convey their purpose, values, and expectations? Stories are also a great way to ensure the larger public- potential employees, clients, vendors- understands the story of your business, and, when used correctly, can help potential employees connect with your values.

Now, I love sharing stories, and here's one for you that has a little history for you—after all, I'm sharing about my cooperative that has shaped my understanding and the way I work, so grab a glass of sweet tea, and I'll plunge in.

Electric cooperatives have done an extraordinary job of creating and sharing their story, and their culture positions them to be highly competitive going forward. Their origin story allows you to root for a group of self-resilient underdogs who took on big corporations to do something that improved the lives of their friends and neighbors.

Until the mid-1930s, nine out of ten homes in rural America functioned without electricity. No electricity made life even more challenging on the heels of the *Great Depression*.

The lack of electricity kept these communities almost entirely dependent on agriculture for income. Now there's nothing wrong with that, but to move into more opportunities, technology, like electricity, can speed things up.

Those not able to access electricity were left in the dark. So much so that factories and businesses chose to locate in cities where electric power was accessible and stay out of the communities that lacked electricity.

Whether you agree with it or not, in the 1930s, The New Deal, provocated by President Franklin D. Roosevelt provided the backbone for groups of residents to join together to form each local electric cooperative to bring power to the under-served areas big, investor-owned organizations wouldn't touch.

It wasn't about generating profits. It was about powering the lives of their members and giving them access to technology that allowed them to work more efficiently and change their economic outlook and opportunities. Electric cooperatives are service providers that level the playing field.

Cooperatives are member-owned and member-governed. Profits aren't shipped off to investors who don't even live in the communities receiving power. These purpose-driven initiatives are still vital almost 100 years later.

The *National Rural Electric Cooperative Association*™ is a trade association representing over 900 local electric cooperatives that power 42 million Americans. *Touchstone Energy*™ is a national network of 700 electric cooperatives across 45 states providing research, communication resources, and employee training programs to help their members better engage and serve their members.

As national associations representing electric cooperatives, they are uniquely positioned to talk about the culture, strengths, and challenges facing their members because, remember, electricity is a service that allows people to improve their lives, just like running water and good food.

At this time, I think it's crucial to bring my friend Jana Adams back from section two to the interview chair. Jana Adams is with *Touchstone Energy Cooperative™*, a huge part of America's electric cooperative, to ask her some key questions and share the secrets of cooperative culture with you.

Q. Jana, what are the challenges facing America's electric cooperatives today?

The workforce is aging, and many co-op employees across all levels are either within five years of retirement or past their eligible retirement age. From a practical matter, you have to create an environment that new generations want to come to because there's a need, just out of sheer numbers.

My friend Scott Peterson, at the *National Rural Electric Cooperative Association (NRECA™)*, said, "There's so much transition in our workforce, as there is in so many other workforces, that I think the big challenge for us is having that *co-op culture permeate that transition and workforce*. Not so much at the upper levels, but as folks come into the co-op."

Q. That is telling, Jana. How do electric cooperatives change?

Well, co-ops haven't been immune to workforce challenges, especially following the Covid-19 pandemic. Personally, I was a very early adopter of remote work. I have worked from home multiple days a week for nearly three decades.

I believe that it can have an incredibly positive influence on culture. Here's why. When you are no longer working at the same desk, five days a week, eight or nine hours a day, *work becomes your output, not your environment*. Too often, when you've got a traditional structure where everybody comes to the same office five days a week, work is simply being there.

You can see productivity drops because it doesn't matter

what you're doing; you're there and working. You can see a very positive shift simply by opening some flexibility. Covid-19 has made that a requirement. I don't see a scenario that goes back to the predominant model, being five days a week sitting in an office or a building.

Q. Jana, Doesn't that open new challenges?

Yes, the challenges that you face are in building connections and collaborating across projects. We've got a bunch of tools, collaborative tools. We are big users of the office tool, Slack™. I can get a response from any team member a thousand times faster than if I had to stand up and walk to an office on the other side of the hallway.

It's an immediate collaborative tool that works well for us. We've got other productivity tools that help keep us aligned on what everyone's working on. You don't have to all be sitting in a room sharing here's my update on the big things I've got going on. It's all in our system.

We use a system called *Monday.com*™(²). It is flexible and helpful to build those collaborative teams around different projects. One area where I think it's important to have an in-person process is in managers. It's hard to manage remotely fully.

Q. Jana, if you can't fully manage it remotely, what do you do?

Well, that's an area that we've been evolving. I need to have a better connection with those management points. So, we all come into the office on Tuesdays. We do all our in-person stuff, then. It gets us connected. We see each other. We have those conversations that are incredibly important in developing a shared culture.

It's not just about the work. It's a balance of having that in-person time. Obviously, things like Teams™ and Zoom™ have made remote face-to-face much easier and more successful. One of the challenges I think everybody's going to have to get better at, ourselves included, are hybrid meetings, where there's a big chunk of people in-person, and a chunk of people are virtual.

I don't think those are as effective for the virtual folks because the regular banter happens in person, and it's hard to engage. Technology has enabled it. Circumstances with Covid-19 have required it. I think co-ops, and every industry, must embrace the ability to have different workplace models.

Jana mentioned our friend, Scott Peterson, now retired from the *National Rural Electric Cooperative Association (NRECA)*™, and I wanted to ask him a similar question.

Q. Scott, one success factor of how effective electric cooperatives have been is to tie their origin story with what's important to today's workers and members. Do you feel that's true?

Having come into the cooperative world from another part of the utility sector, I know it's very different. Everybody says they have a customer focus, but when you have a member focus, it drives a different set of behaviors and commitments you're making.

With the spotlight on broadband access or the lack of access, electric cooperatives are primed to be again the ones who deliver a vital service to underserved areas. I think that's no more evident than in broadband.

Where other companies have come in and taken big census blocks and provided broadband and left those lower population areas out of the mix, and here come co-ops again, eighty years later from providing electricity, trying to reach that end-of-the-line member. I think what that does from the member's standpoint is build credibility and trust.

Many other entities would love to have that relationship, but they don't demonstrate what it takes to get it. And at a time when trust is lagging, and distrust, I would say, is the predominant emotion in the relationship that we have with many of our providers or other companies.

That trust factor from the cooperative to the member is such a fundamental point of building and maintaining that relationship. And that only works if you're [new employees] coming into the cooperative and being sort of inducted into that cooperative system of values.

I believe the fact that cooperatives are formed on a set of principles allows them to connect with their membership and with potential employees. After talking with Scott, I wondered what Holly Wetzel, the senior director of marketing for *NRECA*™, would say if I asked her a few questions about future workforce challenges cooperatives could face.

Q. Holly, what is the one challenge that electric cooperatives face?

That's simple; it's the longevity found in our workforce. It's challenging and also a good problem to have. The tenure of employees in the cooperative network is so long because people who came into it fell in love with the culture. They fell in love with the community focus. They fell in love with what they were doing and the values and principles that drive the work.

You have people who've been in these positions for decades,

and then as large swaths of them are retiring, you have a new crop of folks coming in. We're also seeing the general shake-up and reshuffling of the workforce that has followed the pandemic. So, many new people are coming in, and there's a pull between the tenured and the new.

Q. Holly that is interesting. It feels like if we could appease both groups then there might be some hope.

True. Learning how to get those groups working together and ensuring an effective knowledge transfer is key. It's an issue other industries are dealing with also. I mean, how do you get a new crop of employees to buy into that aspect of cooperatives that makes us unique?

Our community focus, our difference of culture, it's probably something new to them. We've built our young adult member engagement program to address all the things that matter to today's employees and members. For employees, one key aspect we focus on is this opportunity to be part of a mission-driven organization that shares its values.

Being a mission-driven organization is something people, especially those newer to the workforce—like Millennials—and even Gen X care a lot about and are looking for when they are choosing where to work. We want the tools we need to do our job and leadership opportunities, but we also want to work for a place we really can get behind and believe in if we spend more than half our lives there. Co-ops have that quality.

Yet, we must modernize how we present that to potential employees. As we're out there telling that story to potential hires in the marketplace, employer branding is important. We have to not only reiterate the cooperative difference and community focus but couple that with the story of innovation that's happening in the industry.

That's a potent combination. We must mix it correctly to make that secret sauce and live up to our ideals and make them relevant for the next generation of employees coming in. And once we get them in, we have to walk the walk. We have to welcome new perspectives, make collaboration easy, engage employees in innovation, and provide the flexibility and community folks of all ages are looking for. I think that's the challenge, finding a secret sauce that works across the generations and the tenures of the people already in the industry. As the workforce continues to get younger, I see great opportunities for us to adapt while still holding on to what makes a co-op unique.

Millennials, also known as *Generation Y*, are often characterized as a generation that prioritizes work-life balance and purpose in their careers. Purpose comes when they find alignment with their personal values and beliefs and those of the company they choose to work for. By understanding and addressing these priorities, employers can create a work environment that appeals to the Gen Y demographic and attract top talent from this generation. I asked Scott Peterson, with *NRECA™*, what he thought about the idea of electric cooperatives being well-positioned for the future workforce.

Q. Scott, how are electric cooperatives positioned to be aligned with the wants of the next-generation workforce?

The *next generation workforce is coming in with those mission-driven values.* So, we're fortunate with recruitment to have that alignment. I think the difference and the opportunity for that group of employees coming in are they understand the needs and desires, particularly from a member outreach perspective of where many co-op members are now.

While their expectations of what the co-op is delivering, regarding reliability, transparency, and honesty, how that's delivered to the members is changing. And it's changed rapidly. It's gone from a lot of face-to-face interaction to a lot of interaction on digital platforms. How you manage that and keep that relationship becomes critical.

Just as Scott alluded to, I believe electric cooperatives are uniquely positioned to appeal to the next generation worker especially when cooperatives build internal cultures that address career development and work-life balance concerns that allow employees to manage their work and personal lives effectively. Jana, with *Touchstone Energy*™, also had some insights on the next generation of workers and how to find out what works for them.

Q. Jana, what is one thing you do well when it comes to the next-generation workforce?

One of the things we do well is to collect examples of what works. We partnered with *NRECA*™ to create the framework for young adult member engagement, which looks externally at your member-owner base and internally at your employee base.

With that framework, we've got good materials to help drive those initiatives forward. At *Touchstone Energy*™, what we do best is connect people. We're all about relationships, whether it's internally within the co-op, between co-ops, or between co-ops and their member-owners.

Q. Jana, have you had an aha moment with the concept of culture?

You bet I have. Just last August (2021), I had an "aha moment" at the CEO *Close-Up Conference*. There was a breakout session just for new CEOs to chat. And being a new CEO and wanting to hear from them, I joined in.

By a huge margin, the number one issue that they knew they needed to address was the culture of their co-op. Co-ops are positioned for the future, and I think it's happening almost organically because of new employees, whether it's CEOs or others coming into co-ops. There's a good foundation there. I think the co-op model is very relevant today.

It works. It's attractive across generations. But just like any organization, things get stuck. And you don't always incorporate new ways of thinking, ideas, or processes. They recognize they need to take that foundation of goodness, a cooperative business model, and make it relevant to today's workforce.

Q. What would you say comes first?

Culture comes first. Everybody says it, *but the strategy is downstream of culture.* You can have the best idea and the best strategy in the world, but if you don't have a culture that's receptive to that new way of doing things, it's going to fail. They know to be successful; they've got to have a culture that's willing to try new things and one that's willing to make mistakes. Going forward, how to best serve member-owners today may not be how we served them fifty-plus years ago.

As a leader, *knowing your purpose* allows you to stay relevant for years to come and appeal to today's workforce. That allows you to attract the type of people you want to employ who will continue your values and mission. I know because, in my career, I have seen how the people who keep a member-first mindset are the most successful. When I interview, I always include questions that reflect our core values to see how a potential candidate demonstrates those currently in their life.

Being able to shift the narrative in a way that doesn't change what you do or the heart of what you're about but reframes it in a way that speaks to today's world will be a huge benefit as companies compete for talent. Learning how to balance the fundamental understanding of the core values with the excitement of a changing industry will be a challenge that leaders must face head-on. When I asked Scott Peterson about the challenges leaders in the electric cooperative industry face, he had this to say on the topic.

> **Q. Scott, for electric cooperatives, how do you shift the narrative in a way that doesn't change the heart of what you do?**

For electric cooperatives, when you're talking about reframing it for potential employees to get the workforce you want, I think it is the same story presented through a different lens. It must be mission-focused and mission-driven. It must be focused on providing full value to the member at the end of the line. I think a big difference is now we want you to think innovatively about how to do that.

While so much of what we're doing is changing, the fundamentals are the same. We're still delivering the same product, electricity, with the same level of expectation that our members want and expect. What's changing is how we manage the relationship. We must continue giving employees a fundamental understanding of the cooperative mission while giving them the excitement of coming in and changing the way that we engage. I think that's a challenge for leadership.

Q. Scott, what is a big part of that challenge?

The challenge is providing new employees with the foundation of what the co-op mission is all about, but also giving them the sense that this landscape has changed. It's changed quite a bit. It's going to continue to change as our industry does.

We need leaders who can think differently about how to engage our membership and how to engage our communities in ways that are different today than they were ten years ago, and they will be different ten years from now than they are today.

It is up to today's cooperative leadership to tell the cooperative story in a way new employees connect with the co-op mission. I needed to get back to *Touchstone Energy's*™ Jana Adams and find out if she thought that our cooperative culture was value-based.

Q. Jana, Do you think that culture is value-based?

I honestly think our culture is 100% value-based. I don't know how you can have a positive culture without looking at the values that you share. And fundamental is trust, honesty, and loyalty; all those base needs that everyone has to be able to come together and be productive and successful as a group.

If you don't have those, you can't build a culture. I think the first step is defining that culture. I fear we're at a point where it means something different to everyone. You must have a shared definition among your leadership team.

If you're hearing and seeing there's an issue with culture,

you need to get the stakeholders within your organization together and define what that means to everybody. It could be a productivity issue.

There could be some negative undercurrents of people not being honest, or people not being good stewards of their resources or their job. You must figure it out and then you have to define what it is you want.

Once you understand and define that cultural challenge, then you can start to address it because it would be aligned. We're stronger if we work together and collaboratively. And here's our plan to make that happen. But it starts with digging in on that shared definition of what the challenge is.

Q. Jana, how do you define your culture?

You begin defining your culture by pulling people from across your organization. It can't be led from the top. It's got to be up and down the organization. To borrow social media language, who are the influencers in your organization? Who are the ones that people listen to?

You know the ones the room quiets down for when their hand goes up. You need to get those folks together, but also the quiet people who are the ones absorbing some of the potentially negative cultures that are happening.

Then you've got to get everybody on board with that shared understanding of exactly what we are trying to do here. Have that group be your ambassadors within your full employee base. Without that, it's very, very hard to be successful.

I agree that successful culture implementations can't only be driven from the top. You need to bring in people from across the organization if you want buy-in to be successful. After listening to Jana, I had another question for Holly Wetzel, with *NRECA*™, about whether today's leaders understand what today's workforce values.

Q. Holly, do you think that part of that leadership shift is knowing what today's workforce values and making sure the words and actions match?

I think we have to look at what today's employees value and how they look at work. Wanting work that aligns with your values is important. The opportunity to innovate is exciting. I think the energy industry is exciting. That helps in positioning. It depends on where the co-op is on that spectrum of evolution when we talk about innovation.

In terms of walking the walk, we can look at the research that we have done and our ACSI (American Consumer Satisfaction Index™) scores. There is a ton of research out there about what folks are looking for in work.

Ours is not a different story at its core; it's just shifting the way we talk about it. And when we shift the way we talk about it, to focus a little bit more on community, to focus a little bit more on innovation, to focus more on values, I don't think we're alienating our older audiences. We're telling the same story in a slightly new way.

The community focus is a key component of the cooperative culture. Holly's words made me think of something Jana said in her interview I needed to bring to your attention.

Q. Jana, in all the studies out there about millennials and Gen Z coming into the workforce, what is it they want more of?

In all of these studies, their *number one need* is to feel like they're doing *meaningful work*.

Co-ops have that, and I think it is an unused attractor. I don't think that we leverage that nearly enough. We focus more on providing essential services to our community. We don't talk about all the other things that co-ops do, but I think we should.

I think that is a huge part of what makes this community so special. You have your day job, and your day job might be keeping the lights on or whatever your role is in the co-op. Yet there are so many other ways you touch and embrace your community that we should honestly lead with that.

The fact that electricity is the base, but it's all the other things the local cooperative does that share that story of why it's a special business model. That's one of the things that certainly comes out in our research at *Touchstone Energy*™; we need to be more forward-looking with those activities.

I hope you're taking in all of these amazing lessons. Our conversation on the newest generations entering the workforce reminded me of something Adam Schwartz said. He said, "Leaders must always be enforcing the why we're doing this. It's not just about kilowatt hours, it's about quality of life. And I think we can make that connection that we're here for, you know, a slightly larger purpose than just selling a commodity. I think we will do better with productivity and connection with employees."

That "why" is what creates the personal connection and attracts people to your organization.

MY WORK MAKES A DIFFERENCE

I know my cooperative world positions employees to see how their work impacts the lives of members and the communities served. Our purpose is key to growing employee engagement. Engagement turns your employees into brand ambassadors and is what keeps them fully vested in the day-to-day activities of work. Yet, there are some areas where work still needs to be done. I wanted to get more of Holly Wetzel's insights on how electric cooperatives are engaging their workforce.

Q. Holly, how does the cooperative world position employees to make sure they engage?

One key is employee engagement. *You can't attract new people into your culture if it isn't real.* You may talk about a great game and sell this great brand, but if it's not real, they will not stay.

Q. Holly, who are your biggest ambassadors?

That's easy. Our employees are the biggest ambassadors for the co-op brand, with potential employees and our members because they're in the community alongside them. They're talking about how it is to work at the co-op. If the personal experience doesn't match the story that we're telling, we're not going to have much luck getting the type of people that we want.

I couldn't agree more with Holly on how our story has to match the experience an employee has when they join the ranks of an electric cooperative. Matching the experience is one of the keys to building strong engagement. I asked Scott Peterson from the *NRECA*™ to share his own challenge with building employee engagement as a manager.

Q. Scott, how do you keep your employees engaged at NRECA™?

Well, that's a great question. Employee engagement is a challenge here (*NRECA™*) as well as at a lot of cooperatives in terms of professional growth or movement.

It's usually our weakest rating in terms of how we advance people. When you look at other workplace cultures, it's not so much moving up as it's moving laterally and giving employees new experiences and other leadership opportunities.

Q. Scott, what does recruiting for the sake of culture require?

Recruiting for culture requires a shift in thinking and for management to do some great modeling. I mean. It's a good thing to shake up an organization occasionally, whether that's from the top or somewhere in the middle. You have to have people think differently.

People will only change if the culture is supportive of that change—and that comes from leadership modeling it. *If the leadership doesn't model it, there's no change coming.* I've seen that happen. Leadership must drive it down, modeling it every year.

I think there is an opportunity in the co-ops for that to happen. Tenure makes it difficult if your leadership is on a forty- or forty-five-year run. That typically is not going to happen until there's a leadership change.

For some co-ops, we're seeing stagnation in leadership, and when that leader retires, then that co-op jumps forward. Why? Because of new leadership coming in and driving innovation, challenging staff to think differently and behave differently. Then suddenly, you see a co-op starts to move quickly.

Tenure is a big issue with some co-ops, particularly small-size co-ops. Numbers matter in terms of what you can do there from a transitional standpoint and a change management staff standpoint.

I've seen longevity in the electric co-op world since I began my career there. It's not unusual to have employees with 35, 40, or even 50 years of service. That makes it difficult to convince younger employees there is an opportunity for advancement inside our walls which is one of today's worker key drivers. Scott made me think of more Holly had to say when it came to retaining and attracting great talent.

Q. Holly, can you tell me how taking a critical look at internal culture is a must as companies prepare to compete for talent today?

Absolutely. We need to be looking critically at our internal culture as it is and how we can enhance it. We need to increase connections across departments, increase communication, and increase people's connection to a shared mission. People feel galvanized around a shared mission when they understand where the connection points are between the work that they're all doing and the people they are serving.

We need to pay attention to where we're out there recruiting, too. Because if people come in and reality doesn't match what we sold, they are going to leave.

After what Holly said, I thought about how cooperatives and other industries must understand how culture impacts the member or customer experience. It is the key to recruiting new leadership. I went back to ask Scott Peterson what he thought about it.

Q. Scott, I want to know how culture creates amazing customer experiences. What do you have to say about it?

Well, for cooperatives, and other industries, understanding how culture impacts the member or customer experience is key as new leaders are recruited.

We've done a lot of research, and the core values in terms of what members want are reliability and low cost. But then it's transparency and honesty they want from their co-op. If there's a third factor I would be recruiting for as a leader, it would be a demonstration of being responsive to your members.

If you think about the experience, or at least the experience that I have now in any relationship with a merchant, its customer responsiveness is sorely lacking. We've heard that responsiveness is key and that transcends all ages.

Q. I agree. It is not associated with only this generation or that generation. People want responsiveness.

Right, all generations want to be heard and responded to. That's just humanity. They don't want to deal with a *bot*. It's insulting, and it's not a satisfactory experience. So, even in engineering, the experience still needs to be as personal as it can be with your members.

You need to have responsiveness as a core value, whether that's timing or whether that's a personal experience. That's one of the elements if you're a member-driven organization you better have.

One way to show all generations *they have value in the workplace is to invest in their personal and professional development.* It's been commonplace for electric co-ops to provide training for their line crews, research and development, engineering departments, and other technical areas, but today's workers want to see themselves as part of the organization's success.

Now there is a movement to focus on better communication and leadership skills throughout the co-op. We need to learn our leadership, and we need to be able to spread it throughout the organization.

I wanted to know more from Scott Peterson about this, so I asked some more compelling questions.

Q. Scott, do you think that there is greater attention being invested in employees than before?

Yes, I do. I think there is greater attention being paid to development further down into the organization than there has been in the past. We've seen that here at *NRECA*™, just through greater attendance at lower levels of training, there is more diversity of groups coming into our Management Intern Program.

We're being asked to train on a more diverse set of topics across the board. I want to go back to a point on identifying the roles of more junior people in the organization. One of the things I was thinking about was we ask our employees [at *NRECA*™] to find themselves in our strategic plan. It's designed to orient some of their individual goals around meeting our strategic plan goals.

We drill that into our employees but seldom do we go back to those employees and recognize how they fit those successes in the strategic plan. We do that at the macro level. And we may even identify the leadership of a project that has succeeded. But I'm admitting this, as a manager, rarely do I go down to that individual level.

I rarely go up to someone and say, "Hey, Joe, that was a great job or piece of work you did on that project. I know you led that one piece that was fundamental to the success, what a great job."

We don't do that. I think that's a missed opportunity in

terms of highlighting the individual roles and having people feel they're a part of the success of the organization at a fundamental level. I think we all try to have those one-on-one opportunities with employees, but I'm counting the missed opportunities there because, as senior leaders, we stay at such a high level in those things.

It's true, unfortunately. It can be hard for leaders to stay in touch with each level of the organization because they do get stretched in many different directions. Time becomes a scarcity the further up the management ladder you move. To be a strong culture-building leader it's important you recognize the limitation and make an effort to make the time you do have with each employee meaningful.

Q. Scott, with that in mind, how can leaders effectively cast a vision for the future that excites employees and helps them feel valued and connected to the outcome?

I think a big part of that is repetition, and how you talk about priorities. How do you talk about your employee's role in those priorities? We do it in a department setting. I do it with a weekly priorities note.

Every Monday morning, I send a note that lists the weekly priorities for my groups. The team gets it, so they know the priorities we're working on. It shares some successes and some challenges. Since the shift due to the pandemic, it changed.

Now, I probably make thirty-five percent of those notes, non-goal notes. I add personal things I'm seeing in the industry, health, and wellness. I focus on making that a part of the overall approach to the team and bringing those non-project issues into those conversations. So doing that collectively as a team, down to the department level, down to the individual workgroup unit, and then one-on-one, to the extent you can do that.

I think all that repetition matters. It takes a lot of time. But as a leader, if you're going to build your team and embrace those strategies and demonstrate how you want them to work collaboratively within your group and with other groups, you've got to deliver that message consistently.

We must be intentional about the training and leading teams in the direction we want them to go. We need to be acknowledging success to the larger group of people within our group or within the collaborative teams that they're working in. I think it's an ongoing opportunity that we have as leaders to continuously communicate that in just about every way we can.

Q. How do you manage a culture change shift to help move the needle in your favor?

One way to move the needle in your favor is by looking at roadblocks you might encounter and planning for ways to move past them. Culture itself is one of them. And, if your overall culture isn't aligned with the steps you need to take to be successful in recruiting, onboarding, and maintaining the employees you want, that's a challenge as an individual leader.

You can take all those steps down that path to be successful. But if other senior leaders are acting in opposition to that, it makes it very difficult to be successful. So, having that commitment and alignment throughout the organization is key.

If you're going to build and maintain a culture conducive to recruiting and maintaining the workforce you want, this thousand feet view of your organization is an important thing from a leadership perspective. The other is investing in the team and time allocation.

It takes a while, but the results go back to the concept of human collateral and that we all want to be heard and responded to. Employees should never be looked at as just assets to be managed. This concept can lead to the creation of workplace silos if leaders are not mindful of how they treat their employees. When workers are used for short-term gains, or put into positions that do not match their skillset, morale can suffer and individuals may stop feeling like important members of the team. This can lead to conversations being cut off and a sense of disconnect from the rest of the organization. Over time, these silos can become more entrenched as workers begin to feel isolated and disregarded by their supervisors—thus leading to further fragmentation within the workplace and a lack of collaboration between different departments. I knew I needed to return to Holly and get the final insight from her about the challenges in leadership.

Q. Holly, I know one of the challenges you feel leaders face is the creation of silos in the workplace. Can you share what you mean by that?

Organizational silos are when we accidentally or purposefully have groups of experts separated by department, specialization, or location. I mean, it's a very common approach. However, the problem starts when employees not only have physical separation but when they also pursue department goals instead of company goals.

Q. Can it happen with co-ops?

Sure. It can happen within any organization and especially in utilities, or cooperatives, where there's an inside workforce and an outside workforce. But it could be that you've got technical people and non-technical people. Individuals can get in their world, with their people, or their tribe easily.

Fostering collaboration and breaking down those silos, starts with being clear about a vision, and the roles of everyone fulfilling that vision. It's the understanding of how departments connect. It goes back to how all our work supports the work of each of the other departments.

Driving toward this shared vision is creating opportunities for the departments to better engage and work with each other and understand the value that each department brings is one of the challenges and opportunities to create the culture that we want to have at our co-ops.

We asked our CEOs that attended *Power Exchange* one year, and that was the number one answer they gave. It happens naturally, without even really trying because of the nature of the work. It's very hard to get them to cross over and interact.

I'm not gonna lie. It is the challenge that's out there. Committing what you're going to try to address is the first step because it's easy to just keep going and let everybody do their job. If leadership acknowledges this is something we should address, that's the first step, at least.

I think Jana, Scott, Holly, and Adam shared a lot of thoughtful ideas and comments. I'm sure you had a few *deer-in-the-headlight* looks if you saw your organization in what these leaders have shared. The great news is you know where to begin making changes to have some massive impact. The biggest key to take away from the cooperative success model is a *member-first, service mindset*. Holly, Jana, Adam, and Scott gave some great solutions, and you now have the awareness to address any issue that arises in your culture-build.

Jana had some great closing words, so I thought I'd leave them here for you to ponder.

"Culture has to be fun. It's got to be a part of your job—underlying everything you do. It's not just another activity. It's not *on my 11 o'clock window, and now I'm going to think about culture.* It's how you work, not what you work on. It means that anytime you're engaging with others you're doing it with a good heart, an honest voice, and you're proud that's how you work. It doesn't become a to-do list. It's not the thing you shove aside because you finished with it. It is ingrained in all you do. That's when you know you've been successful."

With the member-first, service mindset top of mind for cooperative leaders, the Electric Cooperatives of America are positioned perfectly to attract today's workforce and build a bright future.

CHAPTER 17:

Unexpected Moments of Happiness

You've seen how a V.A.L.U.E. Culture works for a global manufacturing company and a not-for-profit electric utility, but I couldn't leave our culture discussion without sharing how an entrepreneur can build a successful internal culture for their business. I believe building a well-defined culture helps entrepreneurs attract talent and can also serve as a competitive advantage and help differentiate the company from others. As you'll hear in the *King of Pops™* story, building a successful business and a strong culture doesn't happen overnight and requires the buy-in of everyone, especially when your business grows and begins offering franchise opportunities.

What turns a prosecutor into a popsicle peddler? According to Nick Carse, Co-Founder of *King of Pops™*, it's rum and a summer trip with his anthropologist brother. I met Nick Carse and knew him, and his brother Steven, had a story to tell that will make you appreciate your summer treat more than ever before because they took an idea and built a culture that stems from the idea of creating unexpected moments of happiness for both their customers and employees.

Q. Steven, how did <u>King of Pops</u>™ get started?

We started in 2010. I had been laid off from my insurance job and had the idea with my two older brothers to start this business after several trips throughout Latin America. My brother and I traveled through Central America and watched the locals use leftover fruit from the markets to create sweet treats before they were ruined. They used everything! These Mexican frozen treats were called paletas.

Q. Steven, How did you start to grow the business?

Like anyone, we had to start somewhere. We went from a single used ice cream pushcart purchased from *Craigslist*™ to a family-owned company which includes *King of Pops*™, where they grow some of the great ingredients used in their pops and share the message of sustainable farming, a Christmas tree delivery service called *Tree Elves*, and *Perfect 10*™ Foods which is a regional distribution company. All of this is because of a desire and a dream, something we can all relate to—the American dream.

Together with their tenacity, many say the two brothers spearheaded Atlanta's food truck movement. And they did it in a way that highlighted their unique brand of culture.

Q. It is amazing to go from idea to opportunity, to full business. Nick, how have you created a culture around this?

We created a culture centered called, *Unexpected Moments of Happiness—UMoHs*. This theme is central and focused on our culture. From their hiring philosophy to giving back to the community, *King of Pops*™ isn't focused on gaining customers, rather they are focused on creating fans. It's not about doing something fancy; it's about doing something special.

Q. Steven, tell me about the philosophy and if it carries over from your work with employees to your contractors.

I think the obvious one is being nice to folks. For employees, I think it carries over most directly when they stop and think about the person that's receiving help or the one that is getting the benefit.

There are a lot of positive feelings to creating that as well. We encourage them to find things that they're passionate about and help provide the opportunity for them to do it. [*King of Pops*™ donates pops to numerous charitable events and activities in the southern region.]

Sometimes they're on the receiving end. We try to do it for each other. We all need a little nudge to do things that we know we should do or want to do or would be important to do. And so, we're trying to nudge people a little bit, including myself.

Q. Steven, do you think it's important for everyone to see the leaders doing their part as well?

Of course! We have to be examples. When we do something, we have to make sure we're communicating it. If I'm doing it, and if other people are doing it, I make sure to celebrate them and appreciate their generosity.

Q. Steven, what do you compare workplace/business culture to?

There are years and months when you do an amazing job.

Then there are years and months where you do a poor job. Then maybe somewhere you just do an average job. It's like a bank account, always making deposits and withdrawals.

You can build up a lot of goodwill and people appreciating you by doing things the right way. Then if you let it slack, you start making withdrawals from the culture bank. You can get by for a while, but at some point, if you don't invest back into that, it runs out.

I think Covid-19 did that for a lot of companies. We had to make a lot of difficult decisions. But I think because we had invested so much for the decade before that we got the benefit of the doubt a lot more than people who didn't. I think another piece to consider is it's just enjoyable. Hopefully, we're working on that.

Q. How do you keep your culture front and center?

One way we at *King of Pops*™ keep culture front and center is in our people processes. Whether that's in hiring their cart-repreneurs or in determining if someone is a good fit for a franchise. It's about the experience. When we hire someone, we look for someone who will laugh and share a joke and make the interaction with our guests a great guest experience.

Q. Steven, do you think that the age of your workers makes a difference?

The age of workers does make a difference. Many of them are in school and haven't had a lot of exposure to workplace expectations.

We hire a lot of young people. There's a lot of just learning about what life is like. We have six core values we interview on.

King of Pops™ core values:
- Get sweaty.
- Get it done.
- Wear the shirt.
- Be thoughtful.
- Stay hungry.
- Good vibes only.

We try to put things in terms of core values. It's the same working with a supplier or with a contractor or really anybody. It's always a conversation.

Q. Have the core values helped you to set expectations right from the beginning?

Our company started as a popsicle cart business. That's very much from the hiring side. If you hire somebody that thinks they're just going to be in an air-conditioned room and a desk, it's over before it starts. We put "get sweaty" because this business requires a lot of physical effort. Working hard, enjoying working hard, is a bit more of a rare trait, but something that we appreciate.

I like to be clear about expectations. Big egos and lack of humility are red flags. We have a lot of things to offer but big salaries aren't one. You'll get to influence the future of something and build something special and make people happy. You have a lot of flexibility. But we certainly don't have a corporate cafeteria with sushi.

If I'm talking to people, and I feel like they are only focused on the financial piece of it, I would suggest to them, they probably wouldn't be a good fit. That doesn't happen that much. But I think that is one thing on the franchising side, sometimes we've been dealing with is this a good opportunity to make money.

Yes, but it's probably not the fastest or easiest one.

Q. How did you both make their dream a reality?

We spent time mapping out our vision. I was inspired by a company called *Zingerman's*™ out of Ann Arbor, Michigan. They have a training business that we went up to fairly early on, probably our third year in business.

It's about visioning. We wrote a vision and it's something we still refer to today. It comes back to why are you in this. Are you in it to exit and get a nice multiple and find some other business? Are you trying to have it be your life's work?

Q. Steven, can you explain the Zingerman process to us?

It involves picking a point in time in the future and then you write your vision like you are writing it from that point of view rather than a strategic plan.

I think we get caught up in how we're going to do stuff. They have a great process to get you out of that kind of limited perspective and think of the big picture. We went to their training. They're in a book called *Small Giants*, that's how I found them.

The tagline is businesses that choose to be great instead of big. We wrote a draft there and then we came back and took that draft and a committee of interested people from different parts of the company and at different levels. We spent a couple of months building that together so people would have buy-in.

Q. What if you write it out and then just stick it in a drawer somewhere? Will that work?

The goal is that we read it in our quarterly meetings. Then

at our annual symposium. We read it every month on our training calls for our franchisee's cart-repreneurs. It's a good thing because it sets people in a common starting place, and they understand where the heart of the business is.

Q. Steven, do you feel that having others be a part of the vision process is invaluable?

I think sharing is certainly important. People are more connected to things they helped to create. They were there. They bought in if they were creating part of it. Having a great vision doesn't mean those people will stick around forever.

That's the nature of this business. But having a good group of people that are connected with it and talking about it, is important.

Q. Should you reevaluate the vision along the way?

In this style of visioning in particular you're setting a date and time. At some point, you get to that date and time. If you set it five years in advance as they recommend, you have to start writing your next vision before that date gets there.

Ours is fifteen years. It's a 2030 vision and we're halfway to where we are right now. Some of the things we've already eclipsed and done better than we had imagined that we would do.

I think that's why I wanted to rewrite it. There were things that I didn't quite understand and that we couldn't contemplate in the business fully back in the beginning. I don't think there is or should be a single vision. I also think there are departmental visions. There can be a quarterly vision.

I don't like the idea of visioning being confined to the company as a whole. From the top, I think it's valuable to think about being in charge of the cart at the park. What would be great this year for us to do with this single cart? What would be meaningful? How would our core values be displayed? How would it impact me personally?

Most of our people's goal isn't to be a cart-repreneur their whole life. I think it's important to realize the goal isn't for everyone to work here forever. I think when you're when you're visioning, a powerful part of the way I think visioning works is when it includes some bits and pieces of your personal life. That's realistic and important as well.

Q. Nick, does the vision tie into the King of Pops™ flavorful roadmap to success?

It sure does.
- First, set a date. It's important to give yourself a set time in life when you are going to do something.
- Secondly, embrace the unknown. Don't worry about everybody else, they don't know what they are doing either.
- Third, you've got to rely on people. It's okay not to know everything. Just find folks who know what you don't.
- Fourth, keep growing. Our philosophy is "if you aren't growing, you're dying."
- Fifth, create a culture uniquely yours. Don't just exist. Know who you are and create a vision that gets you where you want to be.

Q. Steven, what do you think about the community, and do they matter?

The thing that stands out the most to me, it's if people buy a popsicle, they might like it, and they might buy another one. But I think when people buy a popsicle at a community event we're hosting for a cause or they're just really having fun, it builds relationships.

They get to meet someone and uniquely connect with them. I think instead of maybe buying another product, they'll buy ours because they feel good about the company. Remember we spent a lot of time mapping out our vision. We've been asked to expand to other markets, but we are committed to staying in the south. We're passionate about supporting the community and of course, we have our Unexpected Moments of Happiness. And we do it all while having fun.

You have seen a prime example of a business that started literally from a *Craigslist*™ push cart to what it is today. The Carse brothers are so passionate about culture and the secret that they discovered was that it was like a bank account. You must make your deposits so that you are ready to handle the cultural crisis that happens.

Whether you love *King of Pops*™ or not, you can't knock their philosophy and the success they are achieving by building a brand based on happiness and community. Knowing their team members, addressing their needs, and serving in a unique way has allowed them to turn a one push cart business into a thriving franchise and influence not only their workplace culture, but society, in a positive way.

I shared these examples so you could see the concepts which make up the V.A.L.U.E. Culture formula work no matter the industry or size of your organization. All of these companies created a vision based on a set of core values built around their own identity. They incorporated accountability from the top down to ensure everyone was committed to their culture program. Leaders used a coaching style to motivate and grow their employees so they felt valued and an integral part of the company. Their recognition program took into account the unique qualities and skills of their employees. Finally, they encouraged multiple ways employees could take part in activities that increased their engagement and satisfaction with their job.

Creating a culture of value requires more than just implementing a few initiatives. It must be an ongoing effort that is part of the organization's core beliefs and practices. Leaders should create clear goals for their employees, encouraging them to strive for excellence in all aspects of their work. They should also actively listen to employee feedback and use it to improve processes or develop new ideas. Additionally, providing incentives such as rewards or recognition can help foster loyalty and motivation among staff members and emphasize the importance placed on their contributions. Finally, developing opportunities for meaningful engagement with colleagues can further strengthen employees' sense of purpose within the company culture.

CHAPTER 18:

People-First Cultures Create Thriving Environments

I want you to imagine walking into the workplace and hearing happy chatter as teams work on projects that add to the company's profits. Visualize walking into the break room and hearing employees sharing stories about the family activities they enjoyed over the weekend. I want you to have this experience every day in the workplace.

Feel the joy in knowing your human resource manager has an abundance of qualified candidates clamoring for the position you posted. Revel in the newfound confidence your employees feel when they are receiving promotions and sharing ideas that help streamline processes and boost productivity. Picture your board's reaction to reduced insurance premiums, less turnover, and higher productivity when you report quarterly updates.

All these things are within reach when you implement a people-first V.A.L.U.E. Culture in your workplace. Transitioning to a V.A.L.U.E. Culture mindset will be the beginning of a transformation, and it will provide you with increased positive morale among team members, improved productivity, better customer satisfaction ratings, and more meaningful relationships throughout the organization.

As you enter the workplace tomorrow morning, think about how you can strive to create an environment of mutual respect and support, regardless of title or position. Consider what actions you can take to ensure that everyone is included and valued while working together towards a common goal. Build upon this idea and work to foster an atmosphere that encourages collaboration, creativity, and innovation. Celebrate successes together as a team and acknowledge the efforts of all individuals. Create an environment where everyone feels heard, respected, and valued for their contributions. Encourage open dialogue and honest feedback, knowing that different perspectives create better solutions and stronger results. With everyone's unique abilities driving the success of the company forward, you can take your organization to heights you never thought possible.

As you begin to create your own culture and take all that you have learned back in the office, consider ways to implement trust and help build relationships within the team. Encourage employees to express themselves openly, while giving them the tools they need to succeed. Inspire a sense of positive energy in staff with tangible rewards and recognition for hard work. Above all, foster an atmosphere of belonging and inclusion so everyone feels safe and supported in their endeavors. How you show up is how your team will show up. How you execute is a sign to your team as to how you want them to operate and perform. As the leader, it is up to you to set the tone and provide a vision for how everyone can work together. Demonstrate respect and appreciation by recognizing individual strengths and weaknesses, helping them grow and develop. Show your team that their success is yours too, and empower them with autonomy to make decisions on their own. Take an active role in understanding each member's needs and passions, so that you can create an environment where everyone can thrive. Give your staff permission to fail without fear of judgment or repercussion; encourage innovation by allowing mistakes as opportunities for learning.

As we close out the book, here are a few words of encouragement and advice from the business leaders you've met on these pages, so you too can create a thriving culture inside the walls of your business.

DON'T GO AT IT ALONE

Daniel Lawrence said, "*I think that the most important thing I did is I didn't just sit down and do it by myself.*" I asked him to share more about that.

> *Q. Daniel, in regards to creating the <u>Bots For That</u>™ culture recipe what did you do?*

I got everyone to sit down. We made these observations together. It was a joint initiative. Everyone came up with ideas and contributed to them, as opposed to me sitting down, writing it up as a typical management consultant, and saying this is our culture tomorrow.

It was more a case of everyone making observations on what they'd learned, what was working and what wasn't, and what they wanted. I think that's probably the most important thing, don't sell a culture, ask.

This cross-company involvement is such an important piece of a successful culture program. It's one of the main ways you'll create a culture that addresses employee and company value components.

VALUE ALL OF THE TEAM

I wanted to share one last thing from Mark Allred, director of Talent Development and Growth at *Reveal Global Intelligence™*, as every business leader will be adding members of Gen Y and Z to their workforce.

Q. Mark, what about <u>younger</u> generations? Do you need to have buy-in at all levels?

As younger generations are entering the workforce, the definition of loyalty is changing. I've had the chance to do a little studying on Generation Z and what's happening with them in the workplace. An *Indeed™* survey showed fifty-eight percent of them are already saying that they're burned out at work. They've only been in the workforce for just a little while. So, I think there's a lot of pressure when you're the new person coming in. There's a lot to learn. We've all been through that, but it seems to be a little bit more rampant with them.

There are other interesting things, like the fact that their attention span is quick. They've been raised on things like Instagram™ and *Facebook™*, and now you have TikTok™ where they're just flipping through things very quickly. It's tough to engage them.

Q. Mark, what do you think is the leading cause of loyalty decline?

That is simple, the lack of engagement is a leading cause of the loyalty decline. Fifty-five percent of them said they plan to look for a new job in the next three years. Only two in ten plan to stay with their company for seven years. If you compare that to Gen-Xers when they were asked the same question seventy-two percent of Gen-Xers said they plan to stay at least seven years.

Forty-six percent of Millennials said they would accept a job offer if the opportunity arose, even if they were not actively looking for one. Culture is also a huge driver in whether they will take a position offered or not. In fact, it outperforms salary. Employees don't leave when they care about the success of an organization and feel positively challenged in their position.

ENGAGEMENT BUILDS CULTURE

I've been on the flip side of that and worked in an environment where employees felt unappreciated and unheard; I know the morale killer that can be. Everyone is doing the bare minimum, and no one is generating new ideas. It becomes stagnant.

Q. Mark, what is the key?

Engagement is the key. Building a V.A.L.U.E. Culture is a new approach to employee engagement. Your team is a very rapidly moving group of individuals. They are a lot sharper and more connected than a lot of folks give them credit for.

It seems like every generation is saying about previous generations, nobody wants to work hard anymore. They're getting blasted with that moniker. But it's funny, there was another study I read recently that said if you go back and look at newspaper articles over a century, they're all saying the same thing about those generations.

The more things change, the more they stay the same. This generation is coming into the workplace and what we need to understand is that they do have short attention spans. We need to learn how to refine those and work on them.

But here's the surprising thing that I'm finding personally about them. They are very receptive to coaching and mentoring. I think that surprises folks. I'm a Gen-Xer, and if you kind of consider what our generations were like, we were very much a generation who felt like we had to get it right.

Asking for help was a sign of weakness. That's not the case for Gen-Z. They will take help. Now here's the difference—they won't necessarily ask for it. But, when it's offered, they tend to take it and really lean into it.

> *Q. Mark, how can we dial in the engagement factor so that it will also help you keep those employees instead of looking for replacements?*

I think organizations really need to think a lot more about how they're pouring into their employees. They can't let the day-to-day busyness get in the way of employee development. I'm with a recruiting company and part of what our recruiters do all the time is look for employees who aren't happy.

Then we can introduce new opportunities and bring them on this wonderful golden bridge to the new opportunity. The only way that's going to be stopped is if you've already made your employees happy employees, and they're thrilled with where they are, and they're happy to say no thank you to those opportunities.

Think of the competitive advantage you will gain and how you will outpace your competition if your workforce feels invested in and feel their personal mission is tied into that of your company.

BE ORGANIZED AND SUCCINCT

An organization's culture reflects the environment, behaviors, and values of everyone in the workplace. Your organization has the power to build a high-performance V.A.L.U.E. Culture. When you set goals, define responsibilities, create trust, and encourage employee development, the pieces form a thriving culture.

Throughout the information-gathering process for my book, everyone agreed that no culture initiative would be successful if you didn't think about the people. Garry Ridge put it most succinctly.

Q. Garry, what is the workplace all about?

To get straight to the point, it's all about the people. It's defining and creating a workplace culture that works for your business. Doing that is one of the more challenging tasks for a business owner. The most successful ones keep people at the center.

Remember, it's all about the people. You've got to start with your people. What are you going to do? How are you going to behave? How will you make sure that people go home happy? I think we get that right. The other reason why it's so rewarding, if you think of it, you extend that out a little bit.

Happy people create happy families. Happy families create happy communities. Happy communities create a happy world. And by golly, we need a happy world. Business has a huge opportunity to make a positive difference in the world today. If we just create cultures that treat people with respect and dignity, that gives them the opportunity to learn.

They feel like they belong. We have a huge opportunity to make a positive difference in the world. It's our responsibility. We better do it.

EFFICIENCY IS KEY

Creating an effective culture for your business is one of the best ways to raise the odds of your company succeeding in the future. Let's see what Adam Schwartz has to say about this topic.

Q. Adam, do you see more emphasis on culture in the workplace?

I'm definitely seeing more emphasis and efficiency when it comes to culture. One of the questions I ask supervisors is, have you ever gotten this question from an applicant, "What's the culture like around here?" Some organizations are getting ahead of the culture issue by making it a priority in hiring and onboarding.

I talk about an organization called *Vancity*™. It's a credit union in Vancouver, British Columbia. They have an orientation and immersion program all their employees, within the first month, must go through it. They allowed me to participate in it five years ago, so I spent the whole week up there, learning how they do it. It's all taught by fellow employees.

Employees from their departments come in, then they spend a day and a half in the field at a credit union branch and with members of the credit union, learning all about the operation and how members feel. At the end of the five days, every new employee is offered $2,000 to leave.

Just take the check. No hard feelings. Goodbye. They have found, as I'm sure you would attest to, that getting rid of an employee who's not going to be a good fit for $2,000 is the best bargain you'll ever have. The overwhelming majority don't take the money.

It has the added impact of after you've said yes to the job

and refused to take $2,000 you've essentially bought your job. You know you're obviously part of this tribe. This is another thing that we all share now. I think there are ways that we can do that that make sense and hopefully help build relationships.

Another is giving every employee the opportunity to select an educational opportunity that they would like to engage in every year. One that helps make them better. There should be some connection to their job, but it could be a very loose connection. Whatever it might be, it shows folks that you value them. I think it's an important thing.

UPLIFT FROM WITHIN

What happens to the people you already have? You have to focus on the recruitment process, and you also have to remember the people you already have. I talked to Mark again about the importance of re-recruiting your current employees.

Q. Mark, what happens to the people you already have?

When you get the V.A.L.U.E. Culture right, your retention numbers will outpace your need to recruit and hire. One way to ensure your people continue to feel valued is to spend time each year re-recruiting them. We have a process around our company called Re-recruiting You to Reveal.

We do it yearly. Some companies really need to consider doing it quarterly or at least twice a year. We take that career driver conversation, and you find out how your folk feels. Find out what motivates them about their work. It's important to understand what those things are. You can't ever be fully accommodating, but you do the best you can to really meet people where they are. You motivate them through what motivates them, not what you think. Then you need to check in every so often and say how are we doing.

Q. Mark, do you think re-recruiting is a way to get everyone on the same page?

I think what makes folks vulnerable to losing somebody for two extra dollars an hour is they either forget why they chose to work there in the beginning or nothing they were told came to fruition.

When you start, we get on the same page about what we're offering. As far as culture goes, here's what it looks like. Your leadership interaction will look like this. Your compensation is this. How does that all sound? That sounds great. You join the organization. If we never talk about that again, and that's never revisited, then a lot of the things just never happen. Then when somebody comes to offer two more dollars and I say to him, "Well remember all the reasons why you signed up. You know we were going to do this and this." But they never saw those things, or we've never done those things.

That's why they leave. That's why it's important to have that sit down. Because sometimes you think you're providing them or in your mind's eye you think I am taking care of my employees. But if you can have the courage to sit down and find out you're not doing as good a job as you thought that's important.

Q. Mark, you remind them of the culture you're creating. You talk about the type of leadership they were hoping to have. You share company goals and paint a picture of the future. It's about helping them see real possibilities?

Yes. It's about keeping everyone moving forward. It's about

being very willing to have a real conversation with them. This isn't about kowtowing to every whim your employee has.

I give people more credit. Most people are reasonable. I think you can have that conversation and you can say we're not able to do the work-from-home thing, and here's why.

I think people get that. That's what I would say is the biggest thing, making sure that you've got a touch point where you can do a quick pulse check.

I know the V.A.L.U.E. Culture will be a benefit for any company when it comes to retaining and hiring new talent. This formula turns leaders into coaches which also helps you keep the great talent you hired.

CULTURE BENEFITS

Before I close out this chapter, I want to get Harry Hynekamp's insight on the benefits of culture. His are the last words I'll leave with you.

> *Q., Harry, what do you think about this statement: Culture doesn't spontaneously combust.*

I love the statement. In fact, as I've mentioned before, *great culture doesn't just spontaneously combust or appear out of thin air.* You have got to work at it all the time. You have to create new and different ways to connect with your associates, your team. Not only listening and responding to them but also more specifically and importantly, implementing the team's ideas as to what would make it an even greater place to work.

Q., What do you do in your organization to make it a greater place to work?

There are a bunch of ways, one is our *Fun Committee*. It's got probably twenty or thirty associates from all across the business involved and what they do is they decide for the whole year what are the things that we can do differently this year to create an even greater place to work.

What are the new things that we can do this year to connect one another to a common purpose and understanding, as well as create the space for people to share their perspectives and their opinions?

I would say each month we have something different and new that we haven't ever done before to kind of kickstart our culture in a new and different way. *Walk in My Shoes* will always be a staple of our culture. *Skip-level* meetings will always be a staple of our culture. *Huddles* with the executives will always be a staple of our culture.

Our recognition appreciation ceremony will always be a staple of our culture. Discussions and sharing openly the results of our associate survey, as well as sharing the feedback that associates provided to us, will always be a part of our culture.

These are some of the foundational elements that will never go away. But we've been really good at involving associates to come up with new things like the *Lunch Lottery program*, to do something different. The goal of the Lunch Lottery program was simply connect all associates in a new, fun, and creative way to further drive networking and collaboration.

You have to actively work on culture. Culture is embedded in everything you do. Culture is defined by the policies and processes that you put in place. It's in the written words and documents, you define it everywhere, all over the place. Culture is slightly different from team to team, but that doesn't make it bad.

Finance folks probably have a slightly different cultural feel, then a marketing culture. That doesn't mean they're misaligned, just means they're a little bit different. Everything in and across the business is a reflection of your culture. From your accounts payable process, IT request form to your onboarding process.

From what your associate communications email looks like to how your town hall meetings are structured. I've been around the block long enough to be able to distinguish good and bad cultures. So the point is if we take care of our culture, our associates, one another, we're going to be able to take care of our business. Because then we are going to take care of our fans, guests, customers, and community.

Culture isn't something that just happens. It's something you work on and nurture. Culture is something to be celebrated in both big and small ways in the workplace. And when done correctly, culture will be your big success driver. You'll create an organization in which both the employees and the company's bottom line thrives.

LEADERS LEAD

The secret is out and it's all about the impact of a V.A.L.U.E. Culture brings to your organization. I've shared inside information from amazing business leaders located all over the world. We covered what they did to find culture, figure out what was missing, how they implemented it, and infused their unique cultures into the lives of the people that work for them. Now it's up to you to be the leader your cooperation needs and bring these same values to life inside of your organization.

I believe that it is the leaders, like you, that will shape the future of work and build companies that are not only successful financially, but have thriving people-centered cultures that have job seekers clamoring to be a part of. Showing our teams we value their ideas and recognize their dreams, brings people together and forges relationships and connections that can help to create an atmosphere of collaboration, understanding, and appreciation. It encourages team members to work together and makes space for new possibilities, which can ultimately drive innovation and help businesses reach their goals more efficiently. Our jobs are meant to bring out our potential and help us reach new heights and options. Our leaders are called to foster an environment that encourages and supports this growth, enabling each team member to thrive in their own way. By providing a platform for collaboration, understanding, and appreciation for our teams we create an atmosphere of trust and respect, allowing members to feel comfortable expressing their ideas with confidence—resulting in increased creativity and productivity.

When you think about the people in your organization, think about their unique skills and talents, their potential for growth, and what value they can bring to the team. Recognizing each individual's worth is the foundation of any successful business, and by stressing the importance of collaboration and support within your team, you create an environment that encourages creativity, productivity, and success. You never know who is capable of great feats, or who needs a little extra motivation to reach their full potential. By creating an atmosphere of understanding and appreciation for each team member, you can foster an environment that encourages everyone to strive for excellence. Employing strategies that recognize the contributions and successes of individuals, teams and departments will lead to higher engagement levels and help your organization flourish.

The culture you create gives *everyone* in the organization a sense of belonging and the purpose they need to thrive. Cultivating a team environment that values growth and encourages creative problem-solving instills confidence in employees and helps build trusting relationships. Through communication, collaboration, and effective feedback, your team will be empowered to make great strides as individuals, teams, and as an organization. In the modern world, CEOs and managers represent the highest category of leadership. Allowing them the opportunities to be role models, inspire others, and mentor their team. They can instill a sense of trust and confidence in their team members and have the ability to influence positive change throughout the organization.

By learning what you have, you now possess the tools to create a culture that values relationships and encourages collaboration. You can foster an environment that builds connection and trust between everyone, enabling them to reach their highest potential both together and individually. It is only through cultivating a people-centered workplace culture that true success and achievement can be achieved.

IT'S NOT A SECRET AFTER ALL

It's been an honor bringing all of these stories, ideas, and frameworks to you. We embarked on a journey together, and I hope it is just the beginning of how we can each impact one another. If you want to dive deeper and become a more visionary leader, or you need help identifying your current workplace culture and how to begin building a stronger, more vibrant one, visit my website at www.chelliephillips.com and I am happy to make time if you book a call with me.

As a speaker for many years, I'd enjoy the opportunity to

come and speak and share more insights with you or your organization or workplace because culture is such a passion of mine. I'd be delighted to see your people and your structure, and share whatever I can to make your culture as engaging and beneficial as it can be.

Albert Einstein said it best: "When you add value, it leaves a trail of value in its wake. Strive not to be a success, but rather to be of value."

That is the best *Culture Secret* to end on. You are my greatest value. You picked up my book wanting to know more about the secrets to having a great workplace culture—and I hope you found exactly what you were needing to build the culture you desire! I can't thank you enough for investing in your future and the future of those you work with. Your work family will appreciate all the insight you have gained to make coming to the office feel more like a "get to" instead of a "got to." Remember, if your workplace culture is improving, your people will stay loyal, and your organization becomes more than a job to people; it becomes a way of life.

As an added bonus, you can access these incredible interviews, and the many people who were so kind to be part of this book, by following the link to the *Culture Secrets Podcast* I have at the back of this book. I wanted to make these available to you so that you can have access to all the great discussions and can hear straight from these amazing business leaders themselves. It's powerful to take the information you have read about and reinforce it with their interviews. There will also be several follow-up episodes you can use as resources while you investigate your current company culture and begin building a new one. Just keep reading, and at the back of the book, you'll find a way to subscribe to the *Culture Secrets Podcast* and keep the conversation going.

I have also included on the following pages the references and links to all the research used in compiling this book. If you want to read the full articles or learn more about a particular topic, simply follow the link and enjoy the many resources available to help you learn more about creating an impactful workplace culture.

Throughout this book, I also included the names of many other publications and articles of interest that both myself and the other CEOs have utilized. Books are a wonderful source of information and the stories imparted bring the ideas to life. I have added a powerful reading list for you to continue learning from some of the best in their field. I encourage you to pick up any one of them to further your understanding of culture and its impact on employee engagement. Of course, you can always contact me should you need a good recommendation or specific suggestion to supplement the learnings you have gained here.

As you found out, culture is ever-evolving, it is never stagnant or asleep. As you immerse yourself into building a dynamic culture your needs, wants, and learning level will need to grow exponentially; as fast as your culture does. Take the time to listen, learn and understand your team members' perspectives. And, know that as you work on becoming a better leader, and grow in understanding and empathy for others, you will build a workplace culture your entire company will be proud to be a part of. Your workplace culture will become everything you aspire for it to be.

References

INTRODUCTION

1. The Great Resignation Didn't Start with the Pandemic https://hbr.org/2022/03/the-great-resignation-didnt-start-with-the-pandemic
2. Dore, Kate, "Toxic Company Culture is the Number 1 Reason Workers are Quitting Jobs," CNBC, April 13, 2022, https://www.cnbc.com/2022/04/13/toxic-company-culture-is-the-no-1-reason-workers-are-quitting-jobs.html.
3. Woodruff, Judy, "Why Millions of Older Americans are Retiring Early in the Wake of the Pandemic," February 23, 2022, https://www.pbs.org/newshour/show/why-millions-of-older-americans-are-retiring-early-in-the-wake-of-the-pandemic.
4. Ferguson, Stephanie, "Understanding America's Labor Shortage the Most Impacted Industries," Oct 31, 2022, https://www.uschamber.com/workforce/understanding-americas-labor-shortage-the-most-impacted-industries.
5. Smith, Morgan, "Gen-Z and Millennial Workers are Leading the Latest Quitting Spree," September 3, 2021, https://www.cnbc.com/2021/09/03/gen-z-and-millennial-workers-are-leading-the-latest-quitting-spree-.html.

6. Allcott, Dawn, "Gen-Z Millennials Rather be Unemployed than Unhappy Work," April 6, 2022, https://www.gobankingrates.com/money/jobs/gen-z-millennials-rather-be-unemployed-than-unhappy-work/.
7. Glassdoor Team, "New Survey: Company Mission & Culture Matter More Than Compensation," July 10, 2019, https://www.glassdoor.com/employers/blog/mission-culture-survey/.
8. Harter, Jim, "Is Quiet Quitting Real," September 6 2022, https://www.gallup.com/workplace/398306/quiet-quitting-real.aspx.

CHAPTER 2

1. Arne Gast, Aberkyn McKinsey, Pablo Illanes, Nina Probst, Bill Schaninger, Bruce Simpson, April 22, 2020, Corporate purpose: Shifting from why to how | McKinsey https://www.mckinsey.com/capabilities/people-and-organizational-performance/our-insights/purpose-shifting-from-why-to-how
2. Bryant Somerville, August 25, 2021, "Ohio nurse's facebook page goes viral over vaccine choice" https://www.10tv.com/article/news/health/coronavirus/vaccine/ohio-nurse-facebook-post-announcing-job-loss-due-to-vaccine-choice-goes-viral/530-b8274b0c-dc36-44d8-a1a3-2523ec074a4f

CHAPTER 3

1. Three reasons why Value matters Forbes (https://www.forbes.com/sites/garypeterson/2013/08/14/three-reasons-why-values-matter-and-im-not-talking-the-money-kind/?sh=343ae5a11d93)

CHAPTER 4

1. Scott Miller, "How to Win the Great Retirement," Gallup, Nov 1, 2021, https://www.gallup.com/workplace/356729/win-great-resignation.aspx

CHAPTER 5

1. Pat Blackstaffe, *It's Not All Strawberries and Cream*, Darkstick Aug 16, 2021.
2. Dewitt Jones, "Celebrate What's Right," https://celebratewhatsright.com/profile/dewitt-jones.
3. Aaron De Smet, Bonnie Dowling, Marino Mugayar-Baldocchi, and Bill Schaninger, "Great Attrition or Great Attraction; The Choice is Yours," Mckinsey, September 8, 2021, https://www.mckinsey.com/capabilities/people-and-organizational-performance/our-insights/great-attrition-or-great-attraction-the-choice-is-yours
4. Alok Patel, Stephanie Plowman, "Increasing the Importance of a Best Friend at Work," August 17, 2021, https://www.gallup.com/workplace/397058/increasing-importance-best-friend-work.aspx

5. Tim Hodges, "School Engagement is More Than Just Talk," October 25, 2018, https://www.gallup.com/education/244022/school-engagement-talk.aspx

6. Bridget De Maine, How Many Good Experiences Finally Outweigh a Good One," May 15, 2017, https://collectivehub.com/2017/05/how-many-good-experiences-finally-outweigh-a-bad-one/

CHAPTER 6

1. Simon Sinek, "How Great Leaders Inspire Action," September 2009, Ted, https://www.ted.com/talks/simon_sinek_how_great_leaders_inspire_action?language=en

SECTION 2

1. Peter F Drucker, Amazon Author Site, https://www.amazon.com/Peter-F.-Drucker/e/B000AP61TE.

2. Peter Senge, *The Fifth Discipline: The Art & Practice of The Learning Organization.* Crown Business, a Division of Penguin Random House LLC. March 21, 2010.

3. Tom Peter, *Compact Guide to Excellence.* Amazon.com Service LLC. November 1, 2022.

4. Davitsahakyan, "IDEO Shopping Cart Design Process," YouTube Video. September 29, 2017. https://youtu.be/izjhx17NuSE.

5. John Brownlee, "Why Steve Jobs drowned the first iPod prototype," Cult of Mac, November 18, 2014, https://www.cultofmac.com/303469/steve-jobs-drowned-first-ipod-prototype/

6. Waltere Issacson, "The Real Leadership Lessons of Steve Jobs," Harvard Business Review, https://hbr.org/2012/04/the-real-leadership-lessons-of-steve-jobs#:~:text=He%20made%20products%20that%20he,thousand%20songs%20in%20his%20pocket

7. Simon Sinek, "The Optimism Company," https://simonsinek.com/

CHAPTER 9

1. Garry Ridge, Ken Blanchard, *Helping People Win At Work*, Person Education 2009.

2. Collaboration, "What is the RACI Model?" Monday.com https://monday.com/blog/project-management/raci-model/.

3. Tom Smith, Roger Connors, *The Oz Principle: Getting Results Through Individual and Organizational Accountability*, Portfolio Publisher. October 1, 1998.

CHAPTER 12

1. Jim Harter, "U.S. Employee Engagement Data Hold Steady in First Half of 2021", April 8, 2022, https://www.gallup.com/workplace/352949/employee-engagement-holds-steady-first-half-2021.aspx

CHAPTER 16

1. "Cooperative identity, values & principles," ICA, https://www.ica.coop/en/cooperatives/cooperative-identity.

2. Monday.com https://monday.com/

CHAPTER 18

1. What is the King of Pops? https://kingofpops.com/.
2. Green, Josh. "Local brothers become kings of the popsicle world." Gwinnett Daily Post. Mar 8, 2013 Updated Jan 22, 2016. https://www.gwinnettdailypost.com/archive/local-brothers-become-kings-of-the-popsicle-world/article_f2a43981-2c12-55c7-bf5d-2fa9f6ce82ad.html.

Suggested Reading List

Joy, Inc.: How We Built a Workplace People Love by Richard Sheridan (https://richardsheridan.com/books)

Chief Joy Officer: How Great Leaders Elevate Human Energy And Eliminate Fear by Richard Sheridan (https://richardsheridan.com/books)

Helping People Win at Work: A Business Philosophy Called "Don't Mark My Paper, Help Me Get an A" by Ken Blanchard and Garry Ridge (https://www.amazon.com/Books-Garry-Ridge/s?rh=n%3A283155%2Cp_27%3AGarry+Ridge)

Tribe Culture: How It Shaped WD-40 Company by Garry Ridge (https://www.amazon.com/Books-Garry-Ridge/s?rh=n%3A283155%2Cp_27%3AGarry+Ridge)

THE UNEXPECTED LEARNING MOMENT: Lessons in Leading a Thriving Culture Through Lockdown 2020 by Garry Ridge and Martha I. Finney (https://www.amazon.com/Books-Garry-Ridge/s?rh=n%3A283155%2Cp_27%3AGarry+Ridge)

Not All Strawberries and Cream, But There's Some Wonderful Moments by Pat Blackstaffelt (https://www.amazon.com/Its-Not-All-Strawberries-Cream/dp/0986750336)

Made to Stick by Chip and Dan Heath (https://heath-brothers.com/books/made-to-stick/)

The Effective Executive, The Definitive Guide to Getting the Right Things Done by Peter Drucker (https://www.amazon.com/Peter-F.-Drucker/e/B000AP61TE)

*The Five Most Important Questions You Will
Ever Ask About Your Organization* by Peter Drucker
(https://www.amazon.com/Five-Important-Ques-
tions-About-Organization/dp/0470227567/
ref=asc_df_0470227567/?tag=hyprod-20&linkCode=d-
f0&hvadid=312106851030&hvpos=&hvnetw=g&h-
vrand=7339737221747674390&hvpone=&hvptwo=&h-
vqmt=&hvdev=c&hvdvcmdl=&hvlocint=&hvloc-
phy=9010899&hvtargid=pla-493812575668&psc=1)

*The Fifth Discipline: The Art & Practice of The Learning
Organization* by Peter Senge (https://systemsawareness.org/
person/peter-senge/)

*In Search of Excellence: Lessons from America's Best-Run
Companies* by Tom Peters (https://tompeters.com/) ,

*The OZ Principle: Getting Results Through Individual
and Organizational Accountability,* by Tom Smith and
Roger Connors (https://www.amazon.com/Oz-Princi-
ple-Individual-Organizational-Accountability-ebook/dp/
B0012M2IX2).

*Small Giants: Companies That Choose to Be Great Instead of
Big* by Bo Burlinghman (http://www.smallgiantsbook.com/
about.html)

Good Company by Arthur M. Blank (https://www.harper-
collins.com/pages/arthurblank)

*Driven to Delight: Delivering World-Class Cus-
tomer Experience the Mercedes-Benz Way* by Joseph
A. Michelli (https://www.amazon.ca/Driven-De-
light-Delivering-World-Class-Mercedes-Benz/
dp/007180630X)

About the Author

Chellie Phillips is a sweet-tea-sipping, sassy Southerner with a passion for helping dynamic, career-minded professionals stand out for all the right reasons. She's used her Successfully Ever After formula to coach hundreds of clients through the process of creating a personal brand designed to make them irresistible in the workplace.

Throughout that process, Chellie realized her clients shared a common thread. The majority of her clients didn't necessarily hate the work they did; they just didn't enjoy the people and atmosphere they did it with or in. From micromanaging bosses to watching lackluster employees get the same raises as the ones who were going above and beyond, it became clear that the culture inside an organization was a vital component needed for an employee to feel successful.

That became even more apparent when Chellie experienced her own workplace culture nightmare. The management changed at an organization she had worked with for over 20 years after the retirement of a long-tenured leader. In the span of six months, she went from feeling she had a seat at the table and voice in the direction the company was taking to doubting her own abilities and feeling totally devalued.

The final straw came when she received an email one evening from her new general manager implying her skills came from a box of cereal (like the prize inside, all of us Gen Xers fought our siblings over as kids). That caused her to look deep inside, and she was amazed at how quickly she had let one person make her doubt her own abilities and the value she had contributed for years.

A bookcase full of industry awards didn't keep the self-doubt from creeping in. That email became the kick in the pants she needed to walk away from that career and find a place where employees feel valued and invested. Now she makes sure others don't stay in an environment where their talents and skills aren't recognized and celebrated.

Today she works with business leaders to improve and boost employee engagement. Her coaching helps leaders create a culture that stops turnover, highlights problem solvers, and shines the spotlight on rising stars. Research shows companies who invest in their employee's development are generally 202% more profitable than their competitors (source Forbes).

When employees leave her event they have the clarity of knowing how they play a role in the success of your organization, no matter the position they hold. Through workshops and one-on-one experiences, Chellie helps employees and leaders gain great self-awareness and, together, create an actionable plan designed to create a culture where employees and businesses thrive.

Chellie knows that by providing an employee-focused culture and setting up structures that foster career development opportunities through training, you reduce turnover and build loyalty.

She uses her 25+ years of corporate experience to build solid result-driven programs based on a background in communications and public relations, which has been recognized on a state and national level. This includes recognition such as Outstanding Alumnus of the Year in Public Relations field from Troy University in April 2000, the 2022 LaBerge Award for Strategic Communications from the *National Rural Electric Cooperative Association™ (NRECA™)*, Alabama Rural Electric Association (AREA) Communicator of the Year, and the Cooperative Communicators Association (CCA) Graznak Award. She's appeared as a guest on over 50 podcasts (and counting).

She's presented programs on stage for the National Rural Electric Cooperative Association, Cooperative Communicators Association, the Fayette County Chamber of Commerce Diversity and Inclusion Summit, the University of West Georgia, USAC & Material Advantage Group, Georgia Tech University, the West Georgia Technical College Foundation, and others on topics related to workplace culture and employee development including, *Beyond Organizational Effectiveness: What Extraordinary Executive Assistants Really Do, Building Women Leaders in the Workplace, When In Doubt, Delete It!, Engaging Multiple Generations in the Workplace and Community*, and *3 Secrets to Landing A Job You Love*.

When she's not spreading the word on creating irresistible workplace cultures, she serves as the current board chair for Elevate Coweta Students. She's also on the board of the Coweta Community Foundation and the Coweta Chamber of Commerce. She and her husband reside in Moreland, GA, with their two furry mutts, Roxie and Izzy.

Chellie has been lucky enough to turn her passion into a career. She calls herself blessed to have a supportive, loving group of family and friends by her side from the beginning.

www.chelliephillips.com
chellie@chelliephillips.com
chelliep
chellie_phillips
chellie-phillips

Other Books by the Author

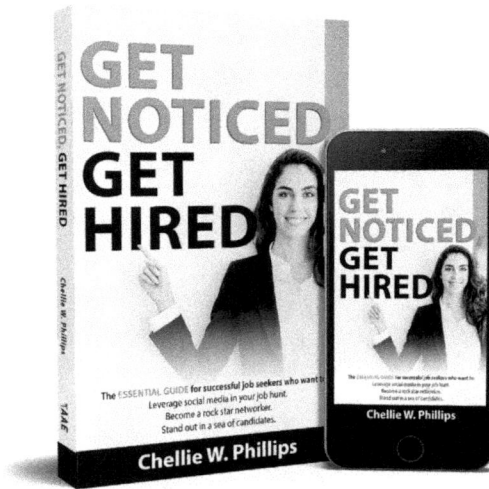

BUILD A PERSONAL CAREER BRAND THAT GETS YOU NOTICED!

AVAILABLE ON AMAZON, AUDIBLE, OR AT YOUR LOCAL BOOK STORE

If you can't get noticed, you won't get hired!

Get Noticed, Get Hired is the definitive guide to showcasing your experience and skill, while offering tips and strategies to land you in the interview seat.

Learn how to:
- Build a career brand designed to make you stand out throughout your career.
- Create a power resume designed to get results.
- Maximize your LinkedIn profile for optimum discoverability.
- Build and utilize your personal and digital network for career success.

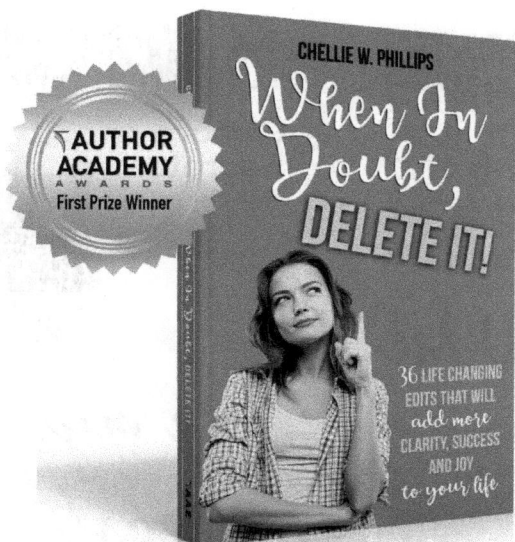

AUTHOR ACADEMY AWARDS
First Prize Winner

CHELLIE W. PHILLIPS

When In Doubt, **DELETE IT!**

36 LIFE CHANGING EDITS THAT WILL *add more* CLARITY, SUCCESS AND JOY *to your life*

WHAT'S YOUR PERSONAL SUCCESS STORY?

AVAILABLE ON AMAZON, AUDIBLE, OR AT YOUR LOCAL BOOK STORE

Just as an editor uses proofreader marks to make stories more readable and understandable, we can use those same edits in life to add more clarity, success and joy to our stories.When In Doubt, Delete It! shows you how to change your life with five proofreader marks – delete, insert, move, begin, and stet.

Learn how to:

- Delete things holding you back.
- Insert qualities and ideas that help you grow.
- Move toward what brings you happiness.
- Begin adding new experiences to stay out of a rut.
- Remain true to yourself.

SCAN ME

Culture Secrets
Hosted By Chellie Phillips

Culture Secrets, the podcast that uncovers the secrets to creating a people-centered workplace culture that drives success. Are you ready to unlock the power of a culture that inspires and motivates your team? Then hit that subscribe button and join me, the author of the Culture Secrets book, for insightful conversation with business leaders who have cracked the code to building high-performing cultures.

From fostering a sense of belonging and inclusion to nurturing growth and development, we'll cover all things people-centered workplace culture. You'll discover practical tips and strategies for creating a culture that attracts and retains talent, fosters innovation, and drives business growth.

But that's not all. We'll also dive into the nitty gritty of organizational culture, exploring the latest trends and best practices for creating an irresistible workplace people love. So what are you waiting for? Join me for Culture Secrets, the podcast that reveals the secrets to creating a culture that inspires and transforms your workplace. Hit the subscribe button now and never miss an episode!

Join my podcast and let's keep the conversation going!

www.chelliephillips.com/

GENERATE EXCITEMENT IN YOUR EMPLOYEE BASE

BUILD A CULTURE WHERE YOUR PEOPLE THRIVE!

Book your next company workshop or training event today!

www.chelliephillips.com/corporate-training

BIG STAGE OR SMALL, IT'S TIME TO IGNITE THE IMPACT OF YOUR EMPLOYEES

AUTHOR, SPEAKER, MOTIVATOR

Do your employees look at your company's purpose as just a faded poster on the wall? Let's talk about how you can align both company and personal values for success!

Start the conversation today.
contact@chelliephillips.com/speaker

Design a life (or workplace) you love.

Keynotes

If you want to create an irresistible workplace and have a lasting a impact on employee behavior, I'll serve as that motivator and change agent. My authenticity and passion will have your audience engaged from start to finish and ready to act.

Workshops

When you assist your employees in creating their personal career brand, you become a partner in their career development. You enable them to recognize their strengths and contributions they bring to your organization. It's a strong signal that you value what they bring to the table.

Coaching

Together, we design a career strategy with your vision of success in mind. Along with crafting attention getting online profiles, you'll implement tactics to become more visible in the workplace so decision makers take notice.

Online Courses

In 30 days, you can create a personal brand designed for career success. This self-paced course walks you step by step through the creation process. You'll even find information on how to prepare for evaluations and interviews too!

www.chelliephillips.com
contact@chelliephillips.com

SCAN ME

Back Ads

Career PROgressions
PODCAST

Mark Allred,
Director of Talent Development & Growth

Reveal Global Intelligence, Charlotte, NC

R E V E A L
GLOBAL INTELLIGENCE   www.RevealGlobal.com

"Finding the right career path shouldn't be a mystery. At **REVEALTalent**, our goal is to help you tap into your professional work talent so you can land a career that transforms your life and ultimately aligns with who you are."

the
CareerPRO
PATHWAY

Career PROgressions
PODCAST

Convert Your Knowledge into
Streams of Passive Income

DAVID
BRANDERHORST
COACHING

Every single day people buy online courses to help them improve their skills and solve problems.

Countless people have taken advantage of this opportunity to generate streams of passive income.

If you're ready to take charge of your future and create a financial breakthrough...

Download Your Free Guide Below

https://davidbranderhorst.com/knowledge/

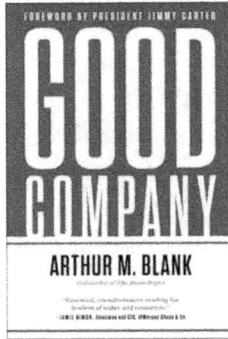

FOREWORD BY PRESIDENT JIMMY CARTER

GOOD COMPANY

ARTHUR M. BLANK

A must read for anyone who wants to be in Good Company!

-Harry Hynekamp, VP Guest Experiences, AMB Sports & Entertainment

Get Your Copy Today!

GRATITUDE CHANGES
EVERYTHING!

For people to feel fully recognized and appreciated, we have to create a significant moment. This doesn't mean expressing gratitude needs to be complicated, but it does need to be sincere. "I'm Grateful for You" gives us all an easy way to show people we are thankful for them.

It all starts with a card that says "I'm Grateful for You". Take a moment to write a short note acknowledging why you are grateful for this person. Give the card to your friend or colleague. Watch everything change.

HOW IT WORKS

Order cards and start expressing gratitude this month. If gratitude is something you want to add to your daily routine, we challenge you to share our cards with 10 people each month making a bigger impact in your community. Keep the cards on your desk or in your car and share your appreciation with those around you.

ORDER YOUR CARDS ->

KEVIN MONROE
GRATITUDE CONSULTING

IMGRATEFULFORYOU.CO
KEVIN@KEVINDMONROE.COM
(404) 713-0713

KING OF POPS

HOWDY!

WE'D LOVE TO BE
A PART OF WHAT YOU
HAVE GOING ON.

BOOK A KING OF POPS
CART TO COME TO
YOUR NEXT EVENT

LEARN MORE ABOUT
OUR CARTREPRENEUR®
PROGRAM

LEARN MORE WHAT AN
UMOH IS ...

@ KINGOFPOPS.COM

Making Work Better For People, Profit & Planet

BOTS FORTHAT

botsforthat.com

www.ingramcontent.com/pod-product-compliance
Lightning Source LLC
Chambersburg PA
CBHW062111020426

42335CB00013B/924